Organized Complexity

Organized

Ronald D. Brunner
Garry D. Brewer

 The Free Press · New York
Collier-Macmillan Limited · London

Foreword by Harold D. Lasswell

Complexity EMPIRICAL THEORIES OF
POLITICAL DEVELOPMENT

THE FREE PRESS
A DIVISION OF THE MACMILLAN COMPANY
866 Third Avenue, New York, New York 10022

Collier-Macmillan Canada Ltd., Toronto, Ontario

Library of Congress Catalog Card Number 79-141936

Printing number 1 2 3 4 5 6 7 8 9 10

Contents

22905

Foreword

In the grand division of labor among scholars the responsibility of political scientists is to examine one among the several interdependent, though often distinctive, processes of society. The scope of the subject has not always been delimited this way. At one extreme the whole of the social process is allegedly swallowed in the science of the state ("The Queen [or King] of the Sciences"). At the other extreme the discipline has faded into a descriptive and formalistic specialty whose practitioners have lost sight of the links between public law, for example, and the whole life of society.

The inclusive version of political science appears to have come into existence very early with the advent of urban civilization. Urban civilization was invented in the fourth millennium B.C. or earlier in the Nile, Tigris-Euphrates and Indus valley cultures. The political thinkers of record were evidently identified with the formal claims of Imperial authority. It is not credible, however, that they should have failed to recognize the factual limits on government and law. Records of the three *r*'s—revolt, rebellion revolution—suggest that the established elite, exercising power in the name of one or many Gods, or of one or many people, were caught in a two-way relationship. To "have" power is to "be empowered," to obtain from the environment the flow of behavior and resources necessary to carry on. The leaders of the new territorially organized, city-based empires were undoubtedly aware—only too aware, in fact—of the persisting autonomy drives of the tribes, families, cults, guilds or localities that were the component members of pre-territorial communities.[1]

During times of surface calm, thinkers and active politicians tend to play down, to ignore or even to forget some fundamental facts of life. The focus of attention is allowed to narrow until it deals almost exclusively with the active members of the official elite and with strategies for scoring relatively minor league triumphs over one another.[2] The accepted ideology shifts from faith, belief and loyalty to ritualized phraseology.

Until the "behavioral revolution" in modern political science the dominant tradition for several decades was legalistic and descriptive. World events are among the factors that explain why it became obvious once more that the institutions conventionally called "government, law and politics" are interactive with the socio-historical context as a whole. The reference is to the de-stabilizing impact of world war, revolution and de-colonization, and the cumulative results of a universalizing pattern of science-based technology.

The intellectual challenge to political science is to devise analytic, descriptive and manipulative concepts and procedures that provide a durable reorientation of the profession toward contextual, problem-oriented and versatile methods. The phenomena of "modernization" or "development" are appropriate testing areas for a configurative approach.

In the unfamiliar setting of an African, Asian, or Pacific anti-colonial power the Western-trained scientist is thrown back on fundamentals. He must locate himself in reference to the phenomena to be investigated and take responsibility for defining the "political." Since it is evident that political events are interwoven with all events in the social process, distinctions are

---

[1] There were formal as well as factual qualifications on Imperial power. See Mario A. Levi, *Political Power in the Ancient World* (1955, 1965).

[2] A masterly analysis of self-preoccupation in politics is the study of the election of René Coty to the Presidency of France by Constantine Melnick and Nathan Leites, *The House Without Windows*.

understood to be matters of relative emphasis, not dichotomous exclusion. Differences are acknowledged between "government, law and politics" in "conventional" and in "functional" usage. The conventional usage, for example, may continue to speak of a "chief" long after it is apparent to all that the official in question has no role whatever to play in making or executing important decisions. The political scientist who would collect "conventional" labels alone would be wasting his time, since his responsibility is to identify and compare genuine patterns of authority and control.

The delimitation of an appropriate frame of reference is the beginning, not the end, of the political observer's role. As a scientist he tries to explain what he finds. He searches for the constellation of factors that accounts for winning (or losing) votes and fights (inside the body politic; between the body politic and other entities). The observer also asks the historical question, hoping to find his way to a perspective that aids scientific analysis. He may seek to forecast the emerging future, partly because it provides a means of testing his grasp of significant determiners of the situation. He may also postulate the desirability of seeking to realize a democratic and relatively non-violent public order and may consider the lines of policy development that point in this direction.

In any case the systematic political scientist is seeking to orient himself in context. If we explore the conception of "context" itself, it is helpful to take the term as referring to the field of events with which a scientific observer concerns himself. Strictly, it is the *observer-and-field* that defines the relevant manifold of events. Clearly any particular context is within the hypothetically universal manifold of past, present and future. A context is chosen in reference to a set of problems growing out of and relevant to the observer's orientation in the overriding manifold. If the scientific observer is identified with political scientists, the common orientation is toward what is conventionally called "government, politics and law," and this frame of reference must be delimited by the observer in functional terms.

A context is expected to exhibit "order" rather than the "disorder" of an utterly random pattern. The observer detects "order" when he identifies a "process," which is a pattern of (non-random) recurrence. In a social process the recurring patterns are regularities of interaction among human beings, such as giving or receiving (withholding or rejecting) love, gestures of respect, claims to productive or consumable resources, and the like. Most particularly, political scientists are focused on the giving or receiving (withholding or rejecting) of support in the making and execution of important decisions. Importance is estimated in terms of the significance of the "values at stake" or the probable consequences of the decision for the participants in the context.

It is evident that the "social process" involves "structures" and "functions." The observer becomes oriented toward a social process when he becomes interested in the interplay of structural and functional patterns within it. The structures are the features that remain constant in the field of observation during the period of study. "People" are relatively unchanging "structures" in the social process, because they are perceived by the observer as a stable configuration. They can also be said to perform "functions" to the extent that they are the locus of change during the period. What is defined as structure or function depends on the observer's problem. Thus some patterns are candidates for the "function" category if they exhibit a changing feature that the observer wants to investigate, such as the offering of money for votes. The observer may disregard other "functioning" patterns or treat them as timebound components of the structure (such as "physical growth" or "aging").

The category of "structure" is available to include patterns of inter-action that change so little during a given period that they are not included among the phenomena of interest to the observer. For instance, the grammar and vocabulary of the local language may be treated as structure, while the frequency of positive or negative reference statements uttered about a political figure, issue or organization may be a "function." Or a council of elders may be classified as a structure despite changes in the size or age composition. Its "functions" may be the decisions. However, it may be useful for more refined comparisons to stipulate that a council is only recognized as a structure if it reaches a specified minimum level of "functioning." These are ever-present questions to be settled by each observer or observing team.

It is apparent that no scientific observer can ever make an exhaustive, empirically established inventory of all the "potential" characteristics of a context that enumerates all the features that may be pertinent to a question that will eventually interest him or his colleagues. For instance, the tone of voice accepted as reassuring by the infants and children of today may be modified as phonographic records and radio-TV facilities change the composi-tion of the future environment of children. Hence the tone of voice employed by exponents of the established order may change; or, if changes in the early environment occur rapidly, challengers may sound more trustworthy than established spokesmen. Up to the present no political scientist has described the "predispositions to interpret the political voice patterns" in a developing country or explored contingency models of vocal change. Such predispositions are usually buried among the unspecified features of "language structures" or of "demands." Although a particular political scientist may justifiably decide not to concern himself with this problem, he would no doubt concede that his priorities might not be accepted by all, especially in future decades, when questions may be more differentiated and refined.

In choosing problems an investigator will undoubtedly be influenced by current conceptions of the most important questions, the availability of information, and the adequacy of current methodological procedures. In recent years political scientists have greatly amplified the body of explicit propositions relevant to the scientific explanation of political phenomena. The comprehensive formulations found in the traditional literature have been extended and refined to guide the study of a great variety of contexts defined according to culture, class, interest, personality and level of crisis, and particularized in terms of various aspects of the decision process (such as intelligence, promotion, prescription, invocation, application, termination, appraisal).

The proliferating bodies of articulated theory have not been matched by commensurate progress in data-gathering. Brunner and Brewer properly underline the crucial nature of this constraint on the growth of an adequate theoretical contribution to development planning and appraisal.

Especially germane to the present inquiry is the confusion and uncertainty that is current about the intellectual tools and procedures best adapted to the performance of scientific and related tasks connected with political development. For the moment it is sufficient to distinguish three sets of devices now at the disposal of political scientists who are studying political development in national or urban settings. Brunner and Brewer note that political development is systematically explored by two principal methods to which they propose to add a third. The first can be called "correlational," the second "formal deductive," the third "computer modelling."

Great reliance has been put on the use of statistical correlation as a means of validating propositions formulated by political and social scientists. Brunner and Brewer have enriched the teaching literature of political science by showing in detail that the "correlational" procedure is often misapplied. It is an exploratory *not* a validating instrument.

The second procedure yields to none in formal elegance, since "formal deduction" is equipped to exhibit in detail the consequences of a set of initial rules of interplay among the components of a formal system. The essential objection to giving top priority to this method of studying political development, according to the authors, is that it is diversionary. It diverts the accomplished mathematical model maker toward aesthetically satisfying results that are appropriate for problems other than political development. Here, too, Brunner and Brewer offer sufficiently specific confrontations of model and data to get their message across.

The computer modelling alternative is the affirmative recommendation in the present book. As Brunner and Brewer outline methodology they emphasize the arrow of time and the opportunity to engage in a continuing procedure of model improvement as data become available and as new policy alternatives pose new questions and generate pertinent information. Computer modelling lends itself to the intensive, expanding study of predispositions in an interactive context, in this way avoiding the distortions that come from mistaking cross-contextual correlations or formal beauty for satisfactory results.

The present treatise is an essential instrument of the emerging policy sciences.

HAROLD D. LASSWELL

Preface

Nearly every student of modernization and
its political implications is familiar with Daniel Lerner's book. *The Passing of
Traditional Society.* In one of the early chapters, which has received a good
deal of attention from other scholars, Lerner presents a theory of modernization involving variables such as urbanization, literacy, media development,
and political participation. The theory is focused on the level of the whole
society, it is often stated in terms of cause and effect (even though Lerner
expresses a wish to avoid such terms), it takes into account the temporal
dimension, and it views modernization as a set of systemic relationships.
These things we found fascinating. At the same time, we were somewhat

less captivated by several other aspects of the analysis, including the transition from verbal theory to quantitative analysis, the problem of the "deviant" case of Egypt, and some apparent inconsistencies and omissions. Our fascination and uneasiness led to the development of a small computer simulation model of modernization and mass politics that is the heart of this book.

In the first essay, we suggest some relationships between political development on the one hand and modernization and mass politics on the other, and then trace the development of the model from the work of Lerner and other theoretical and case studies. The behavioral properties of the model are explored by applying it to the experience of Turkey and the Philippines in the decade of the 1950s and by tracing the impact of selected variations in parameters having policy interpretations. The results, we found, were encouraging. Substantively, however, the model is little more than a first approximation that promises to be useful as a guide to the preparation of relevant field research projects and the development of more complex and realistic models.

In the second essay, we use the model as a pedagogical device in the consideration of some issues of scope and method that are raised but not explored in the first essay. More specifically, we contend that the complex nature of political systems and our intellectual habits and limitations have forced upon us certain forms of simplification that have impeded progress in understanding and explaining the behavior of political systems. Foremost among these simplifications are specialization and, within fields of specialization, the extensive use of statistical and simplistic styles of analysis that are only partially appropriate in the study of complex systems. Computer simulation seems promising as one means of facilitating communication and coordination among specialists and the use of process styles of analysis in addition to others.

Beyond these particular issues of substance, scope and method, however, this is a book about organized complexity, a point of view about the nature of social and political problems suggested by Warren Weaver in 1948. Such problems are not problems of simplicity characterized by a few variables, or problems of disorganized complexity amenable to statistical techniques. Rather, they show the essential features of organization among a number of factors interrelated in an organic whole. If we have demonstrated the distinctiveness and the relevance of the viewpoint of organized complexity, our purpose has been fulfilled.

This research began at Yale University and has progressed only through the help and encouragement of many colleagues and financial benefactors. Hayward R. Alker, Jr. and Harold D. Lasswell have provided intellectual stimulation and insightful comments at every stage of this study, and Joseph LaPalombara and Martin Shubik have contributed significantly at several points. Douglas Durasoff, John S. Fitch III, and Raymond F. Hopkins, our colleagues in a continuing seminar on political development, have helped us appraise and modify the study at regular intervals. Research funds have been provided by Yale, The University of Michigan, and the Center for International Affairs at Harvard. We gratefully acknowledge our considerable debts to these persons and institutions.

R.D.B.
G.D.B.
Cambridge, Massachusetts

Contents for Essay I
Modernization and Mass Politics

Essay
I

Modernization and
Mass Politics

Introduction

t is becoming increasingly apparent that the problem of political development in the less developed countries is the creation of strong and legitimate political institutions that can *effectively* direct the course of modernization and at the same time *democratically* absorb the social forces unleashed by it. But the goals of effective and democratic rule seem to be partially contradictory in those countries which have achieved some semblance of democracy. The more effective a government in achieving rapid gains in the social and economic fields, the more it increases the level of services and

Notes to Essay I begin on page 78.

1

benefits demanded of it and the more it multiplies the number of people and the number of diverse organized interests involved in politics. The greater these burdens of government, the more likely they will exceed the capacity of the government to fulfill them, particularly if the pace of economic development temporarily levels off or declines.[1]

The result is often declining popular support and a succession dilemma that becomes particularly acute at election time.[2] Does the government submit to democratic procedures at the risk of being voted out of office, or does it subvert the democratic order to remain in power? Do the opposition groups submit to democratic procedures at the risk of several more years of the same or similar policies, or do they intervene by force to impose their own views? With a strong and legitimate electoral system the dilemma often can be resolved democratically. But political institutions such as electoral systems tend to be weak in the less developed countries. Moreover, these institutions grow slowly,[3] and are often challenged and subverted before they can take root.

We do not propose to consider directly the problems of political institutionalization and the succession dilemma. We do propose, however, to explore in the light of recent theory some of the social, economic, and mass political roots of these problems. Among those aspects of modernization and mass politics that are relevant to institutionalization and the succession dilemma are political polarization, in which patterns of mass support for the government differ markedly among sectors of the society; decreases through time in economic effectiveness and mass support for the government; and rapid social and economic change. To the extent that polarization between social and political groups increases, the chances that growing conflict among them can be contained and resolved within the framework of relatively new and fragile political institutions are diminished.[4] To the extent that sectors of the population are suffering declines in the standard of living and the government is losing support, the chances that those deprived the most will allow their political responses to be constrained by democratic institutions are decreased.[5] To the extent that economic growth and social change in general are rapid, economic rewards and burdens are rapidly redistributed and traditional constraints on individual and group behavior are weakened or destroyed.[6] The probability that existing political institutions can function effectively under these circumstances is reduced. With sufficient insight and understanding of these trends in modernization and mass politics, perhaps both popular and effective government can be achieved and strong institutions can be built.

Much of the recent theoretical work on modernization and its political impact in the less developed countries draws upon or has been stimulated by Daniel Lerner's excellent study of modernization in the Middle East.[7] Drawing on Lerner's work, McCrone and Cnudde[8] have stated alternative causal models of national political development and then used correlation coefficients to discriminate among them. Schramm and Ruggels[9] have attempted "to seek out hypotheses, rather than to test hypotheses in any definitive way,"[10] through the analysis of cross-national and time-lagged data. Two of three hypotheses selected from Lerner's study are not supported by their data.[11] In a study intended in part to determine the relevance of quantitative techniques and mathematics in the study of political development, but also intended in part to verify and discover theory, Tanter[12] has used causal modelling to test a version of Lerner's theory. Other studies by Alker,[13] Berman,[14] and Domingo[15] draw on Lerner's work to illustrate mathematical modelling techniques or points about the philosophy of science.

Given their different purposes and methods, these studies have contributed to our understanding of the political impact of social mobilization in the less developed countries, and we shall use these studies to explore the research problem outlined above. The first section of this essay introduces the essentials of Lerner's theory and considers in some detail the different types of questions he has posed, their methodological treatment, and their implications for our study. The second section develops some modifications of the substance of Lerner's theory based on additional theoretical literature and case studies of Turkey and the Philippines. In the third, fourth, and fifth sections we state a model based on this modified theory, apply it to the case of Turkey and the Philippines, and explore its implications for the trends underlying political institutionalization and the succession dilemma. In the concluding section we reconsider the problem of institutionalization and the succession dilemma, comment on the limitations of this analysis, and summarize the uses of the model.

1. A Reconsideration of Lerner's Theory: Method

FORMALIZATION OF RELATIONSHIPS

Lerner has summarized the basic relationships in his theory in the following terms:

> The secular evolution of a participant society appears to involve a regular sequence of three phases. Urbanization comes first, for cities alone have developed the complex of skills and resources which characterize the modern industrial economy. Within this urban matrix develop both of the attributes which distinguish the next two phases—literacy

and media growth. There is a close reciprocal relationship between these, for the literate develop the media which in turn spread literacy. But, historically, literacy performs the key function in the second phase. Not until the third phase, when the elaborate technology of industrial development is fairly well advanced, does a society begin to produce newspapers, radio networks, and motion pictures on a massive scale. This, in turn, accelerates the spread of literacy. Out of this interaction develop those institutions of participation (i.e., voting) which we find in all advanced modern societies.[16]

Relationships such as these can take several different forms in the course of further analysis, and these forms may be distinguished according to their interpretation. As an example, consider the relationships between urbanization and literacy. In one interpretation it is a relationship that attempts to explain changes in urbanization and literacy in individual countries through time. Thus Lerner writes that "increases of urbanization tend in every society to multiply national increases in literacy and media participation. By drawing people from their rural communities, cities create the demand for impersonal communications. By promoting literacy and media, cities supply this demand."[17] More succinctly, "Everywhere . . . increasing urbanization has tended to raise literacy. . . ."[18] The relationship in this interpretation can take several different mathematical forms. One of the simplest is

$$Y_t - Y_{t-1} = \alpha (X_t - X_{t-1}) \qquad (1.1)$$

or

$$Y_t = Y_{t-1} + \alpha (X_t - X_{t-1}) \qquad (1.2)$$

where X is the per cent urban, Y is the per cent literate and the subscripts refer to time periods. Thus for any country, a change through time in urbanization produces a change through time in literacy, or equivalently, literacy at one time period is increased by a change in urbanization to give literacy at the next. α, which reflects the magnitude of the impact of urbanization on literacy, is simply a function of the appropriate changes through time:

$$\alpha = \frac{Y_t - Y_{t-1}}{X_t - X_{t-1}} \qquad (1.3)$$

In this interpretation, α can be estimated from time series data for each country.

In another interpretation the relationship between urbanization and literacy is an attempt to explain differences in urbanization and literacy among nations at a cross-section in time. Thus after considering a set of data for 73 countries Lerner writes that "[After urbanization reaches 10%] urbanization and literacy increase together in a direct (monotonic) relationship, until they reach 25%, which appears to be the 'critical optimum' of urbanization. Beyond this literacy continues to rise independently of the growth of cities."[19] In Lerner's analysis the relationship in this interpretation is represented implicitly as a regression equation. Within the specified limits of urbanization, the form of this equation is

$$Y = a + bX \tag{1.4}$$

where again X is per cent urban and Y is per cent literate. The parameter a, the intercept, gives the expected level of literacy when urbanization is zero. The parameter b, the slope, gives the expected difference in literacy for a given difference in urbanization. Thus for countries i and j represented as two points on the regression line

$$b = \frac{Y_i - Y_j}{X_i - X_j} \tag{1.5}$$

In contrast to α in (1.3), b is defined in terms of differences between countries at a cross-section in time rather than in terms of differences through time for a single country. In this interpretation b is estimated from data on a large number of countries.

APPLICATION TO INDIVIDUAL COUNTRIES

Lerner's application of this interpretation of the relationship to the cases of Turkey and Egypt is not entirely successful. In 1950 urbanization and literacy levels were 15% and 30%, respectively, in Turkey, and 28% and 15% in Egypt.

> Since Egypt was twice as urban as Turkey it should, on our analysis, be something more than twice as literate. But its literacy was, in fact, half as high as Turkey's in 1950—i.e., to match Turkey's urbanism–literacy ratio, Egypt would require over 400% more literates than it had. This conforms to the global ratio [which is based on the slope b] . . . which showed that when urbanization exceeds 25% literacy should be over 60% and growing.[20]

Since the ratio between urbanism and literacy in Turkey in 1950 conforms to the global ratio derived from the regression analysis, Turkey is considered a case of balanced growth. Since the ratio in Egypt does not conform, the case of Egypt cannot be explained by the cross-national relationship and Egypt, consequently, is considered a case of unbalanced growth. The relevance of the cross-national regression relationship as an explanation of urbanization and literacy in Egypt is not reassessed.

McCrone and Cnudde do not explicitly apply their model to specific cases, but their cross-national analysis encounters similar problems.[21] Having found a causal model consistent with correlations among indicators of urbanization, education, communications, and democratic political development, McCrone and Cnudde nevertheless feel that these correlations "leave a significant proportion of the variance unexplained. For this reason, deviant cases (in terms of the model) can be found."[22] In one type of deviant case a nation may be "overdeveloped" with respect to one variable in the model. An example would be the situation where "the democratic political system does not have sufficient communications development to maintain the regime."[23] In another type of deviant case a nation may have "fulfilled the requirements for development, in terms of the model, yet fails to maintain a democratic regime."[24] Germany before the era of the present Federal Republic is cited as a possible example. Like Lerner, McCrone and Cnudde do not reassess the assumptions involved in applying cross-national relationships to the explanation of individual cases.[25] They suggest, however, that more variables might be included in the model.

A MATTER OF INTERPRETATION

The failure to explain the case of Egypt is not proof that Lerner's relationship is invalid, and the existence of deviant cases is not proof that McCrone and Cnudde's model is invalid. Rather these problems are artifacts of the cross-national interpretation of their relationships. For example, when the relationship between urbanization and literacy is construed as *a pattern found in a set of cross-national data*, the explanation of the individual case is relatively insensitive to the peculiarities of that case. The estimation of the slope *b* (from which Lerner derives his global ratio) is based on a sample of countries, and the larger the sample the less is the impact of any individual country on the magnitude of *b*. Although it can be applied to individual countries, the relationship has little meaning apart from the cross-national context from which it is derived. Data reflecting the peculiarities of individual countries can only be re-introduced as residuals or departures from the expectation based on cross-national data. When the relationship between urbanization and literacy is construed as *a process operating in individual countries*, the parameter α is estimated for each country individually. The question is no longer whether or how much an individual country departs from the cross-national standard, but whether the trends in urbanization and literacy for the country can be construed as the inputs and outputs of such a process.

If a basic question of comparative government is how nations are similar and how nations are different, the distinction between these two interpretations of the same relationship is not trivial. In a national as opposed to a cross-national interpretation, countries are not similar to the extent that they conform to the cross-national pattern, but in the processes that operate in each of them individually. Similarly, countries are not different to the extent that they deviate from the cross-national pattern, but in the parameters governing the operation of the processes in each country.

The relevance of either interpretation depends on the purpose of the analysis. Where the purpose, like ours, is to explain the course of change in individual countries over time, the process interpretation and substantive process models are more relevant than the cross-national interpretation and statistical models such as correlation and regression. The pioneers in building process models of political development are Domingo and Berman. Domingo[26] used time series data and a computer-programmed algorithm to develop a model, and Berman[27] stated some of the major hypotheses in Lerner's work in terms of differential equations. Neither, however, analyzed in any detail the models they proposed. In the following sections we develop a process model based on Lerner's theory and other theoretical and empirical work in order to explore trends in modernization and mass politics.

2. A Reconsideration of Lerner's Theory: Substance

SOME SUBSTANTIVE QUESTIONS

The substance of Lerner's theory can be reconsidered from several points of view, but for our purposes two seem particularly relevant. First, is Lerner's theory a conceptually complete or systemic explanation of the political implications of social mobilization? This depends on the way and the extent to which the variables in the theory are interrelated. Second, is it an empirically adequate explanation? This depends on the extent to which this theory, derived from the Western experience, is applicable to the underdeveloped countries today.

Both in general and in terms of his own theory Lerner conceived of each developing country as a system in which changes in one sector produce changes in the others. More specifically he writes that

> our historical forays indicate that the conditions which define modernity form an interlocking "system." They grow conjointly, in the normal situation, or they become stunted severally.
>
> It seems clear that people who live together in a common polity will develop patterned ways of distributing *information* along with other commodities. It is less obvious that these information flows will interact with the distribution of power, wealth, status at so many points as to form a system—and, moreover, a system so tightly interwoven that institutional variation in one sector will be accompanied by regular and determinate variation in the other sectors. Yet, just this degree of interaction between communication and social systems is what our historical exploration suggests.[28]

Lerner investigates the systemic question in terms of his own theory by finding multiple correlations among indicators of urbanization, literacy, media participation and political participation. He finds that "the size of these coefficients demonstrates that the relationship between the four sectors *is* systemic. These independent tests of the participant style of life do in fact 'go together' in 54 extant societies."[29] The developmental sequence by which changes in urbanization bring changes in literacy, and media participation and changes in literacy bring changes in political participation is quite clear in Lerner's theory. It is not entirely clear, however, what changes in the system give rise to urbanization in the first place, and what changes in the system result from changes in political participation. Apparently we need to reconsider what urbanization and participation are, what causes the former, and what impact has the latter.

Lerner is somewhat ambivalent about the extent to which the model of modernization that he proposes adequately summarizes the principal processes operating in the under-developed countries of today. On the one hand he writes that

> the Western model of modernization exhibits certain components and sequences whose relevance is global. . . . That the same basic model reappears in virtually all modernizing societies on all continents of the world . . . will be shown in this chapter. The point is that the secular process of social change, which brought modernization to the Western world, has more than antiquarian relevance to today's problems of the Middle East transition. Indeed, the lesson is that Middle Eastern modernizers will do well to study the historical sequence of Western growth.[30]

On the other hand Lerner notes that "Whereas the modern nations have achieved 'optimum' relations between urbanism, literacy, media participation, the traditional societies exhibit extremely variant 'growth' patterns (deviations from the regression lines). Some are more urban than literate, others more media participant than urban."[31] Lerner attributes the difference to two recent trends in the Middle East. The first is that urbanism no longer means what it used to. Newly urbanized citizens in cities such as Cairo tend not to attend schools, do work, get cash, or buy goods. "It would be more accurate to tally these involuntary urbanites as 'internal rural refugees.' . . ."[32]

> The second postwar trend is the rapid diffusion of cheap (or free) radio receivers among the rural populations of the Middle East. This again is an alteration of the Western model, in which media participation reflected a market mechanism—radios produced privately for profit were bought individually for pleasure. Radios distributed gratis by

government facilitate "social control" rather than "individual participation"; they also explain why most Arab countries show an excess of radio listeners over urban literates.[33]

Apparently some consideration of the systemic links among the variables in Lerner's model is in order, as suggested by differences between Western and non-Western experience.

In order to modify the theory along the lines suggested by these observations and by the research problem, we now turn to some case studies of Turkey and the Philippines and to some additional theoretical analyses of the processes involved.

URBANIZATION

Variation in the amount of urbanization has been attributed to the number of teachers in rural areas, the number of secondary school students in rural areas, the development of communications and transportation systems, the man–land ratio in rural areas, government health, education and welfare expenditures in urban areas, the availability of jobs in cities, and spatial distances involved in migrating from rural to urban areas.[34] Although each of these factors can be considered related in some way to the process of modernization, so far as we know no one has attempted to synthesize them or to categorize their relative impact. It would seem, however, that in an underdeveloped country the number of teachers and the number of secondary school students in rural areas would be relatively small, and that consequently their impact on urbanization in relation to the total number of migrants is apt to be small. Aside from spatial distance, the other factors seem to be closely related to economic performance and particularly to relative economic performance in rural and urban areas. As the standard of living improves in cities relative to the rural areas, urbanization apparently increases. Bruce Herrick has formulated this hypothesis in very explicit terms:

> It seems clear that urban migration as found in the real world results from some combination of the "push" and "pull." These two hypotheses may be unified in one, in which urban migration is a function of expected rural–urban income differences. This of course implicitly makes the motivation for migration wholly economic. Nevertheless the combination of bleakness of rural prospects coupled with a more promising urban future is appealing as an explanation for migration.[35]

Bernard Okun and Richard Richardson apparently agree.

Far from reducing the need for migration, regional patterns of natural population increase and growth of economic opportunity generally enhance the importance of mobility. For while the agricultural regions typically have the higher rate of natural increase, it is in the non-agricultural regions that the demand for labor grows more rapidly.

From what has been said, it is clear that population migration must be the predominant force making for redistribution of human resources in response to changing relative opportunities among regions.[36]

More succinctly, according to Gunnar Myrdal, "the localities and regions where economic activity is expanding will attract net immigration from other parts of the country."[37]

These views are consistent with those of several scholars who have studied the experience of particular countries in some detail. Richard Robinson, for example, very explicitly ties urbanization to the relative economic situation in rural and urban areas in Turkey.

Adding further pressure on the marginal or submarginal farmer to stay on the land had been the deliberate policy of channeling to the farm sector more of the national income than was economically justified in terms of production, the major devices for which . . . were easy credit, tax exemption, public investment, and crop subsidy. Inherent in these programs was encouragement for inefficient agriculture, a situation very much at odds with national development.

On the other hand, if agriculture had been freed of these artificial stimulants, the human flood which would have swept into the cities would have far exceeded the already serious proportions of the rural–urban movement. The resulting political restlessness might have been disastrous.[38]

Urbanization need not be treated as an uncaused cause, but rather may be considered in large part a function of relative economic performance in rural and urban areas.

PARTICIPATION

Lerner operationalizes political participation as voting turnout. However, in many countries that are still considered relatively under-developed there are already very high levels of voting turnout, and there seems to be no clear secular trend toward increasing levels of turnout. In Turkey, for example, the turnout rates were 89%, 89%, and 77% of the eligible electorate in the general elections of 1950, 1954, and 1957, respectively.[39] The Philippine presidential elections of 1946, 1949, 1953, 1957, and 1961 had turnout rates of 89.6%, 67.7%, 77.2%, 75.5% and 79.4% of the registered electorate.[40]

If the phenomenon called participation is increasing in the less developed countries, then turnout rates are not an accurate measure of it. Furthermore, it is not apparent that variations in the turnout rates systematically affect other variables in the system. We propose, as a more useful conceptualization of political participation, the capacity of a group or sector to respond to changes in its life situation by giving or withholding support for the government. More generally, participation is the extent to which stimuli or felt needs can be converted into meaningful responses at the aggregate level. This participant form of group behavior increases with advances in communications and transportation, and more generally, with social mobilization. Karl Deutsch's analysis is similar to this one.

> The increasing numbers of the mobilized population, and the greater scope and urgency of their needs for political decisions and government services, tend to translate themselves, albeit with a time lag, into increased participation.[41]

Mustapha Kemal seems to have taken advantage of gaps in the communication system to restrict the scope of political participation in pre-war Turkey. According to Frederick Frey,

> the communications bifurcation in Turkish society between educated elite and uneducated mass actually provided Mustapha Kemal with a convenient halfway house in the reshaping of the country. He could to a large extent afford to forget about the submerged peasant masses and concentrate his limited resources on solidifying his hold on the dominant intellectual groups. . . . The lack of communications between elite and mass was a vital factor which he used to simplify his task and equate it with his resources.[42]

This is not to say that problems did not exist or were not felt among the peasant masses in Turkey during the Ataturk era. In the Philippines in recent years, according to Caridad Semaña,

> The broadening of political participation among the people as evidenced by the heightened interest in elections in the rural areas inevitably increases the pressure on the part of the politician to allocate his resources on a broader basis.[43]

In this case where participation is broader, peasant needs are translated into peasant political action. Carl Landé's observations of the Philippines lead to similar conclusions.

> The ordinary voter . . . learns that what he does can have a direct effect upon certain substantive "outputs" of government. . . . In short, he is far more aware than his American counterpart that what he does on

election day can have a direct and immediate perceptible effect upon the outputs of government insofar as they concern himself. The high sense of participation in the political process that this engenders accounts in large part for the surprising amount of information about politics possessed by the ordinary Filipino and for the intensity of his interest in politics.[44]

Political participation of this kind—a group's capacity for giving or withholding support for the government—can be negligible among those sectors of the population relatively isolated by communications and transportation barriers even though real needs exist and are perceived.[45] Gaps in the communications and transportation systems, in short, can usefully be conceived of as filters that moderate the extent of a group's impact on the society even when sufficient motivation exists and that are removed in the course of modernization.

Removing the gaps in the communications and transportation system not only tends to increase participation, it also increases expectations.[46]

> Investments in transportation and communication may have marked beneficial effects upon output, expectations, and opportunities, but they may result in serious increases in aspirations due to the demonstration effect.[47]

The demonstration effect assumes that a comparison between the standard of living of one group and that of another increases the economic expectations of the relatively disadvantaged group. Although the original concept derived from consumption studies in the United States,[48] recent formulations have been generalized to international comparisons[49] and to the less developed countries.[50] A complementary formulation assumes that a group's comparison between its current and previous standard of living changes its economic expectations. This formulation provides for decreases in expectations with decreases in actual performance and seems to be more consistent with the onset of economic pessimism in Turkey after the recession of 1954. Regardless of the standard of comparison, the magnitude of the changes in expectations should increase with investments in transportation and communication.

POPULAR SUPPORT

Just as there are many possible causes of urbanization, there are also many factors contributing to the degree of support each sector of the society gives to the government. In general however,

> ... the popular acceptance of a government in a period of social mobilization is most of all a matter of its capabilities and the manner in which they are used—that is, essentially a matter of its responsiveness to the felt needs of its population.[51]

In the underdeveloped countries and elsewhere, the single most important felt need seems to be improvements in the standard of living. As Harold Lasswell and Abraham Kaplan have put it, "Poverty has been held to be the parent of revolution since Aristotle (*Politics*, II, 6) and undoubtedly before. The predisposition to oppose the rule in most cases arises from continued deprivation under the rule."[52]

Survey results reported in Lerner's book suggest that economic considerations were important for a large segment of the Turkish population in the early 1950s. In response to the question, "What is the biggest personal problem for people in the same circumstances as yourself?", 72% of those Lerner considered to be Transitional gave responses classifiable as economic.[53] A. H. Hanson, in discussing the Turkish general election of 1954, notes that

> The decisive factor was the peasant, to whom both parties directed a major part of their propaganda. Usually illiterate, but shrewd in his judgments of economic self-interest, he had evidently come to the conclusion that another dose of Democratic rule was the medicine that he needed. This, indeed, was not surprising, as the agricultural policies of the Democrats, with considerable help from the Americans and the weather, had proved conspicuously successful.[54]

Similarly, Richard Robinson has written that in the late 1950s

> The single most important political issue in Turkey became the availability of such key consumer goods as coffee, tea, sugar, kerosene, radios, batteries, lamps, glass, textiles and shoes. This massive popular demand for rapid improvement in the standard of living existed in part because the ordinary folk were now conscious of the vast difference between their own standard of material well-being and that of Western Europe and North America. The demand for economic improvement, it was safe to say, took easy precedence over interest in maintaining democratic political institutions. ... The masters of Turkey were, in reality, the political slaves of the village farming masses and the new lower class urban group.[55]

Furthermore, in Turkey economic factors also seem to influence significantly the political sympathies of the urban middle class, bureaucracy and intelligentsia. After 1954, the support for the Democrats among these groups declined as salaries remained fixed and inflation accelerated.[56]

Landé, in discussing the parallel situation in the Philippines, writes that

> Unlike the United States, the Philippines is a unitary state and the powers and functions of municipal and provincial governments are very limited, especially with regard to their taxing and spending powers. The national government [is] almost the sole source of numerous benefits sought by the public—education, health care, sanitation, agricultural assistance, as well as numerous "improvements" such as roads,

schools, and artesian wells. . . . Filipinos have long been accustomed to look mainly to the national officials, and especially to their congress-man, for the material benefits available from the government.[57]

More explicitly,

... whole villages or towns may shift the bulk of their votes in the hope of obtaining public works projects from the party or candidate thought most likely to win.[58]

Perhaps one can speculate that "with the development of the industrial economy, the problem of poverty and the distribution of wealth cease to be burning issues."[59] But certainly in the less developed countries today, these economic issues are the important ones for many groups in the population.

GOVERNMENT ALLOCATIONS

As we have noted, political participation as voting turnout seems to have no apparent systematic effect. However, political participation as the capacity of groups or sectors to give or withold support for the government has in general a relatively clearcut impact on the policies of the governing party. Studies of optimum economic investment allocation notwithstanding, governments distribute resources in large part as a response to political pressures. According to Hirschman,

The reasons for which local government and domestic private investors may be unable or unwilling to undertake the kind of development projects that lead to dynamic growth are several. We have already dealt with the reluctance on the part of the government to concentrate its investment effort in a single region or sector when all regions and sectors are clamoring for help and are in fact badly in need of improvement. [Private foreign capital] is less inhibited in picking priorities and in giving one region or one sector a temporary advantage over another. Its availability helps the local government to think in terms of development, rather than in terms of the "pork barrel" type of distribution of public funds.[60]

The "picking of priorities" alluded to by Hirschman has been nicely illustrated in the descriptive literature on Turkey.

The peasants have been given the vote, and the parties assiduously woo them to secure the award of that vote to their proffered candidates. The reaction of the villagers to variations in policy are elaborately dis-cussed and estimated by political leaders. . . . There is a great temptation presented to all parties to pander to short-run peasant greed and political immaturity by promising tax reductions, fiddling with crop subsidies, incorporating many local potentates into top-level party and govern-mental positions, and so on. Fortitude to resist these temptations . . .

has not so far been widely displayed. In fact, the key to Menderes' success, despite his anti-democratic tendencies, lay in just such maneuvers.[61]

Pork barrel is a way of life in the Philippines.

> ... scarce public funds have been expended without regard to the economic and/or social returns of such public investments. The paramount objective of such public outlays is political. ...

> In the face of the growing assertiveness of the legislature *vis-à-vis* the presidency since 1948, the authority of the Chief Executive to withhold pork barrel funds has become a necessary instrument to compel defiant legislators to pass "must" administration measures.

> Pork barrel is also an important component of the politician's supply of resources. He bargains constantly with the national leadership in an effort, among others, to maximize the supply of resources at his command. Because the demand for his resources far outruns the supply, he must skillfully allocate them as *quid pro quos* for his constituents' votes. This exchange of direct economic benefits for votes has provided an avenue for incorporating the personal demands of the mass of citizens into the political process.[62]

Much of the descriptive literature suggests that the government has several policy options to manipulate in an effort to stay in power. But given the importance to the electorate of improvements in the standard of living, the manipulation of economic policies for political purposes seems to be the most direct and possibly the most effective option short of massive propaganda assaults on the population and circumvention of the democratic institutions.

In this section we have outlined and illustrated in verbal form some of the relationships suggested by Lerner and others as critical in modernization and mass politics. Our efforts to eliminate some of the logical and theoretical shortcomings have fallen short of producing a logically complete and operational theoretical system. However, the relationships we have proposed suggest that such a system at the very least must disaggregate the individual nation into rural and urban sectors; into distinct but interrelated demographic, economic, and political subsystems; and into at least three basic dimensions of analysis: *people*, *economic goods*, and *political support*. Furthermore, to make the system logically complete, we must consider how government expenditures affect the economic performance of the rural and urban sectors, and we must provide for the growth of the population, which not only increases the size of the electorate but also increases the number of mouths to feed and therefore puts additional pressure on the maintenance of the standard of living. Finally, to make the system operational, we must translate these relationships into highly explicit forms from which their joint implications can be deduced.

3. A Formal Model of Modernization and Mass Politics

OVERVIEW

Turning to these problems, we state in this section a two-sector model of modernization and mass politics consisting of twelve interdependent relationships which trace through time the size and distribution of population, the value and distribution of economic goods, and the amount and distribution of political support for the government as well as some systemic effects. Through urbanization there is a transfer of people from the rural to the urban sector; through government taxation and expenditures that are transfers of economic goods between the sectors. Furthermore, through net foreign aid, trade, and private monetary exchanges there are transfers of economic goods between the international and the national system.

DEMOGRAPHIC SUBSYSTEM

The amount of urbanization varies with the relative performance of the rural ($i = 1$) and urban ($i = 2$) sectors of the economy, the proportion of the rural population that is participant, and the size of the rural population.

$$U_t = s\left(\frac{C_{2,t} \, N_{1,t}}{N_{2,t} \, C_{1,t}}\right) P_{1,t} \, N_{1,t} \qquad (3.1)$$

where

U_t = the number of migrants from rural to urban areas at time t.

$C_{i,t}$ = consumption in constant currency in sector i at time t.

$N_{i,t}$ = the population of sector i at time t.

$P_{i,t}$ = the proportion of the people in sector i at time t that are participant.

s = the proportion of the participant rural population that would urbanize when economic performance in the two sectors is the same.

In this relationship per capita consumption is the measure of economic performance or the standard of living. Other things being equal, a famine in the rural sector or a boom in the urban sector will increase the amount of urbanization. Similarly, a relatively large increase in rural population or a relatively small increase in urban population will increase the amount of urbanization. The participant proportion is a function of communication and transportation expenditures and will be considered below. When the number of people who participate is low relative to the total rural population, the economic stimulus to urbanize is largely latent. When this number is high, superior economic performance in the urban sector may result in large-scale migration to the cities.

Urbanization redistributes the total population between the rural and urban sectors. The population of each sector also changes as a function of natural increase, the excess of births over deaths.

$$N_{1,\,t} = (1 + a_1)N_{1,\,t-1} - U_{t-1} \qquad (3.2a)$$

$$N_{2,\,t} = (1 + a_2)N_{2,\,t-1} + U_{t-1} \qquad (3.2b)$$

where

$\quad a_i \quad$ = the rate of natural increase in sector i.

ECONOMIC SUBSYSTEM

In order to trace the implications of government expenditures, we have adapted with several modifications Samuelson's classic analysis of the interaction between the multiplier and the principle of acceleration.[63] Whether a model designed to study developed economies can be used to study underdeveloped economies as well is open to question. At least one economist, Albert O. Hirschman, sees some similarities between the problem of moving developed economies out of depression and stimulating growth in less developed economies.[64] This model, like Hirschman's strategy of economic development, assumes that resources are available and can be mobilized if pressures and inducement mechanisms exist.[65] In any case, Samuelson's model is a parsimonious treatment of the relevant macro-economic variables. Other more complex models exist, but as a first approximation we feel his model as modified is adequate for our purposes.

The basic accounting identity (3.3) gives the gross product of each sector as the sum of its consumption, investment, share of government expenditures, and a net contribution from the foreign sector.

$$Y_{i,\,t} = C_{i,\,t} + I_{i,\,t} + G_{i,\,t} + F_{i,\,t} \qquad (3.3)$$

where

$\quad Y_{i,\,t}$ = gross product in constant currency for sector i at time t. Gross national product is the sum of gross product in the rural and urban sectors.

$\quad I_{i,\,t}$ = private investment in constant currency for sector i at time t.

$\quad G_{i,\,t}$ = government expenditures in constant currency in sector i at time t.

$\quad F_{i,\,t}$ = net foreign contribution to sector i at time t, aggregating the value in constant currency of both commodity trade and monetary transfers.

Government expenditures in each sector are determined in the political subsystem which is considered below. These expenditures, however, are based in part on total government revenue, which is a lagged function of the tax base and the effective tax rates.

$$GR_t = \tau_1 Y_{1,\,t-1} + \tau_2 Y_{2,\,t-1} \qquad (3.4)$$

where

GR_t = total government revenue from all revenue generating schemes in constant currency.

τ_i = the effective tax rate in sector i.

Per capita consumption[66] at any time period is a fixed proportion of per capita disposable income in the previous period. Alternatively, consumption at t is a fixed proportion of disposable income at $t-1$, times the proportional increase in population.

$$\frac{C_{i,\,t}}{N_{i,\,t}} = m_i\,(1 - \tau_i)\,\frac{Y_{i,\,t-1}}{N_{i,\,t-1}} \qquad (3.5a)$$

or

$$C_{i,\,t} = m_i\,(1 - \tau_i)\,Y_{i,\,t-1}\,\frac{N_{i,\,t}}{N_{i,\,t-1}} \qquad (3.5b)$$

where

m_i = the proportion of per capita gross disposable income consumed in sector i.

Disposable income is merely income left after taxes $[(1 - \tau_i)Y_{i,\,t-1}]$. According to this relationship, consumption increases as population increases even if disposable income remains constant.

Private investment,[67] the second term in the basic accounting identity, is a function of the investment level of the prior period plus a fixed proportion of the change in consumption from $t - 1$ to t. In per capita terms,

$$\frac{I_{i,\,t}}{N_{i,\,t}} = \frac{I_{i,\,t-1}}{N_{i,\,t-1}} + r_1\left(\frac{C_{i,\,t}}{N_{i,\,t}} - \frac{C_{i,\,t-1}}{N_{i,\,t-1}}\right) \qquad (3.6a)$$

In terms of constant currency,

$$I_{i,\,t} = I_{i,\,t-1}\,\frac{N_{i,\,t}}{N_{i,\,t-1}} + r_i\left(C_{i,\,t} - C_{i,\,t-1}\,\frac{N_{i,\,t}}{N_{i,\,t-1}}\right) \qquad (3.6b)$$

where

r_i = the proportion of the change in per capita consumption which induces additions to (or deletions from) the previous level of investment.

Investment decreases from one period to the next if per capita consumption decreases and increases if per capita consumption increases. Negative investment can be interpreted as withdrawals from the capital stock.

The net contribution of foreign commodity trade and monetary transfers to each sector is exogenous to the model and read in as data. The national economy, in short, is not a closed system but subject to the economic influences of the international system including aid, trade, and private monetary transfers.

POLITICAL SUBSYSTEM

Each sector's support for the government is determined by a scale factor, the penetration of the political system into the sector, the proportion of the sector that participates, the previous level of support, and the change in the sector's economic performance compared with the expected change.

$$V_{i, t} = V_{i, t-1} + \sigma \alpha_i P_{i, t-1} \left[(1 - V_{i, t-1}) V_{i, t-1} \right]^3 \cdot \left[\frac{C_{i, t}}{N_{i, t}} \frac{N_{i, t-1}}{C_{i, t-1}} - E_{i, t-1} \right]$$

$$(3.7)$$

where

$V_{i, t}$ = the proportion of sector i supporting the government at time t.

$E_{i, t}$ = the expected rate of change in economic performance.

σ = the scale of fluctuations in support.

α_i = political penetration, or the proportional extent to which responses to economic performance in sector i are channeled through the government.

Per capita consumption is again taken as the measure of economic performance or the standard of living. Support for the government increases when the rate of change of per capita consumption exceeds the expected rate. Support for the government decreases when the rate of change of per capita consumption falls below the expected rate. The magnitude of fluctuations in support is proportional to the discrepancy between actual and expected changes in economic performance, but the magnitude is also influenced by four other factors. The first is a scale factor which may be given a cultural interpretation. There is no reason to expect, for example, that even under the same circumstances Turks and Filipinos change their support for the government by equal amounts. The second is a political penetration[68] factor which suggests that the giving or withholding of support for the government is only one of many possible responses to changes in the economic situation, but to the extent that the political system is visible in a sector these economic changes stimulate variations in support for the government. The third factor is a participation factor. To the extent that a sector is isolated by gaps in the communications and transportation system, a change in economic performance is only a latent stimulus. The closer α_i and $P_{i, t}$ to their maximum value of one, the larger are changes in support. The fourth factor reflects the idea that both the government and opposition groups have relatively committed reservoirs of support in each sector, and that a part of each sector is relatively uncommitted and therefore more responsive to changes in economic performance. Consequently, larger fluctuations in support occur at the midpoint of the zero (complete nonsupport) to one (complete support) range, and not at the extremes.

Expenditures by the government in each sector vary with the number of people in each sector who support the government, the change in the number of supporters in each sector, and with total government revenues.

$$G_{i,t} = \beta_i \left[\frac{N_{i,t-1}V_{i,t-1} - \Delta(N_iV_i)}{N_{1,t-1}V_{1,t-1} + N_{2,t-1}V_{2,t-1} - \Delta(N_1V_1) - \Delta(N_2V_2)} \right] GR_{t-1}$$

$$(3.8)$$

where

β_i = the relative preference of the government for sector i

and where for convenience

$$\Delta N_i V_i = N_{i,t} V_{i,t} - N_{i,t-1} V_{i,t-1}$$

When the proportions of those in the rural and urban sectors who support the government are approximately equal, the change factors $\Delta N_i V_i$ dominate the allocation of funds. A decline in the number of those who support the government in sector i tends to increase sector i's share of government expenditures. On the other hand, an increase in the number of supporters tends to decrease sector i's share. When the proportions of those in the two sectors who support the government are sufficiently different, the scale factors $N_{i,t-1}V_{i,t-1}$ dominate the behavior of the relationship. Other things being equal, the sector with the higher proportion of supporters tends to receive a larger share of the funds, and the sector with the lower proportion tends to receive a smaller share. It should be noted that total government expenditures equal total government revenues only for very special values of β_1 and β_2. In general, expenditures tend to exceed revenues when support for the government declines.[69] The excess of expenditures over revenues, which can be interpreted as a budgetary deficit, is obtained through borrowing or foreign aid. Thus government expenditures are based on a "pork barrel" rationale, and they are also variable-sum depending on the political situation and the relative preference of the government for each sector.

Government allocations determine immediate political outcomes ("who gets what") in the short run, but they also have cumulative effects, which influence the long-run behavior of the system. Thus a fraction of the funds allocated by the government in each sector is used for the development of the communications and transportation system, as shown in (3.9).

$$D_{i,t} = \gamma_i G_{i,t} \tag{3.9}$$

where

$D_{i,t}$ = government communications and transportation expenditures in constant currency in sector i at time t.

γ_i = the ratio of government communications and transportation expenditures to total government expenditures in sector i.

These communications and transportation expenditures have a direct effect on the proportion of the people who participate in each sector.[70]

$$P_{i,t} = 1 - \left(\frac{\delta_i}{D_{i,\,t-1}}\right), P_{i,t} \geqslant P_{i,t-1} \tag{3.10}$$

where

δ_i = the communications and transportation expenditure in constant currency in sector i at which the communications and transportation system can be maintained with no appreciable effect on participation.

According to this relationship, when the current level of expenditure on communications and transportation in a sector is close to the minimum level, the proportion of people who participate in the sector is close to zero. Equal additional increments in communications and transportation expenditures generate initially large and then diminishing returns in the proportion who participate. At very high expenditure levels, this proportion can approach one. The relationship is constrained such that participation can increase or remain constant, but does not decline: Participation is a one-way street.

Changes in economic expectations in each sector are a function of the difference between actual and expected economic performance among the proportion of each sector that participates.

$$E_{i,t} = E_{i,t-1} + \varepsilon \left(\frac{C_{i,t}}{N_{i,t}} \frac{N_{i,t-1}}{C_{i,t-1}} - E_{i,t-1}\right) P_{i,t-1} \tag{3.11}$$

where

ε = the ratio of the change in the expected rate of economic performance to the difference between the actual and expected rates.

Changes in expected economic performance in each sector are positive when the difference between actual and expected performance is positive, and negative when the difference is negative. For $0 < \varepsilon < 1$, however, changes in expected performance are smaller than the difference between actual and expected performance. Consequently, in periods of relative economic boom, performance exceeds expectations; but in periods of relative recession, expectations exceed performance. Under conditions of long-run stability in economic performance, the expected rate equals the actual rate.

In order to apply the model to historical situations in which changes in government occurred through elections, we have incorporated a crude electoral system, which is summarized in Figure 3.1.

Figure 3.1—A Crude Electoral System

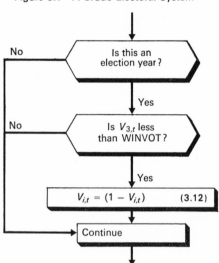

where

> WINVOT = the proportion of aggregate support below which the government loses the election.

At the end of each year's processing, a check is made to determine whether the current year is an election year and whether aggregate support for the government has dropped below the winning level. If both conditions obtain, the former opposition becomes the new government and the support for the former opposition becomes the support for the government according to (3.12). Otherwise, there is no change.

Certainly other variables and relationships (including additional transfers among systems and subsystems) could have been included in the model. But these particular relationships, we feel, constitute a minimal system for the investigation of trends in modernization and mass politics, and additional relationships might significantly increase the complexity of the model without significantly increasing the potential richness of its outputs or its relevance to our research problem.[71]

OPERATION OF THE MODEL

The model stated in this section has been represented as a computer program that calculates time series for each variable given a set of data inputs. This program is listed in Appendix I and examples of its written input display and output are given in Appendix II. The operation of the program is summarized in Figure 3.2. After quantitative values for each of the parameters and each of the variables at $t = 1$ are specified, the program prints these data inputs and then calculates the values of the variables at $t = 2$ and all succeeding time periods. When results for enough time periods have been calculated, they are printed out and processing stops.

4. Turkey and the Philippines: Applications of the Model

PURPOSES AND METHODS

In this section we apply the model to the historical development of Turkey from 1950 to 1960, and of the Philippines from 1951 to 1961. In Turkey the decade of the 1950s began with the electoral victory of the Democratic Party and ended with a military intervention in which the Democratic administration was overthrown. In the Philippines the period from 1951 to 1961 approximates the first decade of effective, independent, mass parties in politics, which developed in the early 1950s with the emergence to national prominence of Magsaysay. Because these are relatively short and politically homogeneous periods, the assumption that the parameters needed to operate the model are constant is a reasonable one.

These applications have three purposes. First, we wish to explore the extent to which the behavior of the model diverges from the historical experience of the political systems it purports to describe. Ideally, differences between generated and historical time series should be attributed to the assumptions in the model alone. But since the behavior of the model in any application depends on its assumptions as well as data inputs, and since the data inputs are often incomplete and to some extent inaccurate, the differences can be attributed to inadequate assumptions *or* to inadequate data. More satisfactory tests must await more complete and accurate data. Second, we need to develop two sets of relatively realistic parameters and initial conditions for the policy explorations described in the next section. In the model as well as in the less developed countries, the implications of similar public

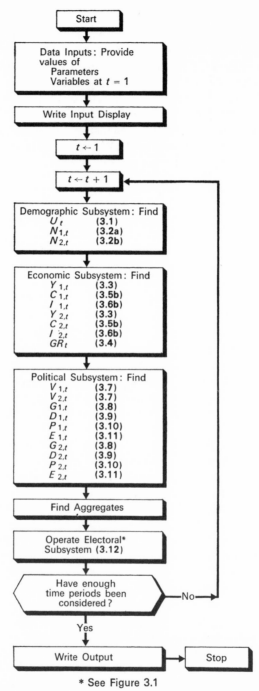

* See Figure 3.1

Figure 3.2—Operation of the Model: Order of Processing

policies are different in different contexts. Given the two sets of data inputs developed in this section, we can use the model to explore tentatively the implications of several policies in countries resembling Turkey and the Philippines. Finally, we hope to illustrate the problems and possibilities of applying the model to historical situations.

The central problem is the setting of parameters. Because much of the relevant data is lacking or inaccurate and because the model's components are interdependent, there is essentially only one way to determine the parameters at this time: Make provisional estimates of the values of the parameters, operate the model using these estimates, and then revise the estimates on the basis of the comparison between the generated time series and whatever time series data are available. Provisional estimates can be made by taking aggregate values based on data and disaggregating them according to known differences between rural and urban areas (as in the case of a_i), or by solving individual relationships for parameters and then plugging in whatever time series data are available (as in the cases of τ_i, β_i, and δ_i, for example). Used in this way the model is a measurement device, and the resulting parameters reflect both the assumptions of the model and the time series data available in each application. In order to disprove the assumptions of the model, it would be necessary to have measures of parameters independent of the assumptions and the historical time series. We shall return to questions of data collection in the Conclusion.

To illustrate the estimating procedure, suppose we have an aggregate growth rate of the population calculated from census data, and we wish to find the rates of natural increase of the rural and urban sectors, a_1 and a_2. Since the rural population is believed to grow faster through natural increase than the urban, a_1 must be greater than a_2. As a first approximation set a_1 slightly higher than the aggregate rate, a_2 lower than the aggregate rate, and set s, the urbanization rate, at a small positive value. Then operate the model to trace out the time series for rural, urban, and total population, and for the number of migrants. Differences between generated and historical time series can then be used to suggest how the original estimates should be modified. For example, if rural population is consistently too high and urban population and the number of migrants consistently too low, then the parameter s should be increased by a small amount and the model operated again to produce a new set of time series. The cycle of comparison and adjustment can then be repeated if necessary.

TURKEY

Population data are available for Turkey for the census years 1950, 1955, and 1960, as shown in Table 4.1a. The urban population is defined as the number of persons living in settlements of greater than 10,000. (We have no explicit sources on the accuracy of Turkish census data.[72]) Accurate data on the amount of natural increase within each sector and migration between them do not exist, but Robinson has estimated that approximately one million people migrated to urban areas from 1950 to 1960 in Turkey.[73]

Data on consumption, investment, and government expenditures in the two sectors are less complete. For each year we know the total value of goods and services produced in the agricultural (including farming, forestry, and fishing) and the non-agricultural sectors of the economy. We have taken these figures as approximations of rural and urban incomes, respectively. In addition, for each year we have estimates of the distribution of the total gross national product in terms of consumption, investment, government expenditures and net foreign trade and monetary transfers. These figures are presented in Table 4.1b. The totals for government expenditures derived from the sources indicated differ considerably from the totals derived from other sources.[74] The maximum discrepancy is about 33% and occurs in 1953. Data on government revenues derived from different sources differ even more and have not been included in this analysis. Finally, we lack data on the amount of consumption, investment, and government expenditures in each sector and the amount of public investment in communications and transportation.

Table 4.1—Data on Turkey

a. Demographic Data (in millions of persons)

POPULATION

	$N_{1,t}$	$N_{2,t}$	$N_{3,t}$
1950	17.024	3.911	20.935
1955	18.640	5.425	24.065
1960	21.697	6.058	27.755

Sources: United Nations, *Demographic Yearbook*, 1952, pp. 194-95.
United Nations, *Demographic Yearbook*, 1962, p. 388.
United Nations, *Demographic Yearbook*, 1963, p. 698.

b. Economic Data (in millions of Turkish Lira at 1948 market prices)

AGRICULTURAL PRODUCT

t	$Y_{1,t}$	$C_{1,t}$	$I_{1,t}$	$G_{1,t}$	$F_{1,t}$	$D_{1,t}$
1950	4,691	—	—	—	—	—
1951	5,659	—	—	—	—	—
1952	6,026	—	—	—	—	—
1953	6,599	—	—	—	—	—
1954	5,306	—	—	—	—	—
1955	5,786	—	—	—	—	—
1956	6,288	—	—	—	—	—
1957	6,450	—	—	—	—	—
1958	7,575	—	—	—	—	—
1959	7,588	—	—	—	—	—
1960	—	—	—	—	—	—

NON-AGRICULTURAL PRODUCT

t	$Y_{2,t}$	$C_{2,t}$	$I_{2,t}$	$G_{2,t}$	$F_{2,t}$	$D_{2,t}$
1950	5,709	—	—	—	—	—
1951	6,329	—	—	—	—	—
1952	6,998	—	—	—	—	—
1953	7,867	—	—	—	—	—
1954	7,839	—	—	—	—	—
1955	8,364	—	—	—	—	—
1956	8,825	—	—	—	—	—
1957	9,618	—	—	—	—	—
1958	10,395	—	—	—	—	—
1959	10,695	—	—	—	—	—
1960	—	—	—	—	—	—

GROSS NATIONAL PRODUCT

t	$Y_{3,t}$	$C_{3,t}{}^*$	$I_{3,t}{}^*$	$G_{3,t}{}^*$	$F_{3,t}{}^*$	$D_{3,t}$	GR_t
1950	10,400	7,800	1,040	1,660	—100	—	—
1951	11,988	—	—	—	—	—	—
1952	13,023	—	—	—	—	—	—
1953	14,467	10,966	1,751	2,098	—362	—	—
1954	13,145	—	—	—	—	—	—
1955	14,151	10,429	2,038	2,066	—382	—	—
1956	15,113	11,229	2,086	2,025	—227	—	—
1957	16,067	—	—	—	—	—	—
1958	17,970	13,747	2,282	2,084	—144	—	—
1959	18,283	13,986	2,560	2,285	—548	—	—
1960	—	—	—	—	—	—	—

*Computed from percentage breakdowns of $Y_{3,t}$.
Sources: United Nations, *Statistical Yearbook*, 1966, p. 540.
  Institute of Statistics, Republic of Turkey, *National Income of Turkey, 1948, 1950-1959*, p. 16.

c. Political Data (proportion of total vote for winning party)

SUPPORT FOR THE GOVERNMENT

t	Winning Party	$V_{1,t}$	$V_{2,t}$	$V_{3,t}$
1950	Democratic Party	—	—	.535
1954	Democratic Party	—	—	.566
1957	Democratic Party	—	—	.478

Source: K. H. Karpat, "The Turkish Elections of 1957," *Western Political Quarterly*, vol 14 (June 1961), p. 459.

Of the relevant political data only the aggregate proportional vote for the governing party is available from election returns for the election years 1950, 1954, and 1957. These are given in Table 4.1c. Direct measures of support within each sector, participation levels, and expectation levels are not available.

Using these data and by the procedures discussed above, we have arrived at the estimates of parameters and initial conditions presented in Table 4.2. These estimates incorporate qualitative constraints reflecting

Table 4.2—Parameters and Initial Conditions for Turkey

a. Parameters

	a_i	m_i	r_i	τ_i	α_i	β_i	γ_i	δ_i
Rural	.029	.935	.200	.020	.800	.500	.120	47.0
Urban	.026	.885	.600	.260	.990	3.60	.120	17.0

$$s = .002 \qquad \sigma = 50.0 \qquad \varepsilon = .100$$

b. Initial Conditions (1950)

	$N_{i,1}$	$C_{i,1}$	$I_{i,1}$	$G_{i,1}$	$V_{i,1}$	$D_{i,1}$	$P_{i,1}$	$E_{i,1}$
Rural	17.024	4090	40	560	.535	70	.60	1.03
Urban	3.911	3610	1000	1100	.535	110	.90	1.03

$$GR_1 = 1400$$

differences between rural and urban areas in Turkey. The rates of natural increase a_i and consumption m_i are believed to be higher in the rural areas of Turkey than in the urban areas. The rates of induced investment r_i, taxes τ_i, and political penetration α_i are believed to be higher in the urban areas than in the rural areas. Furthermore, investment in 1950, $I_{i,1}$, and participation in 1950, $P_{i,1}$, are believed to have been higher in urban areas. Of the initial conditions, only population $N_{i,1}$ has been measured directly, although initial conditions for rural and urban sectors must sum to the national totals given in Table 4.1b. Since the foreign contribution to the economy of Turkey as a percentage of GNP ranges from only -1% to slightly less than -3% during the 1950's, the foreign sector has been excluded from the analysis.

The inputs in Table 4.2 are sufficient to generate time series outputs for any number of years from 1950. However, in order to incorporate into this application the massive effects of some factors not included in the model, we have included an exogenous input that yields a decline in rural income of approximately 1.3 billion T.L. from 1953 to 1954. Prior to 1954, agricultural income expanded rapidly due to an increase in area under cultivation, good weather, and government subsidy, credit, mechanization and land reform programs designed to stimulate the agricultural sector. Much of the expansion was financed by foreign aid. But the boom slowed down as difficulties of repayment abroad mounted, the droughts of 1954 and 1955 drastically reduced the volume of agricultural products available for export, American economic aid failed to reach sufficient volume, and the United States refused a $300 million loan requested by the Turkish government. Farm income, which seemed to be concentrated in the hands of a few large landowners, was spent on luxuries rather than invested, and it remained untaxed. The lack of imported raw materials and spare parts for farm equipment cut into production.[75] "In short, 1954 marked the end of a series of bumper crops and of a relatively easy foreign credit market."[76] "Nonetheless, the government refused to slow down; the investment program had to be maintained or Turkey's economic—and hence, political—future would be imperiled."[77] Aggregate government expenditures in the rural sector have been included in the model; but the expansion of cultivated area into marginal lands, the breakdown of tractors and inability to repair them, and the drop in rainfall are factors not included. Small effects produced by exogenous factors can be ignored, but effects of this magnitude cannot.

Using these inputs, the model generated a set of time series which are listed in full in Appendix 2. Those outputs for which we have comparable historical data are compared with those data in Figure 4.1. Data points are

Figure 4.1—Comparison of Historical and Generated
Time Series for Turkey

a. Population Time Series: Turkey

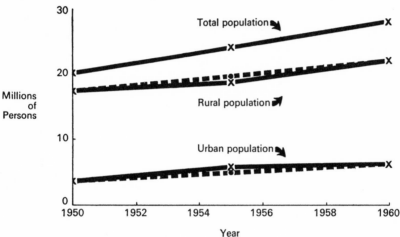

b. Economic Time Series: Turkey

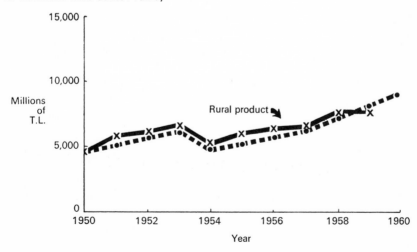

b. Economic Time Series : Turkey (Cont.)

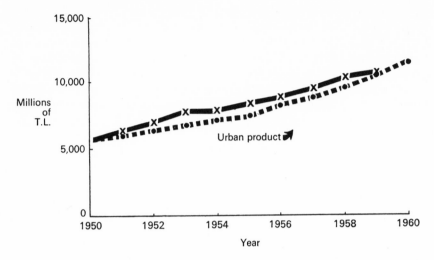

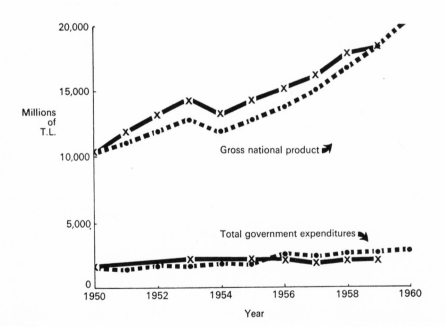

c. Political Support Time Series: Turkey

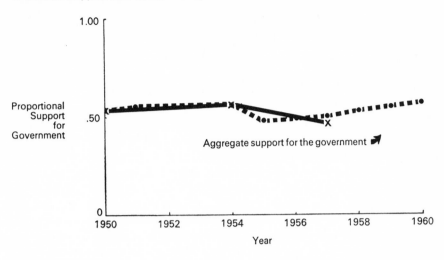

indicated by x's and connected by solid lines; model outputs are connected by dotted lines. The demographic subsystem produces results quite close to the data for 1960, but not quite so close for 1955. The model generates a rural population of 19.232 million for 1955, an error of about 590,000 or about 3% *higher* than the actual population. It generates an urban population of 4.852 million in 1955, an error of about 570,000 or about 11% *lower* than the actual figure as measured in the census. Differences between results and data are less than 50,000 for both the rural and urban sectors in 1960, and errors of this magnitude are probably well within the range of reasonable error in the Turkish census data. The model also generates 863,000 migrants from rural to urban areas in the decade of the 1950's, a result of the same order of magnitude as Robinson's very rough estimate that approximately one million people urbanized in this period.

Differences between the generated and the historical economic time series for which we have data are small by the standards of cross-national, cross-sectional data analyses, but significant in terms of this analysis. As shown in Figure 4.1b, the maximum error of about 12% in rural income occurs in 1954, and the maximum error of about 14% in urban income occurs in 1953. More seriously, the forms of the historical and generated time series are different. For rural, urban, and gross national product, the model underestimates economic gains throughout most of the decade and produces rapid and unwarranted growth near the end of the decade. In broad terms, the data suggest that economic growth in Turkey after 1954 was at best linear and perhaps leveling off. The model on the other hand produces a pattern of increasing gains in economic growth that is almost geometric in form. Furthermore, in the time series data the effects of agricultural problems in 1954 appear in the non-agricultural time series in the same year, but in the results they are lagged by one year. In short, the model produces too great a time lag in tracing effects across economic sectors.

Percentage errors in support for the government in the election years 1954 and 1957 are relatively small, but again the form of the errors appears to be significant. In 1954 the level of support for the governing party produced by the model is .561, which is a change in the right direction from the initial level but slightly less than the level of .566 computed from election returns. In 1957 the level of support produced by the model is .514, a change in the right direction from the 1954 level but still between 7 and 8% more than the actual level of .478. In short, the model slightly underestimates the degree of support for the ruling Democratic Party in the boom years up to 1954, and overestimates the degree of support after the depression of 1954, but the direction of change through time is correct.

These divergences between historical and generated time series for population, economic growth, and political support are interrelated and appear to have a common basis. As we have seen, the rural and urban sectors of the economy in this application of the model grow too slowly in the early years of the decade and too rapidly in the later years. A more realistic pattern of economic growth, in which growth is initially rapid and then levels off, would have increased urbanization by 1955 without necessarily exceeding the urbanization level of 1960, as can be deduced from relationship (3.1). Consequently, the errors in the distribution of population at the middle of the decade would have been reduced. Similarly, a more realistic pattern of economic growth would have increased support for the government in 1954 and decreased it in 1957 according to relationship (3.7), thus reducing the errors in this time series.

The root of the problem seems to lie in the particular pattern of economic growth generated by the model, and this seems to have been a result of the pattern of government expenditures. As we have seen there are at least two rather inconsistent sets of data for Turkish government expenditures in the 1950's. Of the two, we have used the set with consistently higher expenditure levels, and the model produces time series that exceed even these high estimates. The generated level of government expenditures is 2.68 billion T.L. in 1959, which is 17% greater than the high estimate of 2.29 billion for the same year. In short, the model's behavior is such that too much public money is pumped into the agricultural and non-agricultural sectors of the economy and there is no realistic or effective brake on the level of government spending.

This analysis suggests two lines of further work in reducing errors in the application of the model to Turkish time series data. The first is to determine more accurately how much the Turkish government received and spent in the decade of the 1950's. The second is to explore a variety of mechanisms that seem to be plausible constraints on the expenditure of government funds. One such mechanism might reduce the politically desirable level of expenditures as a function of the size of the public debt or the government's national and international credit positions. Such a mechanism seems plausible in the light of the Turkish experience. According to an OEEC mission to Turkey in 1959, " 'The difficulties in which the Turkish economy finds itself today stem basically from an attempt to do too much too quickly.' "[78] But for political reasons, the Menderes government was not inclined to cut back the pace of government expenditures voluntarily. Even a $359 million loan, for which Menderes promised financial reforms of an anti-inflationary nature, proved to be only a temporary measure and was used up by 1960, only two years after it was negotiated. In spite of the pressure to continue the pace of government spending, and some limited international aid to enable the Turkish government to do so, the level of government expenditures as a percentage of GNP dropped from 16% in 1950 to about 12.8% in 1960. In short, the resource constraints operating in the historical situation have no counterpart operating in the model.

THE PHILIPPINES

Population census data were collected in the Philippines in 1948 and 1960, although the 1948 results are likely to contain large errors because the HUKs were almost in control in many parts of the country and a typhoon struck during the census period.[79] These data are presented in Table 4.3a. If we define as urban the number of persons living in a settlement of greater than 10,000 as we did for Turkey, then 85.7% of the Philippine population in 1948 would be considered urban. In fact, in 1948 as well as in 1960 most observers would agree that a majority of the Philippine population did not possess those qualities of modernity associated with urbanism. Both the *poblacion* pattern of settlement and the geography of the land appear to contribute to the maintenance of relatively traditional styles of life in relatively large settlements.[80] Consequently, for the application of the model to the Philippines we have defined urban as the number of persons living in settlements of greater than 50,000. As in the Turkish case, reliable data on differential rates of natural population increase and migration between the rural and urban areas do not exist.[81]

We have again taken agricultural product (including farming, fishing, and forestry) as an approximation of rural income and non-agricultural product as an approximation of urban income. Also, as in the Turkish case, percentage breakdowns of gross national product in terms of consumption, investment, government expenditures and net foreign trade and transfers are available. However, for the Philippines we have in addition some reliable approximations of government expenditures disaggregated into rural and urban sectors. We also have data on government revenue and on government capital outlays that can be taken as an approximation of government development expenditures. These data are presented in Table 4.3b. It should be noted, however, that critics of Philippine national accounts statistics have gone so far as to suggest that these statistics are useless for most purposes of analysis and projection.[82] Disaggregated estimates of consumption, investment, revenues, and development expenditures are not available.

Table 4.3—Data on the Philippines

a. Demographic Data (in millions of persons)

POPULATION

t	$N_{1,t}$	$N_{2,t}$	$N_{3,t}$
1948 *	15.843	3.391	19.234
1951 (est.)	17.020	4.180	21.200
1960†	19.652	7.803	27.455

Sources: *United Nations, *Demographic Yearbook*, 1955, p. 206.
†United Nations, *Demographic Yearbook*, 1962, p. 387.

b. Economic Data (in millions in pesos at 1951 market prices)

AGRICULTURAL PRODUCT

t	$Y_{1,t}$§	$C_{1,t}$	$I_{1,t}$	$G_{1,t}$‖	$F_{1,t}$	$D_{1,t}$
1951	2,780	—	—	164	—	—
1952	2,810	—	—	191	—	—
1953	3,030	—	—	198	—	—
1954	3,110	—	—	199	—	—
1955	3,140	—	—	215	—	—
1956	3,180	—	—	228	—	—
1957	3,250	—	—	243	—	—
1958	3,240	—	—	268	—	—
1959	3,420	—	—	270	—	—
1960	3,530	—	—	300	—	—

NON-AGRICULTURAL PRODUCT

t	$Y_{2,t}$	$C_{2,t}$	$I_{2,t}$	$G_{2,t}$	$F_{2,t}$	$D_{2,t}$
1951	3,707	—	—	562	—	—
1952	3,744	—	—	664	—	—
1953	3,985	—	—	665	—	—
1954	4,035	—	—	819	—	—
1955	4,484	—	—	846	—	—
1956	5,234	—	—	979	—	—
1957	5,568	—	—	1,072	—	—
1958	6,196	—	—	1,058	—	—
1959	6,595	—	—	1,012	—	—
1960	6,962	—	—	1,196	—	—

GROSS NATIONAL PRODUCT

t	$Y_{3,t}$	$C_{3,t}$‡#	$I_{3,t}$‡	$G_{3,t}$	$F_{3,t}$**	$D_{3,t}$††	GR_t‡‡
1951	6,487	5,440	321	726	—	43.4	512
1952	6,554	—	—	855	—	54.4	736
1953	7,015	5,950	491	863	—	53.0	696
1954	7,145	—	—	1,018	—	95.1	733
1955	7,624	6,395	163	1,061	—	96.6	752
1956	8,414	—	—	1,207	—	126.4	809
1957	8,818	—	—	1,316	—	140.1	895
1958	9,436	7,910	—	1,327	—	124.4	854
1959	10,015	—	—	1,282	—	108.1	913
1960	10,492	8,800	196	1,496	—	130.6	1,067

‡Computed from percentage breakdown of $Y_{3,t}$.
Sources: § A. B. Abello, *Patterns of Philippine Public Expenditure and Revenue, 1951-1960* (Quezon City; University of the Philippines, Institute of Economic Development and Research, 1964), Table 5, p. 9 [Hereafter: Abello, *Patterns....*] Cf. also United Nations, *Statistical Yearbook*, 1966, p. 568 for the percentage breakdowns.
∥Abello, *Patterns ...* , Table 1, p. 5 [derived from Budget Commission, *Budget*, FY1953-1960; General Auditing Office, *Report of the Auditor General to the President and the Congress of the Philippines on the Local Government*, FY1951-1960; and, National Economic Council, *Statistical Reporter*, vol. III (April, 1959), p. 12 and vol. VI (April, 1961), p. 9.]
#United Nations, *Statistical Yearbook*, 1966, pp. 553, 559.
**Foreign data are available but were not used in this analysis. Cf. United Nations, *Economic Bulletin for Asia and Far East*, vol. 8, no. 2, p. 33; vol. 11, no. 3, p. 67; and, vol. 15, no. 1, p. 77. The contribution of $F_{3,t}$ in any given year is 4.0% of gross national product for the period of the analysis.
††Abello, *Patterns* .. , Table 13, p. 18 and Table 14, p. 18.
‡‡Ibid., Table 35, p. 49 [derived from *Report of the Auditor General ...* (National and Local), FY 1951-1960].

c. *Political Data (proportion of total vote for winning party)*

SUPPORT FOR THE GOVERNMENT (PRESIDENTIAL ELECTION)

t	Winning Party		$V_{1,t}$	$V_{2,t}$	$V_{3,t}$§§
1949	Liberal	(Quirino)	—	—	.510
1953	Nacionalista	(Magsaysay)	—	—	.670
1957	Nacionalista	(Garcia)	—	—	.413
1961	Liberals—"United Opposition"				
		(Macapagal)	—	—	.535

Sources: §§Carl H. Landé, *Leaders, Factions, and Parties: The Structure of Philippine Politics* (Yale Southeast Asia Studies, monograph no. 6, 1964), Figure I and p. 66; and, Republic of the Philippines, Commission on Elections, *Canvas of Votes Cast for President and Vice President of the Philippines in the Regular Elections Held on November 12, 1957*, NUC 1959/62: 38:23. (Mimeo.) *Ibid., November 4, 1961, Presidential Election*, dated 7/16/64. (Mimeo.) (These latter two documents have been microfilmed as Yale Library #S193#1.)

Of the political data, the aggregate proportional support for the governing party is available from election returns for the years 1949, 1953, 1957, and 1961. These are given in Table 4.3c. We do not have direct measures of disaggregated support, participation levels and expectation levels.

Using these data and the estimation procedures discussed above, we have set parameters and initial conditions for the Philippines as indicated in Table 4.4. These estimates incorporate qualitative constraints reflecting differences between the rural and urban areas in the Philippines. The rates of natural increase a_i and consumption m_i are believed to be higher in the rural area than the urban. The rates of effective tax return τ_i[83] and political penetration α_i are believed to be higher in the urban areas than the rural. Additionally, investment $I_{i,1}$ and participation $P_{i,1}$ in 1951 are believed to have been higher in urban areas. The negative value of r_2, which somewhat implausibly implies withdrawals of investment as demand increases, may be a result of inaccurate national accounts data. One critic of these data has argued that the gross domestic investment component of GNP in the Philippines was underestimated by about 40%.[84]

Table 4.4—Parameters and Initial Conditions for the Philippines

a. Parameters

	a_i	m_i	r_i	τ_i	α_i	β_i	γ_i	δ_i
Rural	.0312	.9497	.0724	.0280	.9200	.4160	.2040	17.75
Urban	.0229	.9146	−1.10	.1410	.9950	5.107	.0805	14.46

$$s = .0055 \qquad \sigma = 80.0 \qquad \varepsilon = .150 \qquad WINVOT = .500$$

b. Initial Conditions

	$N_{i,1}$	$C_{i,1}$	$I_{i,1}$	$G_{i,1}$	$V_{i,1}$	$D_{i,1}$	$P_{i,1}$	$E_{i,1}$
Rural	17.02	2585	31	164	.490	33.4	.57	1.030
Urban	4.18	2855	290	562	.480	45.2	.68	1.035

$$GR_1 = 512$$

These inputs together with the model have generated time series ouptuts which are compared with the available data in Figure 4.2. The demographic subsystem has reproduced results that are close to the published census data for 1960. The model generated a 1960 rural population of 19.655 million, only 3,000 more than the census figure, and an urban population of 7.824 million people, only 21,000 more than the census figure. Neither the size of the population between 1948 and 1960 nor the number of migrants in the decade can be checked directly. However, in this run of the model, migration slowly increased from 240 thousand per year to 334 thousand in 1960. The cumulative migrant population generated by the model from 1951 to 1960 was 2.79 million.

As shown in Figure 4.2b, the maximum error in rural income is −6% (1954), in urban income is 13% (1955), and in gross national product is 10.4% (1954). From 1956 on, the average error between the outputs and data for rural, urban, and total income is on the order of ± 2%. The magnitudes of these errors suggest that the model reproduces the basic trends in the data quite well. However, one aspect of the fine structure of the data series not reproduced by the model is the relative boom in rural income and stagnation in urban income from 1952 to 1954, and the relative stagnation in rural income and boom in urban income from 1954 to 1956.

Figure 4.2—Comparison of Historical and Generated
Time Series for the Philippines

a. Population Time Series: Philippines

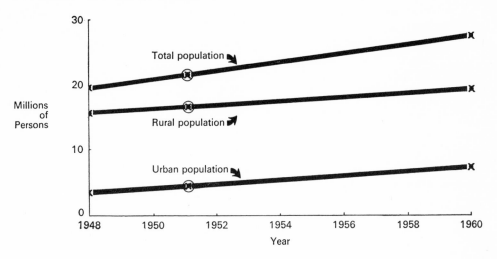

b. Economic Time Series: Philippines

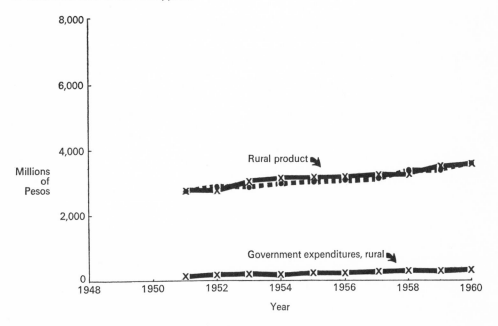

b. Economic Time Series : Philippines (Cont.)

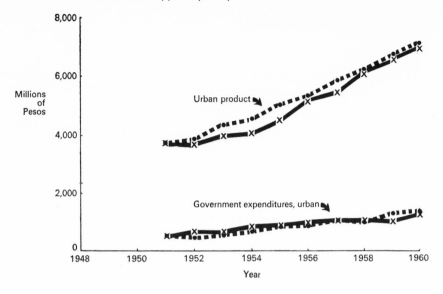

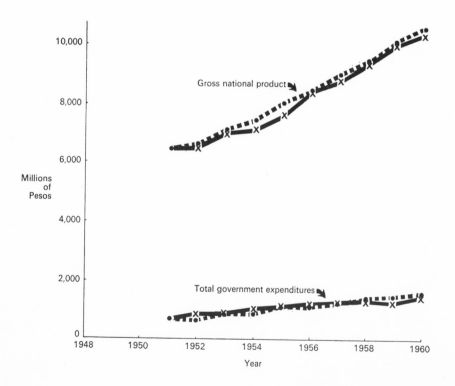

c. Political Support Time Series: Philippines

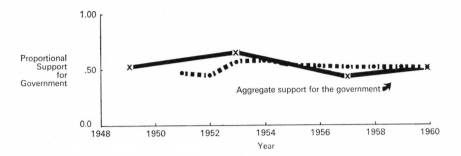

The maximum errors in rural, urban, and total government expenditures are -10.9% (1952), -12.2% (1954), and -13.3% (1952), respectively. Again, the model appears to have reproduced the secular trend. However, there is an interesting pattern in the year-to-year deviations between generated and actual government expenditures in the urban sector. When the data show an increase from one year to the next, the model gives a decrease, and vice versa, producing a "diamond" pattern when generated and data series are plotted together.

The political outputs of the model correspond reasonably well to the actual events. The model reproduced the landslide victory of Magsaysay and the Nacionalista ticket over the Liberals in the election of 1953. Although the precise distribution of support for Magsaysay in this election is not known, Landé suggests that he did well in all sectors, but better in the urban than in the rural.[85] The model produces a support level of .590 in the urban areas and .555 in the rural. The magnitude of the victory is an index of the growing disenchantment felt toward the "old" Illustrado politics and politicians. In 1957, the Nacionalistas were able to maintain control in spite of Magsaysay's tragic death a few months before the election. The Nacionalistas received only 41.3% of the vote, reflecting the hasty entry of several badly divided and ineffective opposition parties. In 1961, the Nacionalistas lost the Presidential election to Macapagal, standard bearer of the Liberal Party, who was supported by the "United Opposition." The model produces a declining level of support in this period, but the level does not drop below a majority. In general, the model tends to underestimate the size of fluctuations in support, as shown in Figure 4.2c.

Although participation data are not available, the model produces trends in participation that are consistent with the judgments of Corpuz and others.[86] The participation rate in the rural sector seems to have been

stable up to 1954–1955 and then increased at a fairly steady rate as the
"Magsaysay Revolution" penetrated into the barrios. In this run participation began to increase in 1954 and by 1961 had grown from .57 to .71.

The errors in the demographic and political outputs of the model as
applied to the Philippines are small enough that they do not require detailed
consideration. The errors in the economic outputs, while small, in one case
highlight some historical events exogenous to the model, and in another
suggest a possible revision of the model. The sharp gain in rural income from
1952 to 1954 is related to growing security in central Luzon as the HUK
rebellion was put down. The decline in urban income in the same period
reflects the general slowdown in economic growth in Southeast Asia following
the end of the Korean War. The diamond pattern formed by the joint plot
of generated and actual government expenditures in the urban sector suggests
that the time lag between the political stimulus for reallocation of funds and
actual allocation is not sufficiently large. If the generated time series is
shifted one year forward, the generated and actual series move into phase.
The larger average errors produced by this shift can be reduced by increasing
β_2. Consequently, $G_{i,t}$ in (3.8) might be advanced another period to become
$G_{i,t+1}$. The Philippine government, in effect, appears to respond more slowly
than the model presently suggests.

COMPARING TURKEY AND THE PHILIPPINES

According to the interpretation presented in section 2, countries are
similar with respect to the processes that operate in each of them and may
differ with respect to the parameters that govern the operation of these
processes in each individual country. Following this interpretation and given
different initial conditions for each country, let us consider differences between Turkey and the Philippines in the parameters that govern the growth
and distribution of the time series we have just described.

A comparison of rates of natural increase a_i in Tables 4.2 and 4.4
suggests that the aggregate rate of natural increase for these two countries
is approximately the same. However, differences in natural increase rates
across rural and urban sectors are much larger in the Philippines. Considering
natural increase alone, the rural population in the Philippines grows at a
rate 36% faster than the urban rate, but the rural population in Turkey
grows at a rate only 11% faster than the urban rate. Taken together with a
much higher urbanization rate s in the Philippines, these parameter settings
suggest that compared with Turkey, the urban population in the Philippines
has grown much more through urbanization than through processes of
natural increase.

Propensities to consume m_i are high in both countries and higher in
rural than in urban areas, but the urban population in Turkey according to

this analysis consumes at a lower rate than the urban population in the Philippines. Rates of induced investment r_i are much higher in Turkey than in the Philippines, possibly reflecting the cross-national differences in perceptions about the climate for investment. Other things being equal, these parameter settings suggest more economic growth potential in Turkey than in the Philippines.

Inequalities in tax rates τ_i and the relative preference of the government for each sector β_i are similar in Turkey and the Philippines. In both countries the urban sector bears a relatively large tax burden, but the urban sector is much more favored in the allocation of government funds as reflected in the magnitudes of β_i. Compared with the Philippines, however, the rural sector in Turkey is taxed relatively less and favored relatively more by the allocation of government funds.

Based on a comparison between σ and ε, which reflect underlying propensities to give or withhold support and to modify expectations about the standard of living, the Turkish electorate appears to be inherently more stable in these aspects of its political behavior than the Philippine electorate.

5. Exploring the Implications of Public Policy

POLICY AND SENSITIVITY ANALYSIS

Having specified a model and developed two sets of inputs, we can now focus directly on the implications of several public policies for trends in modernization and mass politics and indirectly on institutionalization and the succession dilemma. A technique well-suited to this task is sensitivity analysis.

Sensitivity analysis is based on the fact that the behavior of a model of this type in any application is determined by the assumptions built into it and by the inputs that reflect the salient characteristics of each particular case. The inputs may be either initial conditions, the values of variables at the start of the analysis; or parameters, the underlying, unchanging rates and thresholds that govern the operation of the processes built into the model.

The relative impact of the relationships, initial conditions, and parameters can be determined by making systematic changes in them, operating the model, and then comparing the resulting time series with those generated in the reference runs described in the previous section. The major limitation of sensitivity analysis is that there are no obvious bounds to the set of possible modifications. For each relationship there are a large number of possible qualitative alternatives, and for each data input there are a large number of possible quantitative alternatives. Furthermore, for quantitative variations in inputs there may exist scale effects such that changes of different magnitudes in any parameter or initial condition may generate qualitatively different time series or quantitative differences out of proportion to the magnitude of the initial difference. The implications of each unique combination of relationships, initial conditions, and parameters must be traced out individually.

Here we shall explore the implications of 5% changes in those parameters in Table 4.2 and 4.4 having obvious policy interpretations. Birth control programs, for example, could achieve decreases in the rate of natural increase a_i. Austerity programs could effectively reduce the rate of consumption m_i. Variations in τ_i could result from the modification of tax laws or revenue collection procedures or both. Variations in β_i could result from the government's changing its political priorities in favor of one sector or the other. These parameter changes are summarized in Table 5.1. For each individual change, the model is operated from 1950 in the case of Turkey or 1951 in the case of the Philippines to 1965. The resulting time series are compared with those generated by the inputs displayed in Tables 4.2 and 4.4, which we shall call the *reference runs*. The outputs of the reference runs are summarized in Table 5.2 and presented in full in Appendix 2. As a representation of some of the important processes operating in developing political systems, the model suggests that governments respond to problems of political support by allocating public funds; as a tool for the exploration of problems like institutionalization and the succession dilemma, the model suggests and facilitates the evaluation of a broader range of potential policies.

In performing these policy explorations, we are in effect temporarily accepting our initial characterization of Turkey in 1950 and the Philippines in 1951 even though these characterizations are based on incomplete and in some cases inaccurate data. More importantly, we are temporarily accepting the relationships built into the model even though several modifications have already been suggested. Thus strictly speaking, we are investigating situations only resembling those which existed in Turkey and the Philippines, and we are investigating the properties of the model rather than the empirical systems it purports to describe. As each improved set of data is collected and each improved version of the model is constructed, statements about the real world can perhaps be made with some confidence. In the meantime, it is worthwhile to subject our current formulations, both historical and theoretical, to the discipline of these sensitivity analyses in order to generate some provisional answers to our research problem and to uncover additional weaknesses in this analysis.

Table 5.1—Parameter Changes Having Policy Interpretations*

	TURKEY	PHILIPPINES
1. Birth Control Programs		
In rural sector	$a_1 = .0275$	$a_1 = .0296$
In urban sector	$a_2 = .0247$	$a_2 = .0218$
2. Austerity Programs		
In rural sector	$m_1 = .8882$	$m_1 = .9022$
In urban sector	$m_2 = .8407$	$m_2 = .8689$
3. Urban Tax Policy		
Decrease in tax rate	$\tau_2 = .0190$	$\tau_2 = .0266$
Increase in tax rate	$\tau_2 = .0210$	$\tau_2 = .0294$
4. Changed Political Priorities		
In favor of rural sector	$\beta_1 = .5250$	$\beta_1 = .4368$
In favor of urban sector	$\beta_2 = 3.780$	$\beta_2 = 5.362$

*Each entry for each country represents a single run of the model. Parameter settings represent 5% changes from the settings used in the reference runs and displayed in Tables 4.2 and 4.4. All other inputs remain the same.

Table 5.2—Outputs of the Reference Runs

		Turkey			Philippines		
		RURAL	URBAN	AGGREGATE	RURAL	URBAN	AGGREGATE
Standard	1955	229	1007	385	151	691	278
of	1960	344	1188	527	161	728	323
Living *	1965	610	1704	862	187	722	365
Support	1955	.476	.498	.481	.529	.568	.538
for	1960	.585	.529	.573	.510	.519	.513
Gov't	1965	.706	.658	.695	.551	.434	.512

*The standard of living is per capita consumption in local currency in this table and the tables that follow.

BIRTH CONTROL PROGRAMS

Five per cent decreases in the rates of natural increase a_i, the possible effects of birth control programs, have small direct effects on the size of the population in the Turkish sensitivity analysis, and, consequently, small indirect effects on the standard of living and the level of support for the government. These effects are summarized in Table 5.3. A decrease in the rural rate of natural increase a_1 produces a population in 1970 that is only 833,000 less than the population of 36.621 million produced in the reference run. This slower rate of population growth has the effect of slightly increasing the level of support for the government compared with the level in the reference run, but never more than .01. It also has the effect of boosting the standard of living in both sectors, with the increases in the urban sector being somewhat larger.

Table 5.3—Outcomes of Birth Control Programs: Deviations from the Reference Runs

In Rural Sector

		TURKEY			PHILIPPINES		
		Rural	Urban	Aggregate	Rural	Urban	Aggregate
Standard	1955	0	1	1	0	0	0
of	1960	2	6	5	1	1	2
Living *	1965	9	36	19	2	1	3
Support	1955	.000	.001	.000	.000	.001	.001
for	1960	.002	.004	.002	.002	.001	.001
Government	1965	.003	.010	.005	.004	.001	.002

In Urban Sector

		TURKEY			PHILIPPINES		
		Rural	Urban	Aggregate	Rural	Urban	Aggregate
Standard	1955	0	2	0	0	0	—1
of	1960	—1	2	—1	0	0	—1
Living *	1965	—4	1	—6	0	0	—2
Support	1955	.000	.001	.000	.000	.000	.000
for	1960	—.001	.001	.000	.000	—.001	—.001
Government	1965	—.002	.000	—.001	—.002	.000	—.001

*In this table and the following tables, fractions have been ignored in the calculation of deviations from the standard of living in the reference run.

A decrease of 5% in the urban rate of natural increase a_2 generates a total population in 1970 that is only 193,000 less than the total population in the reference run. The lower rate of urban growth slightly improves the support for the government and the standard of living in the urban areas, and it slightly decreases support and the standard of living in rural areas. The differences relative to the reference run are considerably less than 1%.

These small deviations from the reference run make it difficult to trace with confidence the adjustments that underlie the model's behavior. Other things being equal, a decrease in the ratio of population in one year to population in the previous year will decrease the value of consumption according to (3.5b). But a decrease in the same ratio will generate increased difference through time in consumption and therefore increased investment according to (3.6b). In short, a reduction in population pressure both depresses consumption and stimulates investment. Depending on the magnitudes of these two effects income may decrease or increase. When the rural rate of natural increase is lowered by 5%, the relative increases in aggregate investment are sufficient to boost aggregate consumption above the reference level by 1964. But when the urban rate of natural increase is lowered by 5%, the losses in consumption are enough to eliminate potential increases in investment. The magnitude of the decline in population pressure in these runs is influenced by urbanization. Through urbanization, a decrease in the rural rate of natural increase will not only decrease the size of the rural population, it will also decrease the number of migrants and therefore the size of the urban population. These reductions in rural population (523,000 by 1965) and urban population (16,000 by 1965) seem to have beneficial effects. But urbanization does not redistribute population from urban to rural areas. Consequently, a decrease in the urban rate of natural increase reduces rural population by only 3,000 by 1965 and decreases urban population by 120,000 by 1965. The reduction in population pressure in the rural sector seems to have been too small and the reduction in the urban sector too large for wide-spread improvements in the standard of living.

In the Philippine sensitivity analysis a 5% decrease in the rural rate of natural increase a_1 produces a population in 1970 that is only 772,000 smaller than the population of 35.615 million produced in the reference run. As shown in Table 5.3, this change generates very small improvements in both the standard of living and support for the government. A corresponding decrease in the urban rate of natural increase a_2 generates a population in 1970 that is only 199,000 smaller. Economic performance and support for the government either remain the same or decline very slightly.

As in the Turkish sensitivity analysis, deviations from the reference run in the Philippine sensitivity analysis are small, which makes it difficult to trace the pattern of adjustments that account for the model's behavior. The important adjustments, however, seem to be the same as in the Turkish case. When the rural rate of natural increase is decreased by 5%, the relative increases in aggregate investment are sufficient to boost aggregate consumption above the reference levels by 1967. But when the urban rate of natural increase is lowered by 5%, the losses in consumption, although not quite eliminating increases in investment, do effectively neutralize them. Aggregate investment in 1965 is only 2 million pesos greater than the reference level of 373 million pesos. As in the Turkish runs, the effects of a decreased rural natural increase rate diffuse into both sectors through urbanization, but the effects of a decrease in the urban rate are effectively isolated. In the first case, the reduction of population pressures generates very small improvements in the economic and political situation, but in the second case neither the individual sectors nor the government benefits. Five per cent decreases in a_i are not sufficient to produce dramatic changes in time series outputs.

AUSTERITY PROGRAMS

As shown in Table 5.4, decreases in rates of consumption m_i, interpreted as the effects of austerity programs, have generally negative implications both from the political viewpoint of the government and the economic viewpoint of the sectors in the Turkish sensitivity analysis. Compared with the reference run, a decrease in m_1, the rate of consumption in rural areas, generates large declines in support for the government in the rural area and in the rural

Table 5.4—Outcomes of Austerity Programs:
Deviations from the Reference Runs

In Rural Sector

| | | TURKEY | | | PHILIPPINES | | |
		Rural	Urban	Aggregate	Rural	Urban	Aggregate
Standard	1955	—74	4	—57	—28	—12	—22
of	1960	—185	88	—115	—55	5	—25
Living	1965	—310	1729	312	—75	—26	—29
Support	1955	—.123	.003	—.097	.017	—.003	.013
for	1960	—.212	.113	—.137	—.064	.027	—.037
Government	1965	—.105	.187	—.026	.073	—.049	.020

In Urban Sector

| | | TURKEY | | | PHILIPPINES | | |
		Rural	Urban	Aggregate	Rural	Urban	Aggregate
Standard	1955	—4	—273	—59	0	—24	7
of	1960	—71	—982	—268	—1	—35	—12
Living	1965	*	*	*	—3	—7	—7
Support	1955	—.005	—.172	—.039	.002	.035	.010
for	1960	—.080	—.409	—.048	—.001	.033	.008
Government	1965	*	*	*	—.008	.084	.022

standard of living. These two trends reach low points of .353 and 154 T.L. per capita, respectively, in 1955. For the next seven years there are slow annual gains in the rural standard of living and relatively rapid gains in rural support for the government. After about 1963 the standard of living grows rapidly, and gains in support tend to taper off, surpassing the levels attained in the reference run. In contrast, in the urban sector after 1954 both support for the government and the standard of living begin to show large and continuing gains over the levels attained in the reference run. Given the relative weight of the rural population, the aggregate support and standard of living levels remain below those of the reference run at least through 1962.

A decrease in m_2, the rate of consumption in urban areas, has even more serious effects: Political support and consumption per capita at no time exceed the levels attained in the reference run. While the rural sector does experience some moderate year-to-year increases in per capita consumption up to 1962, the urban level of per capita consumption decreases at a moderate rate up to 1954 and decreases very rapidly thereafter. The government maintains a majority in the rural sector up to 1960, but urban support is very low and aggregate support is only .425 in that year. In short, austerity programs according to this model and Turkish inputs generate large costs to the government in terms of political support and unevenly distributed but (even in the aggregate) significant costs to the people in terms of the standard of living.

The direct effect of a decrease in m_i is to decrease per capita consumption according to (3.5b), and this accounts for much of the behavior of the model in this context. Given relationship (3.6a) and positive rates of induced investment r_i, increases through time in per capita consumption stimulate increases through time in per capita investment. However, other things being equal, a decrease in m_i has the effect of decreasing both initial and subsequent per capita gains in consumption, thus reducing gains in per capita investment, and finally reducing the level of income available for consumption in the next period. Since $r_2 > r_1$, a 5% decrease in m_2 has a much greater impact than a 5% decrease in m_1. The general deterioration in both political support and the standard of living are a result of this chain of events.

The relatively good performance of the urban sector after 1954 under conditions of a rural austerity program occurred as a result of a complex series of adjustments, which at least superficially resemble some aspects of Hirschman's theory of economic development.[87] This theory suggests that a serious but tractable nationwide problem may have beneficial long-term effects on national economic development. In our analysis, the sharp exogenous drop in rural income in 1954 generated a redistribution of government funds in favor of the rural sector in 1955. The result was a small gain in rural support from 1955 to 1956 and a large loss in urban areas where the decline in government expenditures had cut into the standard of living. The governmental response was massive: Expenditures in urban areas were increased from 1,058 million T.L. in 1955 to 1,891 million T.L. in 1956, giving rise to a large budgetary deficit. This boost was much larger than the one that occurred in the reference run and sufficient to generate large and self-sustaining gains in consumption per capita. The relatively good performance of the rural sector toward the end of this application of the model resulted from massive urbanization, as much as 458,000 per year, in response to the large inequalities between urban and rural standards of living. Under conditions of an urban austerity program, the long-run decline of the rural sector was caused by the withdrawal of government expenditures, which in turn was caused by a drastic decline in revenues as the urban sector of the economy deteriorated. Deterioration in the rural sector of the economy has little effect on government revenues because the effective rural tax rate τ_1 is very low.

In the Philippine sensitivity analysis, decreases in m_i reduce the standard of living but in some instances increase the level of support for the government.

Compared to the reference run, a decrease in the rural rate of consumption m_1 generates declines in the standard of living in the rural areas. The trend reaches a low point of 104 pesos per capita in 1962 and then increases. The urban standard of living increases and decreases from year to year, but the secular trend is upward at levels slightly below the levels in the reference run. Trends in political support differ considerably from the reference run. In both sectors losses of support are greater from 1951 to the 1953 election, and consequently the former opposition assumes office at a higher level of support. The government retains control in the 1957 election with a small majority of .505, although support in rural areas dropped to .492. In contrast to the reference run the declining support in rural areas caused the government to lose the 1961 election. From this point on support grows in rural areas and fluctuates in urban areas. Neither the economic condition of the people nor the political position of the government improves as a result of a rural austerity program.

A decrease in the urban rate of consumption m_2 has a relatively small impact on the standard of living and support for the government in rural areas. Both trends closely parallel those in the reference run. In the urban area the trends are quite different, however. Compared to the reference run, the standard of living is consistently lower and the level of support for the government consistently higher. In general, the government does better in terms of aggregate support and the people as a whole slightly worse in terms of the standard of living as a result of an urban austerity program.

As in the case of the Turkish analysis described above, the behavior of the model under conditions of an austerity program as compared with its behavior in the reference run is most decisively a function of the consumption and investment relationships. Small decreases in rural consumption as a result of a rural austerity program lead to a declining standard of living and a withdrawal of support for the government in rural areas. However, gains in urban consumption have a different impact, because the urban rate of induced private investment r_2 is negative. Consequently, in the reference run, gains in per capita consumption follow losses and vice versa. An increase in investment causes an increase in income, but the increase in income generates gains in per capita consumption in the next year, and these cause decreases in investment. This oscillating pattern tends to maintain expectations at high levels. A decrease in m_2, however, moderates gains in consumption per capita and the resulting decreases in investment to the extent that the per capita consumption series exhibits slight positive gains from year to year. This pattern tends to generate a secular downward trend in expectations. Since, according to relationship (3.7) economic performance is judged with respect to expected performance in determining the level of support, urban support declines much less rapidly than in the reference run even though, on the whole, the performance of the urban sector of the economy falls below that of the reference run. The role of economic expectations is very important in this complex series of adjustments.

URBAN TAX POLICY

Effective tax rates in rural areas in Turkey and the Philippines are so low that 5% changes in them make very little difference in the behavior of the model over time. Changes in effective tax rates in urban areas, however, make a great deal of difference.

In the Turkish analysis, a decrease in the effective urban tax rate τ_2 generates consistent improvements in both aggregate standard of living and aggregate support for the government, although the rural sector endures slight losses in the short and middle term. Economic performance in the rural sector begins to exceed that of the reference run only in 1961, but grows rapidly thereafter. Economic performance in the urban sector is consistently stronger than in the reference run, exacerbating the inequality in the standard of living from rural to urban areas although improvements through time occur in each sector. Trends in support for the government in each sector roughly parallel trends in the standard of living. The results are summarized in Table 5.5.

The consequences of an increase in the effective urban tax rate τ_2 are quite different. Per capita consumption in the urban areas remains essentially constant until the decrease in government expenditures in urban areas in 1955. From that point on, aside from a slight gain in the period 1956–1957, there are increasingly large annual declines in the urban standard of living. Per capita consumption in rural areas exceeds that of the reference run until 1961, after which it falls below the level of the reference run but continues to increase. As a result, urban support for the government declines to very low levels in the 1960s while rural support reaches high levels and continues to grow slowly. While a tax *decrease* exacerbates economic inequalities and generates widespread political support, a tax *increase* eliminates the initial inequality and generates political polarization.

Variations in τ_2 have two direct effects in the model, and the relative impact of these two effects explains the behavior of the model in these runs. One effect of a decrease in τ_2 is to increase disposable income and therefore consumption, according to (3.5). The other effect is to reduce government revenues and therefore, other things being equal, total government expenditures, according to (3.4) and (3.8). An increase in τ_2 has opposite effects: It decreases disposable income and consumption in urban areas, and it increases government revenues and government expenditures. Under conditions of both an increase and a decrease in the urban tax rate, in the Turkish

Table 5.5—Outcomes of Urban Tax Policies :
Deviations from the Reference Runs

Decrease Tax Rate

		TURKEY			PHILIPPINES		
		Rural	*Urban*	*Aggregate*	*Rural*	*Urban*	*Aggregate*
Standard	1955	—4	83	14	—1	1	—1
of	1960	—2	354	80	—4	—2	—3
Living	1965	70	1344	391	—9	16	—1
Support	1955	—.006	.048	.004	—.004	—.009	—.005
for	1960	.001	.133	.030	—.013	—.012	—.013
Government	1965	.036	.151	.101	—.025	.059	.003

Increase Tax Rate

		TURKEY			PHILIPPINES		
		Rural	*Urban*	*Aggregate*	*Rural*	*Urban*	*Aggregate*
Standard	1955	4	—78	—13	0	0	0
of	1960	1	—310	—68	4	3	4
Living	1965	—71	—1038	—295	9	0	6
Support	1955	.006	—.048	—.005	.004	.010	.005
for	1960	—.002	—.159	—.035	.014	.012	.013
Government	1965	—.043	—.409	—.124	.021	.007	.017

sensitivity tests, the impact of the consumption effect is much greater than the impact of the revenue-expenditure effect. A decrease in τ_2 generates self-sustaining gains in consumption, and by 1955 the economy performs so well that revenues exceed the level attained in the reference run. An increase in τ_2 generates early and self-sustaining declines in consumption, and by 1955 the tax base deteriorates to the extent that revenues and expenditures fall below the levels attained in the reference run. Furthermore, because of growing political polarization, the growing economic inequality between rural and urban areas cannot be reversed through redistribution of government funds. The *scale* of the support in rural areas relative to the urban effectively neutralizes the impact of *changes* in support in the urban areas [see (3.8)]. Consequently, high levels of support are rewarded by high levels of government expenditures, and the proportion of total government expenditures allocated to the rural areas increases. Attempts to adjust the growing inequality in per capita consumption by reducing urbanization are apparent, but are not nearly massive enough.

In the Philippine sensitivity analysis a *decrease* in the effective urban tax rate τ_2 generates trends in the rural, urban, and aggregate standard of living that are slightly lower than the reference run but small in percentage terms. The correspondingly lower levels of support, however, are low enough that the government fails to maintain a majority in either sector in 1961 and loses the election. From this point on, the level of support for the government in the rural sector remains below the level in the reference run but increases from year to year, while support in the urban sector fluctuates but at a higher level than in the reference run. The economic costs to the population are small, but the political costs to the government are significant.

An *increase* in the effective urban tax rate τ_2 generates trends in rural, urban, and aggregate standard of living that are in some cases slightly higher than those in the reference run. The rural standard of living initially shows very small gains over the reference run, but by 1965 has gained 9 pesos per capita or about 4.6%. The urban standard of living remains at approximately the same average level as in the reference run, but the fluctuations are somewhat greater. Support for the government exceeds the levels in the reference run by as much as .021 in the rural sector and .012 in the urban. Both the economic position of the people and the political position of the government improve slightly.

In the Philippine sensitivity tests of variations in τ_2, in contrast to the Turkish, the impact of the consumption mechanism is much *less* than the impact of the revenue–expenditure mechanism. The gains in consumption as a result of a decrease in τ_2 were not self-sustaining: By 1955, aggregate consumption had fallen below the levels attained in the reference run. Decreases in government revenues as a result of the tax persisted throughout the run; but through the mechanism of government deficit spending, aggregate standard of living in 1967 exceeded the level attained in the reference run. The average annual deficit for the three-year period 1964–1966 in this run was 1,030 million pesos; in the reference run it was 895 million pesos. The declines in consumption as a result of an increase in τ_2 were also not self-sustaining: By 1955 aggregate consumption had risen above the levels attained in the reference run. Increases in government revenues and expenditures were sufficient to generate a higher aggregate standard of living than that attained in the reference run.

POLITICAL PRIORITIES

In the Turkish sensitivity analysis, as shown in Table 5.6, an increase in the political priority of the rural sector β_1 improves the rural standard of living and increases the level of rural support relative to the reference run. The outcomes are nearly the opposite in the urban sector: After very small increases in the standard of living and support, both variables fall below the levels attained in the reference run. In contrast, an increase in the political priority of the urban sector β_2 generates improvements in per capita consumption and increases in support in both sectors, although relative to the reference run the changes are larger in the urban sector. In short, a change in political priorities has beneficial outcomes from the viewpoint of the government and the favored sector, but in relative, and in some cases absolute terms, deprives the other sector.

Other things being equal, an increase in β_i according to (3.8) increases $G_{i,t}$ through deficit spending. Income increases in the next period, then revenues and consumption, and so on. The increase in β_1 generates increases in rural expenditures but leaves urban expenditures nearly unchanged until the exogenous sharp decline in rural income in 1954. The initial governmental response is to increase rural expenditures from 1954 to 1955 by an amount greater than that in the reference run. But the governmental response to the problem in the urban area from 1955 to 1956 is less massive than that which occurred in the reference run. Without sufficient government "pump priming" the urban sector suffers accelerating declines. After 1957, revenues fall below

Table 5.6—Outcomes of Changed Political Priorities: Deviations from the Reference Runs

In Rural Sector

		TURKEY			PHILIPPINES		
		Rural	*Urban*	*Aggregate*	*Rural*	*Urban*	*Aggregate*
Standard	1955	8	1	6	1	1	1
of	1960	25	—13	16	5	0	4
Living	1965	53	—81	20	9	—2	5
Support	1955	.011	.001	.009	.002	.001	.002
for	1960	.020	—.007	.014	.010	—.001	.007
Government	1965	.013	—.024	.005	.017	—.002	.010

In Urban Sector

		TURKEY			PHILIPPINES		
		Rural	*Urban*	*Aggregate*	*Rural*	*Urban*	*Aggregate*
Standard	1955	1	38	8	0	5	1
of	1960	12	190	52	1	8	3
Living	1965	73	747	238	2	0	1
Support	1955	.001	.023	.005	.000	—.006	—.001
for	1960	.012	.083	.027	.003	.006	.000
Government	1965	.030	.115	.050	.006	—.020	—.003

the levels attained in the reference run, and by 1967 the decline in revenues cuts into expenditures to such an extent that rural expenditures fail to reach the reference run levels. The increase in β_2 has the opposite effect. With respect to the reference run, moderate gains in revenues and rural and urban expenditures occur up to the sharp decline in 1954. But in this case the governmental response in the urban areas exceeds by a large amount the response in the reference run. This impetus is sufficient to generate self-sustaining increases in economic performance.

In the Philippine sensitivity analysis, as shown in Table 5.6, an increase in the political priority of the rural sector β_1 generates persistent gains in per capita consumption in the rural area, but the small initial gains in the urban area are eliminated and, by 1965, urban per capita consumption declines below the level of the reference run. The trends in support for each area are roughly parallel to the trends in the standard of living. An increase in the political priority of the urban sector β_2 generates small gains in economic performance in the rural sector in the long run, but initial gains in economic performance in the urban sector are eliminated in the long run. Support in the rural sector increases by very small amounts. But support in the urban sector decreases up to 1955 when there are gains in per capita consumption; support then increases and finally declines in the long run.

The behavior of the model when β_i is increased in the Philippine context is similar to its behavior in the Turkish context, except there is no exogenous shock to accelerate growth or decline. When β_1 is increased, expenditures in both sectors increase, but by 1959 the relative preference for the rural sector pushes government expenditures in urban areas below the levels of the reference run. This slow but long-term relative deprivation of the urban sector causes revenues to decline below reference levels in 1958. When β_2 is increased, expenditures in both sectors increase by small amounts, with the urban sector enjoying a larger share. But in contrast to the Turkish case, these increased expenditures in urban areas exacerbate the effect of gains and losses in per capita consumption by maintaining expectations at relatively high levels. Not only does the government lose urban support as a result, but the level of urban support becomes low enough that the urban sector has a smaller impact in the determination of government expenditures.

ON THE BEHAVIOR OF THE MODEL

Before considering the implications of these various trends for the succession dilemma, it is worthwhile to consider in a general way some formal aspects of the behavior of the model. In one sense, its behavior seems realistic: Certain pressures or stresses in the system, such as inequalities in the standard of living, gains in consumption, or changes in support for the government, in some circumstances have a decisive impact on the behavior of the system and in other circumstances make very little difference. One of the best examples is the difference in the behavior of the model in the Turkish and Philippine contexts as a result of the pressures created by a 5% increase in the urban tax rate. In the first case these pressures generated large losses, and in the second they generated small improvements. According to this conception, there are a significant number of alternative pressures and potential adjustment mechanisms in a society, and these pressures and mechanisms may generate diminishing or self-sustaining changes in the behavior of the system.

This form of behavior of social systems has been recognized by several theorists, among them Gunnar Myrdal. According to Myrdal,

> In general there are periods when opposing forces balance one another so that the system remains in rest until a push or a pull is applied at one point or another. When the whole system starts moving after such a shock the *changes* in the forces work in the same direction, which is something different. And this is so because the variables are so inter-locked in circular causation that a change in any one induces the others to change in such a way that these secondary changes support the first change, with similar tertiary effects upon the variable first affected, and so on.[88]

The implications of this form of behavior are not lost on social scientists keenly interested in policy considerations and social reform.

> It is important to keep in mind that, if the hypothesis of cumulative causation is justified, an upward movement of the entire system can be effected by measures applied to one or the other of several points in the system. ... The principle of cumulation—in so far as it holds true—promises final effects of very much greater magnitude than the efforts and costs of the reforms themselves.[89]

In another sense, the behavior of the model is unrealistic. In situations such as the one resembling an austerity program in urban areas in Turkey, the model generates such extreme pressures in the system that the adjustment mechanisms are not sufficient to alleviate them. We know that political and social systems do not always adapt successfully; but we also know that per capita consumption cannot drop to zero in one area of a country and yet remain above subsistence levels in another. In the real world in these circumstances the system itself undergoes profound, second-order changes: Tax structures may be abolished and replaced, political priorities drastically altered, and electoral systems abolished as new ruling groups replace the old ones; birth rates decline and mortality rates increase with widespread instability;[90] and so on. Furthermore, even under more stable circumstances some of the underlying propensities governing the behavior of the system are known to change slowly, and others are suspected to change. For example, birth rates decline slowly with economic development,[91] and in various theories propensities to consume, to invest, and to save are important causes and effects of economic development.[92] In short, the long-run rigidity in the behavior of the model as applied to various situations resembling Turkey in 1950 suggests that, at some point and for some purposes, the exploration of a set of second-order or ultra-stable[93] feedback mechanisms may prove to be worthwhile.

Conclusion

IMPLICATIONS FOR POLITICAL DEVELOPMENT

In the Introduction we suggested that several trends in modernization and mass politics adversely affect the probability of building strong political institutions and the probability of democratic resolution of the succession dilemma. Among these trends are increasing polarization, in which the degree of support for the government differs markedly from one sector to the next; declines in economic performance and support for the government; and very rapid economic growth.

In terms of these considerations, the 5% changes in the Turkish sensitivity analysis have generally negative effects. Austerity programs in either sector generate political polarization between the rural and urban sectors in terms of support for the government, and produce either too rapid growth in one of the two sectors or moderate-to-serious economic declines in both. A decrease in the effective urban tax rate generates extremely rapid growth in the urban sector; an increase in urban tax rates generates both rapid economic decline in the urban sector and political polarization. Changes in political priorities have less extreme effects, but perhaps even the rate of economic growth in the urban sector when it is relatively favored is too rapid. In short, according to this analysis, there seems to have been a high potential for institutional decay in Turkey in the decade of the 1950s insofar as trends in modernization and mass politics are concerned.

In terms of the development of effective and democratic institutions, the 5% changes in the Philippine sensitivity analysis have generally neutral effects. The most extreme economic decline occurs as a result of austerity programs, but these effects are small compared to the effects of Turkish austerity programs. Significant polarization and rapid economic growth do not occur. The relatively greater potential for short-run stability if not long-run political development in the Philippine context seems to be the result of a higher potential for adjustment: Economic booms generate recessions and vice versa through the peculiar pattern of investments; lower urban tax rates and higher urban priorities tend to distribute the burdens and rewards of public policy more evenly; and a higher urbanization rate provides for more massive long-term adjustments toward equality in the standard of living.

Our brief excursion into development policy does more to suggest the complexity of the problems involved than to answer them. We have ignored the relative costs of achieving 5% changes in different parameters. Even though a change in the propensity to consume has a much greater impact than an equal change in the rate of natural increase, the latter may be much easier to achieve in terms of political and economic costs. Furthermore, we have ignored possible scale effects: A 2% decrease in the propensity to consume, for example, may have quite different effects than a 5% decrease. Finally, we have not dealt with the possibilities of implementing several coordinated policies at a cross-section in time or at different points in time. The exploration of these possibilities may be postponed until more confidence in the empirical basis of the model is justified.

SOME QUALIFICATIONS

This analysis of the political implications of modernization has several limitations that suggest qualifications to our substantive conclusions as well as fruitful directions for further work. One set of qualifications derives from section 4 where a confrontation between the model and data suggested some revisions in the model. In particular, the application of the model to Turkey demonstrated both a need for more effective resource constraints on the level of government expenditures, and a need for more direct, immediate influences from either sector of the economy to the other in addition to the indirect, delayed influences through variations in government expenditures. The application of the model to the Philippines suggested the need for increasing the time lag between the political stimulus for reallocating public funds and the actual response. In addition, the sensitivity analysis suggested the need to reconsider the assumption of constant parameters. To the extent that these limitations contribute to the invalidity of the model, our substantive conclusions must be considered cautiously.

Another set of qualifications stems from the ways in which we have simplified the phenomena of modernization and mass politics in order to analyze them. One major simplification is that the principal societal cleavage in these countries is the cleavage between the rural and urban sectors. The city limits constitute the boundaries of agricultural and non-agricultural economies; they divide the population into two groups having different standards of living, participation rates, and propensities to consume and invest; and they define the principal range of choice in the allocation of government funds. For Turkey and the Philippines this particular disaggregation seems reasonable, as we suggested in Section 2. In countries other than Turkey and the Philippines, the principal societal cleavages might exist between two ethnic or tribal groups, or between highland and lowland regions. Situations like these could be analyzed without modification of the model, and situations involving important overlapping cleavages could be analyzed if modifications are made. Nonetheless, to the extent that secondary and overlapping cleavages are important in any particular country, this two-sector model may give misleading results.

A second major simplification is the incorporation of the standard of living as the basic political issue to the exclusion of all others. Again, there is evidence for Turkey and the Philippines that this is a reasonable simplification at least in terms of mass rather than elite politics. The large bulk of the population in both rural and urban sectors seems to respond to the issue of the standard of living and not so much to the issues of democratic rights or the propaganda campaigns of political elites. Nevertheless, in Turkey and the Philippines, as well as in other countries, to the extent that large changes in support for the government are determined by other issues, the model needs further development.

A third simplification has been suggested above: The model focuses on mass electoral politics and power as broad popular support, and excludes elite politics and power as access to decisions affecting specific issues. To the extent that political elites are in fact the slaves of the masses (as Robinson suggested was the case in Turkey), this simplification may be productive. To the extent that political elites can effectively insulate themselves from mass support and opposition, this simplification may give rise to misleading results.

These simplifications define the range of countries to which the model can reasonably be applied. In less developed contexts, such as Turkey under Atatürk and the Philippines under the Illustrados, the course of political change can best be explained in terms of elite politics and in some cases the aspirations and abilities of a single man. In more developed countries the number and complexity of overlapping cleavages and political issues are considerably beyond the scope of the model. The model seems most suited to countries in the transitional period between these extremes. In spite of the simplifying assumptions of the model, its outputs are enormously complex and, in terms of the experience of Turkey and the Philippines, empirically encouraging. However, the present version of the model is believed to be applicable only to the two countries for which it was developed. Its relevance to other countries if any must be documented rather than assumed.

USES OF THE MODEL

The model we have developed to analyze the implications of modernization for the succession dilemma can serve as a tool for the consideration of a number of similar questions from the normative, historical, scientific, and policy viewpoints, and it can also be used to project future developments.[94] Given the current state of our knowledge of politics in the less developed countries, however, the model seems to be most useful at this point as a tool to serve the scientific functions of guiding the collection of data, organizing and integrating the information we have, and considering theoretical alternatives. Substantively, the model is only a first step in a process of developing more adequate scientific formulations that can be used for other purposes.

In order to guide the collection of data, sensitivity tests of the properties of the model can be used to suggest which variables and parameters are worth measuring to discover where the model is inadequate. The rate of consumption m_i for example, has much larger direct and indirect effects on the outputs of the system than the penetration of the political system α_i. Data need not be collected solely because they are available or because they appear to have some relevance to theory; using the model, we can determine the relative importance of a large number of indices before the data are collected.

The model also can be used as an organizing device that enables us to draw together a large variety of qualitative and quantitative information on the problem at hand. As we have seen, general theoretical statements about processes of change, specific statements from the political histories of individual countries, and quantitative data can be integrated into a common framework. The analysis need not rely primarily on theoretical statements or data alone, nor is the link between theory and data a tenuous one. According to Richard Bellman, the problem of building theories of social systems can be defined as follows: "Given some information concerning the structure of a system, and some observations of inputs, outputs, and internal behavior over time, deduce all of the missing information concerning structure, inputs, and outputs."[95] If we accept this working definition, then the role of the model as an organizing device is an important one.

Beyond this, the model can serve as an "experimental animal" on which controlled experiments can be made as suggested by the sensitivity analyses. More importantly, the implications of theoretical alternatives can be determined under the same controlled conditions. It should be pointed out that the controls in the experiments are not of a statistical variety in which, for example, a variable may be controlled by assuming linearity and additivity and then subtracting the variance it explains from other variables. Instead, the controls are similar to the laboratory variety in which experimental inputs are varied from one run to the next and there is some confidence in the *ceteris paribus* assumption from one experiment to the next. Properly used, the model does not confine attention to a particular formulation, but stimulates the consideration of theoretical alternatives.

Appendix I.
A Listing of the Model

```
C  BRUNNER AND BREWER   MODEL OF POLITICAL AND SOCIAL CHANGE IN THE LESS
C  DEVELOPED AREAS, VERSION 10, WITH POLITICAL SUBSYSTEM. 6/28/68
      INTEGER T,TT,START,YEAR,SW1,SW2,SW3,ELECT
      REAL IN,M,N
      DIMENSION N(3,52), Y(3,52), C(3,52), IN(3,52), F(3,52),
     1 V(3,52), D(3,52), P(3,52), E(3,52), U(52), GR(52), CN(3,52),
     2 A(2), M(2), R(2), TAU(2), ALPHA(2), BETA(2), GAMMA(2), DELTA(2),
     3 TITLE(17), LABEL(3), YEAR(52), ELECT(8)
      DATA (LABEL(I), I=1,3)/6H RURAL, 6H URBAN, 6H TOTAL/
500   CONTINUE
C  INPUT
      READ (5,1)  NY, SW1, SW2, SW3, START, (TITLE(I), I=1,17)
      READ (5,2) (A(I), M(I), R(I), TAU(I), ALPHA(I), BETA(I), GAMMA(I),
     1 DELTA(I), I=1,2)
      READ (5,3)  S, SIGMA, EPSILN, GR(1)
      READ(5,4) (N(I,1), C(I,1), IN(I,1), G(I,1), V(I,1), D(I,1), P(I,1),
     1,E(I,1), I= 1,2)
      IF (SW1.EQ.0) GO TO 50
      READ (5,4) ((F(I,T), T=1,NY), I=1,2)
      GO TO 51
50    CONTINUE
      DO 52 I=1,2
      DO 53 T=1,NY
      F(I,T) = 0.0
53    CONTINUE
52    CONTINUE
51    CONTINUE
      IF (SW2.GT.0) READ(5,5) WINVOT, (ELECT(I), I=1,8)
1     FORMAT (4I2, I4, 17A4)
2     FORMAT (8F5.0)
3     FORMAT (3F5.0,F10.0)
4     FORMAT (8F10.0)
5     FORMAT (F5.0, 8I5)
501   CONTINUE
C  INPUT DISPLAY
      WRITE (6,10) (TITLE(I), I= 1,17)
      WRITE (6,11)
      WRITE (6,12)
      WRITE (6,13) (LABEL(I), A(I), M(I), R(I), TAU(I), ALPHA(I),
     1 BETA(I), GAMMA(I), DELTA(I), I=1,2)
      WRITE (6,14) S, SIGMA, EPSILN
      WRITE (6,15)
      WRITE (6,16)
```

Line numbers: 1, 13, 27, 28, 44, 68, 76, 83, 84, 85, 100, 101, 102

```
      WRITE (6,17) (LABEL(I), N(I,1), C(I,1), IN(I,1), G(I,1), V(I,1),
     1 D(I,1), P(I,1), E(I,1), I=1,2)
      WRITE (6,18) GR(1)
      IF (SW2.GT.0) WRITE (6,19) WINVOT
      IE = 1
   10 FORMAT ('1'17A4//)
   11 FORMAT ('0DISPLAY PARAMETERS')
   12 FORMAT ('0' 19X*A          R        TAU       ALPHA        BET
     1A     GAMMA      DELTA')
   13 FORMAT ('0'4X, A6, 8F10.4)
   14 FORMAT ('0'18X*S=', F10.4,'     SIGMA=',F10.3,'     EPSILN='
     1 F10.4//)
   15 FORMAT ('0DISPLAY INITIAL CONDITIONS')
   16 FORMAT ('0' 19X*N          C         IN           G          V
     1D          P           E')
   17 FORMAT ('0'4X, A6, 8F10.3)
   18 FORMAT ('0'17X*GR=*F10.3)
   19 FORMAT ('2THE ELECTORAL SUBSYSTEM IS OPERATING.  A VOTE OF 'F6.3,
     1' IS SUFFICIENT TO WIN.')
C  SET THE YEARLY DO LOOP AND BEGIN PROCESSING
      YEAR(1) = START + 1
      DO 100 T=1,NY
      TT=T+1
      YEAR(TT) = START+ TT
C  DEMOGRAPHIC SUBSYSTEM
      U(T)= S*P(1,T)*(C(2,T)/N(2,T))*(N(1,T)/C(1,T))*N(1,T)
      N(1,TT)= (1.0+A(1))*N(1,T)-U(T)
      N(2,TT)= (1.0+A(2))*N(2,T)+U(T)
C  ECONOMIC SUBSYSTEM
      DO 200 I=1,2
      Y(I,T)= C(I,T) + IN(I,T) + G(I,T) + F(I,T)
      C(I,TT)= M(I)*(Y(I,T)*(1.0-TAU(I))/N(I,T))*N(I,TT)
      IN(I,TT) = IN(I,T)*(N(I,TT)/N(I,T)) + R(I)*(C(I,TT)/N(I,TT))-
     1 C(I,T)/N(I,T))*N(I,TT)
  200 CONTINUE
      GR(TT)= TAU(1)*Y(1,T) + TAU(2)*Y(2,T)
C  POLITICAL SUBSYSTEM
      DO 300 I=1,2
      V(I,TT) = V(I,T)+SIGMA*ALPHA(I)*P(I,T)*((1.0-V(I,T))*V(I,T))**3
     1 *((C(I,TT)/N(I,TT))*(N(I,T)/C(I,L))-E(I,T))
  300 CONTINUE
      DO 301 I=1,2
      G(I,TT) = BETA(I)*((2.0*N(I,T)*V(I,T)-N(I,TT)*V(I,TT))/
     1 (2.0*N(I,T)*V(I,T)-N(1,TT)*V(I,TT)+2.0*N(2,T)*V(2,T)-N(2,TT)*
     2 V(2,TT))*GR(T)
```

```
        D(I,TT) = GAMMA(I)*G(I,TT)
        P(I,TT) = 1.0-(DELTA(I)/D(I,T))
        IF (P(I,TT).LT.P(I,T)) P(I,TT)=P(I,T)
        E(I,TT) = E(I,T)+EPSILN*((C(I,TT)/N(I,TT))*(N(I,TT)/C(I,T))
     1-E(I,T))*P(I,T)
  301 CONTINUE
C FIND TOTALS
        Y(3,T) = Y(1,T) + Y(2,T)
        N(3,T) = N(1,T) + N(2,T)
        C(3,T) = C(1,T) + C(2,T)
        IN(3,T) = IN(1,T) + IN(2,T)
        G(3,T) = G(1,T) + G(2,T)
        F(3,T) = F(1,T) + F(2,T)
        C(3,T) = D(1,T) + D(2,T)
        P(3,T) = (P(1,T)*N(1,T) + P(2,T)*N(2,T))/N(3,T)
        E(3,T) = (E(1,T)*N(1,T) + E(2,T)*N(2,T))/N(3,T)
        V(3,T) = (V(1,T)*N(1,T) + V(2,T)*N(2,T))/N(3,T)
        DO 302 I=1,3
        CN(I,T) = C(I,T)/N(I,T)
  302 CCNTINUE
C ELECTORAL SUBSYSTEM
        IF (YEAR(TT).NE.ELECT(IE))  GO TO 400
        IF (SW2.LT.1) GO TO 400
        N(3,TT) = N(1,TT) + N(2,TT)
        V(3,TT) = (V(1,TT)*N(1,TT)+V(2,TT)*N(2,TT))/N(3,TT)
        IF (V(3,TT).GE.WINVOT) GO TO 401
        WRITE (6,30) YEAR(TT)
        DO 402 I= 1,3
        V(I,TT) = 1.0-V(I,TT)
  402 CONTINUE
        GO TO 403
  401 CONTINUE
        WRITE (6,31) YEAR(TT)
  403 CONTINUE
        IE = IE+1
   30 FORMAT (*0    OPPOSITION WINS THE ELECTION OF ', I5)
   31 FORMAT (*0    GOVERNMENT WINS THE ELECTION OF ', I5)
  400 CONTINUE
  100 CCNTINUE
C END OF YEARLY DO LOOP
C OUTPUT
```

```
303         WRITE (6,20)
304         WRITE (6,21)
305         WRITE (6,22) ((LABEL(I), I=1,3), J=1,3)
            WRITE (6,23) (YEAR(T), (G(I,T), I=1,3), GR(T), (P(I,T), I=1,3),
           1 (V(I,T), I=1,3), T=1,NY)
315         WRITE (6,24)
            WRITE (6,25)
            WRITE (6,22) ((LABEL(I), I=1,3), J=1,3)
335         WRITE (6,23) (YEAR(T), (N(I,T), I=1,3), U(T), (CN(I,T), I=1,3),
336        1 (E(I,T), I=1,3), T=1,NY)
337         DO 6C I=1,3
347         WRITE (6,26) LABEL(I)
            WRITE (6,27)
            WRITE (6,28) (YEAR(T), Y(I,T), C(I,T), IN(I,T), G(I,T), F(I,T),
369        1 D(I,T), T=1,NY)
371   60    CONTINUE
372   20    FORMAT ('1'44X'POLITICAL OUTCOMES AND EFFECTS')
      21    FORMAT ('0'6X'  GOVERNMENT EXPENDITURE  REVENUE          PAR
           1ITICIPATION          SUPPORT FOR GOVERNMENT')
      22    FORMAT ('0'6X,3(4X,A6)'               TOTAL '3(4X,A6),X,3(4X,A6))
      23    FORMAT ('0'I5,1X,4F10.3,1X,3F10.3,1X,3F10.3)
      24    FORMAT ('1'50X'STANDARD OF LIVING')
      25    FORMAT ('0'6X'    POPULATION        MIGRANTS       PER CAP
           1ITA CONSUMPTION                  EXPECTED RATE')
      26    FORMAT ('1'48X'NATIONAL ACCOUNTS - 'A6)
      27    FORMAT ('0'24X'INCOME   CONSUMPTION   INVESTMENT   GOVERNMENT
           1   NET FOREIGN  DEVELOPMENT')
      28    FORMAT ('0'I5,1CX,6F15.3)
            IF (SW3.EQ.1) GC TO 500
C     PARAMETER CHANGES FCR NEXT RUN
            READ (5,6) NC, SW3, (TITLE(I), I= 1,17)
388         DO 5C2 J= 1,NC
            READ (5,7) ID, X1, X2
            IF (ID.EQ.1) A(1)=X1
            IF (ID.EQ.1) A(2)=X2
            IF (ID.EQ.2) M(1)=X1
            IF (ID.EQ.2) M(2)=X2
            IF (ID.EQ.3) R(1)=X1
399         IF (ID.EQ.3) R(2)=X2
            IF (ID.EQ.4) TAL(1)= X1
            IF (ID.EQ.4) TAL(2)= X2
            IF (ID.EQ.5) ALPHA(1) = X1
            IF (ID.EQ.5) ALPHA(2) = X2
            IF (ID.EQ.6) BETA(1) = X1
```

```
IF (ID.EQ.6) BETA(2) = X2
IF (ID.EQ.7) GAMMA(1) = X1
IF (ID.EQ.7) GAMMA(2) = X2
IF (ID.EQ.8) DELTA(1) = X1
IF (ID.EQ.8) DELTA(2) = X2
IF (ID.EQ.9) S = X1
IF (ID.EQ.10) SIGMA = X1
IF (ID.EQ.11) EPSILN = X1
IF (ID.EQ.12) SW2 = IFIX(X1)
502 CONTINUE
6 FORMAT (2I2, 17A4)
7 FORMAT (I5, 2F5.0)
STOP
END
```

....   SECTION   3

ENTRY POINTS

.FRDD.	SECTION	4	.FWRD.	SECTION	5	.EXIT.	SECTION	6
.UNO5.	SECTION	7	.FRTN.	SECTION	8	.FCNV.	SECTION	9
.UNO6.	SECTION	10	.FFIL.	SECTION	11	CC.1	SECTION	12
CC.2	SECTION	13	CC.3	SECTION	14	CC.4	SECTION	15
SYSLOC	SECTION	16						

SUBROUTINES CALLED

EFN IFN CORRESPONDENCE

EFN	IFN	LOCATION	EFN	IFN	LOCATION	EFN	IFN	LOCATION
50C	1A	04156	1	FORMAT	03651	2	FORMAT	03654
3	FORMAT	03656	4	FORMAT	03661	50	55A	04340
51	67A	04361	52	64A	04357	53	62A	04354
5	FORMAT	03663	501	76A	04402	10	FORMAT	03665
11	FORMAT	03667	12	FORMAT	03673	13	FORMAT	03711
14	FORMAT	03715	15	FORMAT	03731	16	FORMAT	03737
17	FORMAT	03755	18	FORMAT	03761	19	FORMAT	03764
100	301A	05543	200	163A	04774	300	181A	05103
301	220A	05312	302	266A	05410	4C0	300A	05543
401	297A	05525	30	FORMAT	04003	402	294A	05522
403	299A	05540	31	FORMAT	04013	20	FORMAT	04023

Appendix II.
Reference Run Outputs

TURKISH REFERENCE RUN

DISPLAY PARAMETERS

	A	M	R	TAU	ALPHA	BETA	GAMMA	DELTA
RURAL	0.0290	0.9350	0.2000	0.0200	0.8000	0.5000	0.1200	47.0000
UREAN	0.0260	C.8850	C.6000	0.2600	0.9900	3.6000	0.1200	17.0000

S= 0.0020   SIGMA= 50.000   EPSILN= 0.1000

DISPLAY INITIAL CONDITIONS

	N	C	IN	G	V	D	P	E
RURAL	17.024	4090.000	40.000	560.000	0.535	70.000	0.600	1.030
URBAN	3.911	3610.000	1000.000	1100.000	0.535	110.000	0.900	1.030

GR= 1400.000

POLITICAL OUTCOMES AND EFFECTS

	GOVERNMENT EXPENDITURE			REVENUE	PARTICIPATION			SUPPORT FOR GOVERNMENT		
	RURAL	URBAN	TOTAL	TOTAL	RURAL	URBAN	TOTAL	RURAL	URBAN	TOTAL
1950	560.000	1100.000	1660.000	1400.000	0.600	0.900	0.656	0.535	0.535	0.535
1951	570.881	929.659	1500.539	1578.400	0.600	0.900	0.657	0.543	0.539	0.542
1952	635.648	1105.577	1741.224	1653.006	0.600	0.900	0.658	0.550	0.518	0.544
1953	673.036	1104.960	1777.996	1766.138	0.600	0.900	0.659	0.562	0.513	0.552
1954	719.018	1181.169	1900.187	1873.624	0.600	0.900	0.660	0.575	0.504	0.561
1955	791.893	1043.420	1835.312	1955.078	0.600	0.900	0.660	0.476	0.498	0.481
1956	761.078	1558.520	2319.598	2031.016	0.600	0.900	0.662	0.499	0.476	0.495
1957	819.992	1407.718	2227.709	2239.796	0.600	0.909	0.664	0.518	0.498	0.514
1958	890.318	1652.978	2543.296	2408.334	0.600	0.909	0.665	0.539	0.500	0.531
1959	966.069	1714.305	2680.374	2638.121	0.600	0.914	0.667	0.562	0.515	0.552
1960	1055.133	1900.279	2955.412	2885.367	0.600	0.917	0.669	0.585	0.529	0.573
1961	1156.315	2061.853	3218.168	3184.333	0.629	0.925	0.694	0.609	0.549	0.596
1962	1274.004	2290.766	3564.770	3532.790	0.661	0.931	0.721	0.634	0.571	0.620
1963	1411.327	2556.490	3967.818	3954.620	0.693	0.938	0.748	0.659	0.598	0.645
1964	1574.680	2898.941	4473.620	4465.904	0.722	0.945	0.773	0.633	0.627	0.670
1965	1770.310	3331.022	5101.332	5094.468	0.751	0.951	0.797	0.706	0.658	0.695

STANDARD OF LIVING

	POPULATION			MIGRANTS	PER CAPITA CONSUMPTION			EXPECTED RATE		
	RURAL	URBAN	TOTAL	TOTAL	RURAL	URBAN	TOTAL	RURAL	URBAN	TOTAL
1950	17.024	3.911	20.935	0.078	240.249	923.038	367.805	1.030	1.030	1.030
1951	17.439	4.091	21.530	0.079	252.435	956.144	386.152	1.031	1.031	1.031
1952	17.866	4.277	22.142	0.077	265.687	955.455	398.916	1.033	1.028	1.032
1953	18.307	4.465	22.772	0.076	282.865	975.211	418.621	1.034	1.027	1.033
1954	18.762	4.657	23.419	0.074	302.840	988.683	439.223	1.037	1.026	1.034
1955	19.232	4.852	24.084	0.102	228.554	1006.840	385.334	1.020	1.025	1.021
1956	19.689	5.079	24.768	0.096	247.162	1000.610	401.677	1.023	1.022	1.023
1957	20.164	5.307	25.471	0.096	265.315	1054.178	429.690	1.026	1.025	1.026
1958	20.652	5.541	26.194	0.093	287.118	1083.078	455.500	1.030	1.025	1.029
1959	21.158	5.779	26.937	0.092	313.329	1135.007	489.604	1.033	1.027	1.032
1960	21.679	6.021	27.700	0.090	344.488	1188.340	527.906	1.037	1.029	1.036
1961	22.218	6.267	28.485	0.092	381.506	1256.637	574.046	1.042	1.032	1.039
1962	22.771	6.522	29.293	0.095	425.300	1336.962	628.286	1.046	1.035	1.044
1963	23.336	6.786	30.123	0.097	477.034	1435.693	693.013	1.051	1.038	1.048
1964	23.916	7.060	30.976	0.100	538.068	1555.833	770.041	1.057	1.043	1.053
1965	24.510	7.344	31.853	0.103	610.095	1703.921	862.273	1.062	1.048	1.059

NATIONAL ACCOUNTS - RURAL

	INCOME	CONSUMPTION	INVESTMENT	GOVERNMENT	NET FOREIGN	DEVELOPMENT
1950	4690.000	4090.000	40.000	560.000	-0.000	70.000
1951	5056.617	4402.260	83.477	570.881	-0.000	68.506
1952	5515.206	4746.686	132.872	635.648	-0.000	76.278
1953	6050.412	5178.329	199.047	673.036	-0.000	80.764
1954	4679.796	5681.832	278.947	719.019	-2000.000	86.282
1955	5187.750	4395.653	0.205	791.893	-0.000	95.027
1956	5700.820	4866.259	73.483	761.078	-0.000	91.329
1957	6318.225	5349.770	148.464	819.992	-0.000	98.399
1958	7062.112	5929.678	242.116	890.318	-0.000	106.838
1959	7954.406	6629.380	358.957	966.069	-0.000	115.928
1960	9026.348	7468.309	502.906	1055.133	-0.000	126.616
1961	10312.679	8476.459	679.905	1156.315	-0.000	138.758
1962	11854.658	9684.400	896.253	1274.004	-0.000	152.881
1963	13703.574	11132.271	1159.976	1411.327	-0.000	169.359
1964	15923.775	12868.380	1480.715	1574.680	-0.000	188.962
1965	18593.975	14953.129	1870.536	1770.310	-0.000	212.437

NATIONAL ACCOUNTS - URBAN

	INCOME	CONSUMPTION	INVESTMENT	GOVERNMENT	NET FOREIGN	DEVELOPMENT
1950	5710.000	3610.000	1000.000	1100.000	-0.000	110.000
1951	5968.744	3911.751	1127.335	929.659	-0.000	111.559
1952	6368.591	4086.297	1176.718	1105.577	-0.000	132.669
1953	6740.830	4354.417	1281.453	1104.960	-0.000	132.595
1954	7159.547	4604.228	1374.149	1181.169	-0.000	141.740
1955	7412.541	4684.701	1484.421	1043.420	-0.000	125.210
1956	8176.075	5082.420	1535.135	1558.520	-0.000	187.022
1957	8776.807	5594.559	1774.531	1407.718	-0.000	168.976
1958	9603.380	6001.504	1948.858	1652.978	-0.000	198.357
1959	10485.689	6558.883	2212.501	1714.305	-0.000	205.717
1960	11553.099	7154.914	2497.907	1900.279	-0.000	228.033
1961	12794.373	7875.617	2856.902	2061.853	-0.000	247.422
1962	14298.182	8719.940	3287.476	2290.766	-0.000	274.892
1963	16122.434	9743.258	3822.686	2556.490	-0.000	306.779
1964	18369.202	10984.462	4485.800	2898.941	-0.000	347.873
1965	21162.478	12513.032	5318.424	3331.022	-0.000	399.723

NATIONAL ACCOUNTS - TOTAL

	INCOME	CONSUMPTION	INVESTMENT	GOVERNMENT	NET FOREIGN	DEVELOPMENT
1950	10400.000	7700.000	1040.000	1660.000	-0.000	180.000
1951	11025.361	8314.010	1210.811	1500.539	-0.000	180.065
1952	11883.798	8832.983	1309.590	1741.224	-0.000	208.947
1953	12791.242	9532.746	1480.500	1777.956	-0.000	213.360
1954	11839.343	10286.060	1653.096	1900.187	-2000.000	226.022
1955	12600.291	9280.353	1484.626	1835.312	-0.000	220.237
1956	13876.895	9948.679	1608.619	2319.558	-0.000	278.352
1957	15095.032	10944.329	1922.994	2227.709	-0.000	267.325
1958	16665.492	11931.183	2191.013	2543.296	-0.000	305.195
1959	18440.095	13188.262	2571.458	2680.374	-0.000	321.645
1960	20579.447	14623.223	3000.813	2955.412	-0.000	354.649
1961	23107.052	16352.077	3536.807	3218.168	-0.000	386.180
1962	26152.839	18404.340	4183.729	3564.770	-0.000	427.772
1963	29826.008	20875.529	4982.662	3967.818	-0.000	476.138
1964	34292.977	23852.842	5966.515	4473.620	-0.000	536.834
1965	39756.453	27466.161	7188.960	5101.332	-0.000	612.160

PHILIPPINE REFERENCE RUN

DISPLAY PARAMETERS

	A	M	R	TAU	ALPHA	BETA	GAMMA	DELTA
RURAL	0.0312	0.9497	0.0724	0.0280	0.9200	0.4160	0.2040	17.7500
URBAN	0.0229	0.9146	-1.1000	0.1410	0.9950	5.1070	0.0805	14.4600

S= 0.0055   SIGMA= 80.000   EPSILN= 0.1500

DISPLAY INITIAL CONDITIONS

	N	C	IN	G	V	D	P	E
RURAL	17.020	2585.000	31.000	164.000	0.490	33.400	0.570	1.030
URBAN	4.180	2855.000	290.000	562.000	0.480	45.200	0.680	1.035

GR= 512.000

THE ELECTORAL SUBSYSTEM IS OPERATING.   A VOTE OF 0.500 IS SUFFICIENT TO WIN.

OPPOSITION WINS THE ELECTION OF 1953

GOVERNMENT WINS THE ELECTION OF 1957

GOVERNMENT WINS THE ELECTION OF 1961

GOVERNMENT WINS THE ELECTION OF 1965

POLITICAL OUTCOMES AND EFFECTS

	GOVERNMENT EXPENDITURE			REVENUE	PARTICIPATION			SUPPORT FOR GOVERNMENT		
	RURAL	URBAN	TOTAL	TOTAL	RURAL	URBAN	TOTAL	RURAL	URBAN	TOTAL
1951	164.000	562.000	726.000	512.000	0.570	0.680	0.592	0.490	0.480	0.488
1952	174.490	472.669	647.159	600.527	0.570	0.680	0.593	0.466	0.467	0.466
1953	196.928	649.310	846.239	623.642	0.570	0.680	0.594	0.555	0.590	0.562
1954	204.866	669.907	874.774	689.239	0.570	0.723	0.605	0.541	0.597	0.554
1955	218.176	841.521	1059.697	730.138	0.575	0.732	0.612	0.529	0.568	0.538
1956	232.435	875.334	1107.770	796.975	0.601	0.767	0.647	0.520	0.570	0.532
1957	245.516	1056.094	1301.610	844.068	0.626	0.795	0.669	0.514	0.542	0.521
1958	262.525	1087.780	1350.305	917.162	0.646	0.830	0.694	0.510	0.543	0.519
1959	275.756	1298.649	1574.404	969.989	0.669	0.835	0.714	0.509	0.514	0.511
1960	296.803	1310.051	1606.854	1053.121	0.684	0.862	0.735	0.510	0.519	0.513
1961	309.857	1574.353	1884.209	1108.369	0.707	0.863	0.753	0.515	0.488	0.507
1962	336.437	1530.197	1866.633	1204.679	0.719	0.886	0.770	0.520	0.499	0.514
1963	347.420	1887.213	2234.632	1256.657	0.741	0.886	0.787	0.529	0.462	0.508
1964	382.467	1722.413	2104.880	1371.726	0.750	0.905	0.800	0.538	0.485	0.521
1965	387.386	2249.683	2637.069	1410.323	0.773	0.905	0.817	0.551	0.434	0.512
1966	436.534	1842.431	2279.965	1555.445	0.775	0.920	0.825	0.561	0.476	0.532

	POPULATION			MIGRANTS	STANDARD OF LIVING PER CAPITA CONSUMPTION			EXPECTED RATE		
	RURAL	URBAN	TOTAL	TOTAL	RURAL	URBAN	TOTAL	RURAL	URBAN	TOTAL
1951	17.020	4.180	21.200	0.240	151.880	683.014	256.604	1.030	1.035	1.031
1952	17.311	4.516	21.827	0.251	150.778	696.740	263.731	1.027	1.033	1.028
1953	17.600	4.870	22.470	0.247	150.097	672.268	263.264	1.024	1.026	1.025
1954	17.902	5.229	23.131	0.260	150.446	696.706	273.923	1.022	1.027	1.023
1955	18.201	5.608	23.809	0.263	151.027	690.696	278.144	1.021	1.024	1.021
1956	18.506	6.000	24.505	0.285	152.104	708.395	288.307	1.020	1.024	1.021
1957	18.798	6.422	25.220	0.296	153.699	703.734	293.766	1.019	1.020	1.019
1958	19.088	6.866	25.954	0.313	155.741	718.674	304.654	1.018	1.020	1.019
1959	19.371	7.336	26.707	0.321	158.401	712.786	310.675	1.018	1.017	1.018
1960	19.655	7.824	27.479	0.334	161.479	727.857	322.744	1.018	1.017	1.018
1961	19.935	8.337	28.271	0.337	165.325	719.134	328.634	1.019	1.014	1.017
1962	20.219	8.865	29.084	0.348	169.541	736.637	342.390	1.020	1.015	1.018
1963	20.503	9.415	29.918	0.346	174.726	722.511	347.116	1.021	1.010	1.017
1964	20.797	9.977	30.773	0.355	180.142	745.482	363.423	1.022	1.013	1.019
1965	21.091	10.560	31.651	0.346	186.837	721.840	365.334	1.024	1.007	1.018
1966	21.403	11.148	32.551	0.356	193.444	755.434	385.914	1.025	1.012	1.021

NATIONAL ACCOUNTS - RURAL

	INCOME	CONSUMPTION	INVESTMENT	GOVERNMENT	NET FOREIGN	DEVELOPMENT
1951	2780.000	2585.000	31.000	164.000	0.000	33.400
1952	2814.767	2610.128	30.149	174.490	0.000	35.556
1953	2868.475	2641.762	29.785	196.928	0.000	40.173
1954	2928.963	2693.347	30.749	204.866	C.000	41.793
1955	2999.057	2748.854	32.027	218.176	0.000	44.508
1956	3081.211	2814.770	34.006	232.435	0.000	47.417
1957	3171.462	2889.232	36.714	245.516	0.000	50.085
1958	3275.446	2972.818	40.102	262.525	0.000	53.555
1959	3388.567	3068.384	44.427	275.756	0.000	56.254
1960	3520.112	3173.851	49.458	296.803	C.000	60.548
1961	3661.258	3295.689	55.713	309.857	0.000	63.211
1962	3827.151	3428.033	62.681	336.437	C.000	68.633
1963	4001.060	3582.383	71.257	347.420	0.000	70.874
1964	4209.270	3746.371	80.432	382.467	0.000	78.023
1965	4419.732	3940.553	91.793	387.386	0.000	79.027
1966	4680.135	4140.213	103.388	436.534	0.000	89.053

NATIONAL ACCOUNTS - URBAN

	INCOME	CONSUMPTION	INVESTMENT	GOVERNMENT	NET FOREIGN	DEVELOPMENT
1951	3707.000	2855.000	290.000	562.000	0.000	45.200
1952	3864.030	3146.251	245.111	472.669	0.000	38.050
1953	4318.593	3273.852	395.430	649.310	0.000	52.269
1954	4596.645	3642.741	283.997	669.907	0.000	53.928
1955	5056.747	3873.529	341.697	841.521	0.000	67.742
1956	5374.428	4250.340	248.754	875.334	0.000	70.464
1957	5874.904	4519.615	299.195	1056.094	0.000	85.016
1958	6228.908	4934.117	207.012	1087.780	0.000	87.566
1959	6796.038	5228.691	268.699	1298.649	0.000	104.541
1960	7161.745	5694.814	156.880	1310.051	0.000	105.459
1961	7816.762	5995.254	247.155	1574.353	0.000	126.735
1962	8152.458	6530.128	92.134	1530.197	0.000	123.181
1963	8934.017	6802.654	244.150	1887.213	0.000	151.921
1964	9166.409	7437.381	6.615	1722.413	0.000	138.654
1965	10153.846	7622.535	281.629	2249.683	0.000	181.099
1966	10150.288	8421.498	-114.640	1843.431	0.000	148.396

NATIONAL ACCOUNTS - TOTAL

	INCOME	CONSUMPTION	INVESTMENT	GOVERNMENT	NET FOREIGN	DEVELOPMENT
1951	6487.000	5440.000	321.000	726.000	0.000	78.600
1952	6678.797	5756.379	275.259	647.159	0.000	73.646
1953	7187.067	5915.614	425.214	846.239	0.000	92.443
1954	7525.607	6336.088	314.745	874.774	0.000	95.720
1955	8055.804	6622.383	373.724	1059.697	0.000	112.250
1956	8455.639	7065.110	282.760	1107.770	0.000	117.881
1957	9046.366	7408.847	335.909	1301.610	0.000	135.101
1958	9504.354	7906.935	247.114	1350.305	0.000	141.121
1959	10184.605	8297.075	313.126	1574.404	0.000	160.795
1960	10681.857	8868.665	206.338	1606.854	0.000	166.007
1961	11478.020	9290.943	302.868	1884.209	0.000	189.946
1962	11979.609	9958.161	154.815	1866.633	0.000	191.814
1963	12935.076	10385.037	315.407	2234.632	0.000	222.794
1964	13375.679	11183.752	87.047	2104.880	0.000	216.677
1965	14573.579	11563.088	373.422	2637.069	0.000	260.126
1966	14830.422	12561.710	-11.253	2279.965	0.000	237.449

Notes

[1] For similar generalizations see K. W. Deutsch, "Social Mobilization and Political Development," *American Political Science Review*, vol. 55 (September 1961), pp. 493–514; and S. P. Huntington, "Political Development and Political Decay," *World Politics*, vol. 17 (April 1965), pp. 386–430.

[2] According to M. C. Needler, "the likelihood of a coup d'etat [in Latin America] could be expected to increase as a president's term wears on, reaching its high point prior to a scheduled election but remaining high until the inauguration of a new president. . . ." See "Political Development and Military Intervention in Latin America," *American Political Science Review*, vol. 60 (September 1966), p. 621.

[3] See S. M. Lipset, *Political Man: The Social Bases of Politics* (Garden City, New York: Anchor, 1958), p. 70, and Huntington, *op. cit.*, pp. 417–18. In Lipset's analysis a legitimate political system is the *result* of prolonged economic development; in Huntington's analysis effective political institutions are a *precondition* of sustained economic growth.

[4] See Lipset on cleavages and intolerance, *op. cit.*, pp. 74–79.

[5] See *ibid.*, pp. 68–69, on the crisis of effectiveness.

[6] *Ibid.*, pp. 53–57. See also Huntington, *op. cit.*, pp. 406–407, and Mancur Olson, Jr., "Rapid Growth as a Destabilizing Force," *Journal of Economic History*, vol. 23 (December 1963), pp. 529–52.

[7] Daniel Lerner, *The Passing of Traditional Society: Modernizing the Middle East* (New York: The Free Press, 1958).

[8] Donald J. McCrone and Charles F. Cnudde, "Toward a Communications Theory of Democratic Political Development: A Casual Model," *American Political Science Review*, vol. 61 (March 1967), pp. 72–79.

[9] Wilbur Schramm and W. Lee Ruggels, "How Mass Media Systems Grow," in D. Lerner and W. Schramm, eds., *Communication and Change in the Developing Countries* (Honolulu: East-West Center Press, 1967), pp. 57–75.

[10] *Ibid*, p. 59.

[11] *Ibid.*, pp. 64–67.

[12] Raymond Tanter, "Toward a Theory of Political Development," *Midwest Journal of Political Science*, vol. 11 (May 1967), pp. 145–72.

[13] Hayward R. Alker, Jr., "Causal Inference and Political Analysis," in J. Bernd, ed., *Mathematical Applications in Political Science* (Dallas: Southern Methodist Press, 1966).

[14] Paul Berman, "Systems Theory and Political Development," Committee on Comparative Politics of the Social Science Research Council, 1967.

[15] C. Domingo, "Use of Algorithms to Fit Causal Models to Historical Data," no date (Mimeo).

[16] Lerner, *op. cit.*, p. 60.

[17] *Ibid.*, p. 16.

[18] *Ibid.*, p. 46.

[19] *Ibid.*, p. 59.

[20] *Ibid.*, p. 88. The global ratio is apparently $b = \dfrac{Y - a}{X}$.

[21] So far as we know, no one has yet used a causal model of the type used by McCrone and Cnudde to make rigorous deductions about specific cases. Since their method, like regression analysis, requires the summation of moments of variables across individual cases, this should in principle prove to be difficult.

[22] McCrone and Cnudde, *op. cit.*, p. 78.

[23] *Ibid.*

[24] *Ibid.*

[25] The same can be said of Phillips Cutright, "National Political Development: Its Measurement and Correlates," in N. W. Polsby, R. A. Dentler, and P. A. Smith, *Politics and Social Life* (Boston: Houghton Mifflin, 1963), p. 580: "Under the assumption that the institutions of a society form an interdependent system in equilibrium nations should tend to move to the regression line [of political development on communications] so that their communications development equilibrates with their political development." Others, however, have considered these assumptions. See Hayward Alker, *op. cit.*, pp. 15–17; K. W. Deutsch, C. I. Bliss, and A. Eckstein, "Population, Sovereignty, and the Share of Foreign Trade," *Economic Development and Cultural Change*, vol. 10 (July 1962), p. 354; and, Charles Wolf, Jr., "The Political Effects of Economic Programs: Some Indications from Latin America," *Economic Development and Cultural Change*, vol. 14 (October 1965), p. 3.

[26] Domingo, *op. cit.*

[27] Berman, *op. cit.*

[28] Lerner, *op. cit.*, p. 55.

[29] *Ibid.*, p. 63.

[30] *Ibid.*, p. 46.

[31] *Ibid.*, p. 67.

[32] *Ibid.*

[33] *Ibid.*

[34] James M. Beshers, *Population Processes in Social Systems* (New York: The Free Press, 1967), Chapters 5 and 7.

[35] Bruce Herrick, *Urban Migration and Economic Development in Chile* (Cambridge: M.I.T. Press, 1965), p. 14.

[36] Bernard Okun and Richard W. Richardson, "Regional Income Inequality and Internal Population Migration," *Economic Development and Cultural Change*, vol. 9 (January 1961), pp. 128–43, cite at p. 130.

[37] Gunnar Myrdal, *Economic Theory and Underdeveloped Regions* (London: Duckworth, 1957), p. 27.

[38] Richard D. Robinson, *The First Turkish Republic: A Case Study in National Development* (Cambridge: Harvard University Press, 1965), pp. 211–12. Cf. also Aprodicio A. Laquian, "Manila's Urban Renewal Program," *Philippine Journal of Public Administration*, vol. 10 (April–July 1966), 176–83, for the dimensions of the Philippine problem and some preliminary governmental responses to a rapidly deteriorating situation where out of some "2.7 million people in the Metropolitan Manila area, 160,000 were listed as squatters and another 411,760 classified as living in slum conditions," p. 177.

[39] Kemal H. Karpat, "The Turkish Elections of 1957," *Western Political Quarterly*, vol. 14 (June 1961), p. 459. Different sources give slightly different results.

[40] Data are reported in Hirofumi Ando, "A Study of Electoral Behavior in the Philippines," (University of Michigan, Center for South and Southeast Asia Studies; Working Paper No. 17, Seminar on the Conditions for Democratic Development, Summer, 1968), pp. 33, 35 (Mimeo).

[41] Deutsch, "Social Mobilization and Political Development," *op. cit.*, p. 499.

[42] Frederick W. Frey, "Political Development, Power, and Communications in Turkey," in L. W. Pye, ed., *Communications and Political Development* (Princeton: Princeton University Press, 1963), p. 314. There are conflicting views about the role of communication barriers. See Max F. Millikan and Donald L. M. Blackmer, eds., *The Emerging Nations: Their Growth and United States Policy* (Boston: Little, Brown, 1961), pp. 19–20ff.

[43] Caridad C. Semaña, "Philippine Politics and Economic Development," *Philippine Journal of Public Administration*, vol. 21 (January 1967), pp. 24–40, cite at p. 38.

[44] Carl H. Landé, *Leaders, Factions, and Parties: The Structure of Philippine Politics* (New Haven: Yale University Southeast Asia Studies Monograph No. 6, 1965), p. 115.

[45] See Robert S. Yuill, "A Simulation Study of Barrier Effects in Spatial Diffusion Problems," (Evanston: Northwestern University, Department of Geography Research Report No. 5, November, 1964), for an introductory, albeit rigorous, empirical treatment of the barrier effect.

[46] Lipset, *Political Man, op. cit.*, pp. 47–48.

[47] Ronald G. Ridker, "Discontent and Economic Growth," *Economic Development and Cultural Change*, vol. 21 (October 1962), pp. 1–15, cite at p. 12.

[48] James Duesenberry, *Income, Savings, and the Theory of Consumer Behavior* (Cambridge: Harvard University Press, 1949), pp. 27–32.

[49] W. Arthur Lewis, *The Theory of Economic Growth* (London: George Allen and Unwin, 1955), pp. 29–32.

[50] Charles Wolf, Jr., *Foreign Aid: Theory and Practice in Southern Asia* (Princeton: Princeton University Press, 1960), p. 317.

[51] Deutsch, "Social Mobilization and Political Development," *op. cit.*, p. 502.

[52] Harold D. Lasswell and Abraham Kaplan, *Power and Society: A Framework for Political Inquiry* (New Haven: Yale University Press 1950), p. 264.

[53] Lerner, *op. cit.*, p. 163.

[54] A. H. Hanson, "Democracy Transplanted: Reflections on a Turkish Election," *Parliamentary Affairs*, vol. 9 (1955–56), p. 69.

[55] Robinson, *op. cit.*, p. 13.

[56] See Kemal H. Karpat, "The Turkish Left," *Journal of Contempory History*, vol. I (1966), p. 179; and, A. H. Hanson, "Turkey Today," *Political Quarterly* (October–December, 1955), p. 332.

[57] Landé, *op. cit.*, pp. 79–80.

[58] *Ibid.*, p. 50.

[59] John Kautsky, *Political Change in Underdeveloped Countries: Nationalism and Communism* (New York: John Wiley, 1962), p. 117.

[60] Albert O. Hirschman, *The Strategy of Economic Development* (New Haven: Yale University Press, 1958), pp. 205–206.

[61] Frey, *op. cit.*, pp. 324–25.

[62] Semaña, *op. cit.*, p. 37. See also Mary R. Hollnsteiner, *The Dynamics of Power in a Philippine Municipality* (Manila: Community Development Research Council, University of the Philippines, 1963), for a discussion of the reluctance of village leadership to utilize existing barrio legislation and taxing measures and their continuing dependence on the central government to provide necessary services and improvements for the villages.

[63] P.A. Samuelson, "Interactions Between the Multiplier Analysis and the Principle of Acceleration," *Review of Economic Statistics*, vol. 21 (1939), pp. 75–78.

[64] Hirschman, *op. cit.*, p. 6.

[65] *Ibid.*, pp. 6–7. Cf. the following: "What is gained by considering resources and production factors latent and conditionally available rather than outright absent or scarce? The advantage appears to be that in this way attention is properly focused on the essential dynamic and strategic aspects of the development process. Instead of concentrating exclusively on the husbanding of scarce resources such as capital and entrepreneurship, our approach leads us to look for 'pressures' and 'inducement mechanisms' that will elicit and mobilize the largest possible amount of these resources. . . . The formulation of the development problem which is here proposed calls particular attention to the fact that the use of different economic resources has very different repercussions or 'feedback' effects on the available stocks of these resources."

[66] Charles Wolf, Jr., *Foreign Aid: Theory and Practice in Southern Asia* (Princeton: Princeton University Press, 1960), pp. 321–24 for a discussion of per capita consumption and per capita income as alternative measures.

[67] It is worthwhile to note that, "Investment is still comparatively the most volatile and least predictable among the more important variables that are involved in the growth process." Economists have distinguished between induced and autonomous investment, "But as long as there remains an 'autonomous' investment, i.e., a portion that cannot be convincingly explained by economic variables, we are still without a comprehensive theory of investment." Hirschman, *op. cit.*, p. 33.

[68] See Lucian W. Pye, *Aspects of Political Development* (Boston: Little Brown, 1966), pp. 64–65, for a treatment of the concept of penetration: "The penetration problem is that of building up the effectiveness of the formal institutions by government and of establishing confidence and rapport between rulers and subjects. Initially governments often find it difficult to motivate the population or to change its values and habits in order to bring support to programs of national development. On the other hand, at times the

effectiveness of the government in breaking down old patterns of control [and dependence] can unleash widespread demands for a greater influence on government policies."

[69] For an argument that large-scale government planning and direct state intervention in the economy are based at least in part on domestic political considerations see S. M. Lipset, *The First New Nation* (New York: Basic Books, 1963), p. 46. For some data from Turkey on the same point see Malcolm D. Rivkin, *Area Development for National Growth; The Turkish Precedent*, (New York: Praeger, 1965), p. 96. Public investment as a percentage of total investment in Turkey declined from 1950 to 1954 (a period during which the Democratic government gained in popular support) and increased from 1954 to 1956 (during which the Democrats lost support).

[70] Although this concept bears a close relationship to what Deutsch, *op. cit.*, calls social mobilization, we have continued to call it participation in order to be consistent with the discussion in section 2. To reiterate, however, this concept of participation is *not* voting turnout.

[71] In general, no one really knows the proper scale of models of this sort. How small and simple must a model be in order to be manageable and useful? How large and complex must it be in order to be sufficiently realistic? For some speculations see J. Forrester in M. Greenberger, *Computers and The World of the Future* (Cambridge: M.I.T. Press, 1962), pp. 88ff.

[72] See, however, Irene B. Taeuber, "Population and Modernization in Turkey," *Population Index*, vol. 24 (April 1968).

[73] Robinson, *op. cit.*, pp. 213–14.

[74] See in particular the data in the Public Finances section of several United Nations *Statistical Yearbooks:* 1956, pp. 525–26, 1960, p. 535; 1966, p. 652.

[75] See Kemal H. Karpat, *Turkey's Politics: The Transition to a Multi-Party System* (Princeton: Princeton University Press, 1959), p. 421.

[76] Robinson, *op. cit.*, p. 151.

[77] *Ibid.*

[78] Quoted in *Ibid.*, p. 209.

[79] C. Francis and S. J. Madigan, "Hindsight and Foresight: The Census of the Philippines, 1948 and 1960," *Philippine Studies*, vol. 6, no. 1 (March 1958), p. 91ff.

[80] Empirical work being done on the rural–urban issue would include the following: J. E. Spencer, "The Cities of the Philippines," *The Journal of Geography*, vol. 57 (September 1958), 288–89f; Isao Fujimoto, "The Social Complexity of Philippine Towns and Cities," (Paper read at Meetings, Association for Asian Studies, Boston, March 1969) (Mimeo.); W. A. Withington, "The Intermediate-Size Urban Center: Its Significance and Role in the Developing World of Southeast Asia," (Paper read at AAS, Boston, March 1969) (Mimeo.); Frank M. LeBar, ed., "The Philippines," *Human Relations Area Files*, vol. 1 (New Haven: HRAF, 1955), pp. 367, 375, 409; and Thomas F. Barton, "Rural and Urban Dwellers of Southeast Asia," *The Journal of Geography*, vol. 64 (March 1965), 113–22. That there is little general agreement as to what is in fact "urban" is evidenced in the wide variety of numerical labels used for definition in these papers. Our estimate is within the acceptable range circumscribed by these other efforts.

[81] For some observations about Philippine population data see Amos H. Hawley, *Papers in Demography and Public Administration* (Manila: Institute of Public Administration, University of the Philippines, 1954).

[82] Important contributors to the debate over Philippine national accounts statistics are the following: Emmanuel Levy, *Review of Economic Statistics on the Philippines, Interim Report* (World Bank Resident Mission, Manila, May 1964) (Mimeo.); Clarence L. Barber, "National Income Estimates in the Philippines," *The Philippine Economic Journal*, vol. 4, no. 1 (First Semester 1965), pp. 66–77; and, Ruben F. Trinidad, "Some Proposed Improvements in the Estimation of Capital Formation in the Philippines," *The Statistical Reporter*, vol. 4 (April 1960), pp. 28–40.

[83] See A. B. Abello, *Patterns of Philippine Public Expenditure and Revenue, 1951–1960* (Quezon City: Institute of Economic Development and Research, University of the Philippines, 1964), p. 38: "The National Internal Revenue Code (Sec. 123) levies internal revenue taxes on manufactured products solely and exempts from the sales tax transactions involving specifically agricultural products sold by original producers. . . ."

[84] Trinidad, *op. cit.*

[85] See Landé, *op. cit.*, p. 123: "The most significant characteristic setting Manila off from the rest of the country is that the city traditionally has rallied to opposition parties to a greater extent or earlier than have the provinces. . . ."

[86] O. D. Corpuz, *The Philippines* (Englewood Cliffs: Prentice-Hall, 1965), pp. 119ff.; Corpuz, *op. cit.*, pp. 119ff.; Lande, *op. cit.*, pp. 29ff.; and John E. deYoung and Chester L. Hunt, "Communication Channels and Functional Literacy in the Philippine Barrio," in Socorro C. Espiritu and Chester L. Hunt, eds., *Social Foundations of Community Development: Readings on the Philippines* (Manila: R. M. Garcia, 1964), pp. 262–63, 65.

[87] Hirschman, *op. cit.*

[88] Myrdal, *op. cit.*, p. 17.

[89] *Ibid.*, pp. 19–20.

[90] For example the average annual *decrease* of the Mexican population in the period 1910–21 was 80,000. Howard F. Cline, *Mexico: Revolution to Evolution: 1940–1960* (New York: Oxford University Press, 1963), p. 336.

[91] For a theory about the processes involved, see D. M. Heer, "Economic Development and the Fertility Transition," *Daedalus*, vol. 97 (Spring 1968), pp. 433–46.

[92] Hirschman, *op. cit.*

[93] For an example of an ultra-stable system, see W. Ross Ashby, *An Introduction to Cybernetics* (London: Chapman and Hall, 1961), pp. 241–43.

[94] On simulation models and projections see H. D. Lasswell, "Technique of Decision Seminars," *Midwest Journal of Political Science*, vol. 4 (August 1960), especially pp. 221 and 226; and Daniel Bell, "Twelve Modes of Prediction—A Preliminary Sorting of Approaches in the Social Sciences," *Daedalus*, vol. 93 (Summer 1964), pp. 872–73.

[95] Richard Bellman, "Mathematical Aspects of the Theory of Systems," RAND Corp., P–3032, 1965, p. 3.

Contents for Essay II
Simulation and Complex Political Systems

Essay
II
Simulation and Complex Political Systems

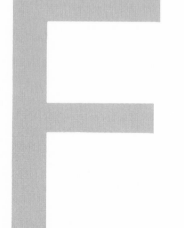

Introduction

ew political scientists would deny the proposition that political
systems are complex. A complex system, in the words of Herbert Simon, is

> ... roughly, one made up of a large number of parts that interact in
> a nonsimple way. In such systems, the whole is more than the sum of
> the parts, not in an ultimate, metaphysical sense, but in the important
> pragmatic sense that, given the properties of the parts and the laws of

Notes to Essay II begin on page 172.

interaction, it is not a trivial matter to infer the properties of the whole. In the face of complexity, an in-principle reductionist may be at the time a pragmatic holist.[1]

Although it is difficult to understand the whole political system in terms of its parts, it is also difficult to understand any of the parts without reference to the whole. In the words of David Easton

> ... each part of the larger political canvas does not stand alone but is related to each other part; or to put it positively, ... the operation of no one part can be fully understood without reference to the way in which the whole itself operates.[2]

Furthermore, few political scientists would deny the proposition that we as human beings have only a limited capacity to deal with complex systems as wholes. As a noted psychologist has written

> It seems to me that the very fact of our limited capacity for processing information has made it necessary for us to discover clever ways to abstract the essential features of our universe and to express these features in simple laws that we are capable of comprehending in a single act or thought. We are constantly taking information given in one form and translating it into alternative forms, searching for ways to map a strange, new phenomenon into simpler and more familiar ones.[3]

In short, the complexity of our subject matter on the one hand and our limited capacity on the other require us to simplify.

One form of simplification in the study of political systems at the national level is specialization through selective emphasis of certain purposes,[4] empirical approaches, and methods, and the de-emphasis of others. By and large the *scientific* purpose of theory-building[5] has tended to dominate our efforts, but there are also examples of the *historical* orientation toward the clarification of past events,[6] the *projective* orientation toward the clarification of future events,[7] the *normative* orientation toward clarification of the goals of political systems,[8] and the *policy* orientation toward the invention and evaluation of policy alternatives.[9] Empirical approaches attempting to deal with systems as wholes include the *cybernetic* approach, which emphasizes communication and control in political systems;[10] the *structural-functional* approach, which emphasizes political institutions, related structures, and the functions they perform;[11] and the *political-cultural* approach, which emphasizes differences in the subjective bases of political behavior both between and within polities.[12] Specialization by methods involves *theoretical* and pre-theoretical studies emphasizing abstractions drawn from other disciplines or generalizations gleaned from the observation of many political systems;[13]

case studies emphasizing information about the richness and variety of political experience in individual countries;[14] and *statistical* studies, which tend to emphasize "hard" quantitative information.[15] No individual study conforms precisely to any one of these types, but in most cases the emphasis is clear.[16]

Another form of simplification is the widespread use, within the areas of specialization, of assumptions and procedures appropriate for the study of some kinds of natural and social phenomena but not sufficient for the study of complex systems.[17] For example, in so far as studies distinguished according to purpose deal with concrete situations, a good case can be made that they tend to attribute uncertainty or unexplained variation in the behavior of political systems to stochastic (random) factors or observation errors. Yet a significant part of the diverse behavior of complex systems at appropriate levels of aggregation is *not* essentially statistical. Furthermore, each of the major empirical approaches proposes basic variables and relationships on the one hand and operational indices of variables on the other as means of studying political systems as wholes. But to the extent that the systems are in fact treated as wholes the connection between the two is not sufficiently close for significant scientific progress. For simple systems the gap between structural parts and the behavior of the whole system may be trivial, but for complex systems, as Simon and Easton suggest in the comments cited above, it is significant. In similar ways it can be shown that each of the three methods in itself fails to cope adequately with the complex nature of political systems.

There will always be a need for specialization and for simplifying assumptions and procedures, but these simplifications are costly. The task of studying complex political systems has a quality of "wholeness" just as the systems themselves do. The scope of analysis cannot be limited to any single purpose since each study specialized to one purpose necessarily makes assumptions about the results of studies specialized to other purposes. For example, rational policy analysis depends either implicitly or explicitly on the clarifications of goals, past and future trends, and the factors conditioning those trends.[18] Similarly, the parts of political systems selected for analysis cannot be limited to those emphasized by any single empirical approach since each approach deals with only a part of the phenomena of importance in explaining the behavior of political systems. If and when adequate theories of political systems are developed, it is a safe bet they will incorporate ideas and insights about communication and control, political institutions and the functions they perform, *and* political culture. Furthermore, most political scientists would agree in principle that information utilized in the study of political systems should not be limited to the type associated with any one of the methodological approaches. Abstractions in themselves tend to be sterile; rich, detailed information about individual countries tends to lack generality; and "hard" quantitative data are in themselves relatively meaningless. Finally, until attempts are made to define the nature of complex political systems and the implications of complexity for political analysis, there is little reason to believe that our efforts ultimately will be successful. Whatever simplifying assumptions and procedures we utilize must be adapted to or consistent with the nature of complex systems. In short, while simplifications are necessary, so are communication and coordination among the areas of specialization and assumptions and procedures that enable us to deal more adequately with problems of complexity.

We have necessarily dealt with large issues in this summary appraisal of the study of political systems at the national level. More detailed consideration of recent studies would no doubt allow us to modify the emphases and qualify the substance of our argument. Other reasons for simplification, other kinds of simplification, and perhaps at some points exceptions to the argument could be found. Nevertheless we believe our major contention is sound: There is a need to take down the barriers separating areas of specialization in the study of national political systems and within each speciality to deal explicitly with the problems of complexity in order to develop empirically adequate theories that are relevant to a number of interdependent purposes.

Computer simulation, a relatively new and unexplored methodology, promises to be of some use in coordinating and fostering communication among the areas of specialization[19] and in coping with the problems of complexity. The promise, in short, is to extend our present capacity to deal with complex political systems as wholes. In the next section we formalize the concept of a political system, investigate the nature of complexity and the role of simulation in coping with it, and summarize a model of modernization and mass politics to be used for illustrative purposes. In Sections 2 and 3 we consider areas of specialization defined by purposes and empirical approaches, respectively, and the role of computer simulation in each. Section 4 deals with the role of other methods. Finally, in the Conclusion we summarize the advantages and limitations of computer simulation in the study of complex political systems.

1. Systems, Complexity, and Simulation

We have asserted that political systems are complex. But what do we mean by "systems" and what are their relevant properties? What makes systems complex? And what is the role of simulation in dealing with complex systems? Our general answers to these questions in this section are reconsidered from several different perspectives in subsequent sections.

David Easton's model of a political system is familiar to most political scientists.

> ... inputs are converted by the processes of the system into outputs and these, in turn, have consequences both for the system and for the environment in which the system exists. The formula here is very simple but, as I hope to show, also very illuminating: inputs—political system or processes—outputs.[20]

Easton summarizes his conception in the diagram presented in Figure 1.1.

Figure 1.1—Easton's Conception of the Political System

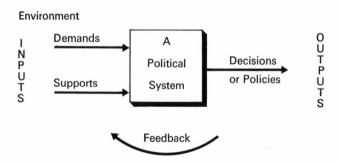

Demands and supports are the inputs to the political system and decisions or policies are the outputs. Political processes convert inputs into outputs, and processes in the environment convert the outputs of the political system into inputs.

A more precise, analytically powerful statement of essentially the same ideas is the following: A political system can be conceived as a state vector $\mathbf{X}_t$ and a set of rules G for determining its values at any time t.[21] The state vector $\mathbf{X}_t$ is really very simple. As shown in (1.1), it is merely the set of variables $x_{i,t}$ and parameters α_j needed to describe the state of a system at any point in time. Both variables and parameters may assume different quantitative values among systems of the same class (e.g., countries in a

$$\mathbf{X}_t = \begin{vmatrix} x_{1,t} \\ x_{2,t} \\ \cdot \\ \cdot \\ x_{n,t} \\ \alpha_1 \\ \alpha_2 \\ \cdot \\ \cdot \\ \alpha_m \end{vmatrix} \tag{1.1}$$

region). But in each individual system, those components of the state vector which are assumed to vary through time we call *variables*, and those which are assumed to remain approximately constant through time we call *parameters*. By specifying the quantitative value of each of the components in $\mathbf{X}_t$ we describe the state of the system at time t. The rule for determining the value of $\mathbf{X}_t$ given information about the system's present and p previous states is a set of functions G as shown in (1.2).

$$X_t = G(X_t, X_{t-1}, \ldots, X_{t-p}) \tag{1.2}$$

($\mathbf{X}_t$ is included on the right hand side of the equation because one component $x_{i,t}$ may be a function of some other component $x_{j,t}$ within the same time period, as in the example to be considered below.) The functions G determine $\mathbf{X}_t$ from $\mathbf{X}_t, \mathbf{X}_{t-1}, \ldots, \mathbf{X}_{t-p}$; they determine $\mathbf{X}_{t+1}$, from $\mathbf{X}_{t+1}$, $\mathbf{X}_t, \ldots, \mathbf{X}_{t-p+1}$; and so on up to the point in time at which the analysis of the system stops. The outputs of the functions G at one point in time become the inputs for the next. In Easton's terms, $\mathbf{X}_t$ is merely the set of variables and parameters needed to describe the demands, supports, and decisions of the system. G is simply the set of processes operating in the political system and the environment.

The *structure* of a class of systems (e.g., countries in a region) is the set of components $\mathbf{X}_t$ and the set of relationships G. Together they constitute a theory of the systems, a temporary commitment to and representation of the phenomena of importance in the class of systems under consideration. A *model* of any one of the systems is the general structure with the magnitudes of the variables and parameters specified to represent the particular context. The *behavior* of a model is the set of time series of the $x_{i,t}$ that are produced as the relationships generate successive state descriptions.

To illustrate these ideas, let us consider the following small structure representing an economic system. It was originally designed to trace the marginal effects of a constant level of government spending on the growth of national income.[22] The state vector X_t consists of five components (three variables and two parameters) as shown in (1.3).

$$\mathbf{X}_t = \begin{vmatrix} x_{1,t} \\ x_{2,t} \\ x_{3,t} \\ \alpha_1 \\ \alpha_2 \end{vmatrix} \tag{1.3}$$

The set of relationships G is given in (1.4).

$$\begin{aligned} x_{1,t} &= x_{2,t} + x_{3,t} + 1 \\ x_{2,t} &= \alpha_1 x_{1,t-1} \\ x_{3,t} &= \alpha_2(x_{2,t} - x_{2,t-1}) \end{aligned} \tag{1.4}$$

For our purposes the substantive interpretation of the structure is not important; we are interested only in its formal properties as a system.

Four sets of time series, which constitute the behavior of the structure in four different contexts are given in Table 1.1. For convenience, the initial

Table 1.1—The Behavior of Four Simple Models Having Identical Structure

	a. Asymptotic			b. Oscillates, Converges		
	$\alpha_1 = .5$	$\alpha_2 = 0$		$\alpha_1 = .5$	$\alpha_2 = 1$	
t	$x_{1,t}$	$x_{2,t}$	$x_{3,t}$	$x_{1,t}$	$x_{2,t}$	$x_{3,t}$
1	1.00	.00	.00	1.00	.00	.00
2	1.50	.50	.00	2.00	.50	.50
3	1.75	.75	.00	2.50	1.00	.50
4	1.88	.88	.00	2.50	1.25	.25
5	1.94	.94	.00	2.25	1.25	.00
6	1.97	.97	.00	2.00	1.13	—.13
7	1.98	.98	.00	1.88	1.00	—.13
8	1.99	.99	.00	1.88	.94	—.06
9	1.996	.996	.00	1.94	.94	.00
10	1.998	.998	.00	2.00	.97	.03

	c. Oscillates, Diverges			d. Quasi-geometric Growth		
	$\alpha_1 = .8$	$\alpha_2 = 1.5$		$\alpha_1 = .8$	$\alpha_2 = 3$	
t	$x_{1,t}$	$x_{2,t}$	$x_{3,t}$	$x_{1,t}$	$x_{2,t}$	$x_{3,t}$
1	1.00	.00	.00	1.00	.00	.00
2	3.00	.80	1.20	4.20	.80	2.40
3	5.80	2.40	2.40	12.04	3.36	7.68
4	9.00	4.64	3.36	29.45	9.63	18.82
5	12.04	7.20	3.84	66.34	23.56	41.78
6	14.28	9.63	3.65	142.61	53.07	88.54
7	15.11	11.42	2.69	298.13	114.08	183.04
8	14.09	12.09	1.00	612.75	238.50	373.25
9	11.04	11.27	−1.23	1,246.30	490.20	755.10
10	6.18	8.83	−3.66	2,518.55	997.04	1,520.51
—	—	—	—	—	—	—

conditions $x_{1,1} = 1$ and $x_{2,1} = x_{3,1} = 0$ are identical in each case; only the parameters α_1 and α_2 differ among the cases. Each set of time series represents a qualitatively distinct pattern of behavior. In case *a*, $x_{1,t}$ and $x_{2,t}$ increase asymptotically to values which in this case are 2.0 and 1.0 respectively. ($x_{3,t}$ is constant and equal to zero because $\alpha_2 = 0$.) In case *b*, the three variables oscillate, but the oscillations are damped and the time series begin to converge. By $t = 22$ the variables reach stable values of 2.000, 1.000, and .000. In case *c*, the time series also oscillate, but each oscillation is larger in magnitude than the previous one. The maximum values attained by $x_{1,t}$ in successive cycles are 15.11 ($t = 7$) and 44.46 ($t = 22$). Similarly, for $x_{2,t}$ successive peaks are 12.09 ($t = 8$) and 35.57 ($t = 23$), and for $x_{3,t}$ successive peaks are 3.84 ($t = 5$) and 15.03 ($t = 20$). The model in this case obviously exhibits explosive behavior. In case *d*, the time series increase smoothly at a rate approaching a geometric rate of growth. For each of these qualitative types of systemic behavior there are an infinite number of quantitative variations, one for each combination of values of α_1 and α_2.

This example suggests several important points about the study of systems in general. First, the qualitative and quantitative differences in behavior among even the small systems in this exercise cannot be attributed to stochastic processes, observation error, or structural differences, all of which have been eliminated. Systems having identical structure produce diverse patterns of behavior in different contexts. Second, the structural and behavioral perspectives on even a small system are at least partially distinct. That is to say, to the untrained observer more inspection of the structural components and the data inputs suggests little about the behavior of the models, and inspection of the behavior of the models suggest even less about the structural components. There is, in short, a gap between the understanding of the structural components and the behavior of the whole system. Third, the structural relationships determine and explain the behavior of the model in each context even though the contexts may differ. For example, in each case $(x_{2,t} - x_{2,t-1})$ causes $x_{3,t}$, even though the parameter α_2 governing the magnitude of the impact of the former on the latter varies from case to case. Conversely, the pattern of behavior of the model does not explain the general structure of the system uniquely. Such a pattern is only one of many possible patterns inherent in the structure. Moreover, models having different structures could in principle produce the same pattern of behavior. The implication is that theory-building, in so far as it is concerned with the parsimonious explanation of a general class of phenomena (e.g., the behavior of political systems), should focus on clarifying their assumed common structure in order to explain their obviously diverse behavior.

COMPLEXITY

Other things being equal, the complexity of a system—in terms of potential diversity of behavior and of difficulty in deducing the behavior of the whole from its structural parts and inferring the structural parts from the behavior of the whole—depends upon its size. The size of a system depends in part on its state vector. As W. Ross Ashby has pointed out

> In the concepts of cybernetics, a system's "largeness" must refer to the number of distinctions made: either to the number of states available, or, if its states are defined by a vector, to the number of components in the vector (i.e., to the number of its variables or of its degrees of freedom . . .).[23]

By the number of states available Ashby means the number of values the components can assume. In this sense a system in which, say, the $x_{i,t}$ can assume only the values 0 and 1 is smaller than a system in which the $x_{i,t}$ can assume any value between 0 and 1. By the number of components in the state vector Ashby apparently means the number of variables and parameters.

> The two measures are correlated, for if other things are equal, the addition of extra variables will make possible extra states. A system may also be made larger from our functional point of view if, the number of variables being fixed, each is measured more precisely, so as to make it show more distinguishable states.[24]

In the small system introduced above, each of the components of the state vector is a continuous measure, and the number of values it can assume is limited only by the accuracy of measurement over the range of reasonable values. Consequently, the number of variables and parameters becomes the more important indicator of the size and complexity of the system.

The size of a system also depends on the degree of connectedness among the components of its state vector. Again in Ashby's terms

> ... there exist factors, such as "height of thresholds" ... which can vary a large system continuously along the whole range that has at one end the totally-joined form, in which every variable has an immediate effect on every other variable, and at the other end the totally-unjoined form, in which every variable is independent of every other. Systems can thus show more or less of "wholeness."[25]

The degree of connectedness among components may depend on structural specifications. Thus where two variables by hypothesis are unjoined or unconnected in a class of systems, there is no direct causal relationship between them in the set of relationships G and the "height of threshold," to use Ashby's phrase, is effectively zero in all systems of the class. The degree of connectedness may also depend on the magnitudes of the components in any particular system. Thus, to take the simplest case, where two variables are linked in a structural relationship, the magnitude of the parameter governing the impact of the cause on the effect may be sufficiently weak to consider the variables unjoined or unconnected in a particular system.

Suppose that the components and relationships of a system S can be grouped into subsystems P, D, and E. Suppose further that—as a consequence of general structure or particular context—the components of P are completely unconnected to the components of D and E. Then it should be obvious that the structure and behavior of P can be studied independently of D and E and vice versa. Compared to a system S', having the same state vector as S but with direct causal connections between P on the one hand and D and E on the other, the system S is smaller and less complex. It is less obvious but equally true that if the connections between P and the rest of S' are *sufficiently weak*, then certain aspects of P's behavior are approximately independent of the behavior of the rest of S', giving rise to the possibility that P can be studied independently. This is the general conclusion of the mathematical work on the decomposability of linear systems by Albert Ando, Franklin Fisher, and Herbert Simon.[26] At subsequent points in this essay we shall consider in detail the implications of decomposability as in the case of system S and near decomposability as in the case of S'. For the time being it is sufficient to emphasize the point that the size of a system depends not only on the number of components in its state vector but also on the degree of connectedness or of decomposability among those components.

The complexity of systems is also influenced by the functional forms of their relationships,[27] the importance of stochastic factors, and errors in the observation of their behavior. These things being equal, however, the complexity of systems is decisively a matter of their size. The greater the number of variables functionally linked together in a system, the greater is the number of possible states it can assume and the greater is the number of interactions obscuring the links between the structure of the system and its behavior as it operates through time.

SIMULATION

As we have suggested, the scientific study of a class of political systems involves the clarification of their assumed common structure in order to explain their diverse behavior. Whether the emphasis is on the clarification of structure or the explanation of behavior, there is a necessary interaction between theory and data. On the one hand, the structure and data inputs are used *to deduce* the behavior of the system in each context. On the other, a lack of fit between deduced behavior and the observed behavior of a corresponding real world system is used *to infer* productive changes in the structure of the model. Verbal, mathematical, and simulational forms of analysis have been used to effect this confrontation between theory and data.

Verbal forms of analysis can be very rich and insightful. However, as verbal formulations of individual relationships are drawn together in an attempt to do justice to the interdependency within systems, they become increasingly cumbersome, imprecise, and in some cases indeterminate. Consider, for example, axiomatic theory, a very simple form of verbal analysis, which deals with the following type of deduction: The greater A, the greater B; the greater B, the greater C; therefore, the greater A, the greater C. It has been shown that even if the premises are true the conclusion may be false.[28] The conclusion is true only if the relationships between A and B and between B and C are sufficiently strong. Axiomatic theory in itself is incapable of incorporating the necessary quantitative precision. In short, deductions based on verbal forms of analysis are not particularly useful in the study of even simple systems.

If verbal statements of theory can be translated into variables and equations, mathematical techniques are sometimes applicable. For example, for the small system (1.4) introduced above, the technique of difference equations can be used to find all possible qualitative patterns of behavior of the system and to calculate any particular pattern given the magnitudes of the initial conditions and parameters. The procedure, in brief, is to transform the set of relationships G through substitution into a set of equations giving each variable $x_{i,t}$ in terms of the same variable at the earlier time periods, $x_{i,t-1}$ and $x_{i,t-2}$. Then for each of the new equations a solution can be found giving $x_{i,t}$ at any time t in terms of a set of parameters and initial conditions $x_{i,0}$ and $x_{i,1}$. Using the solution for $x_{1,t}$ and assuming the boundary conditions $0 < \alpha_1 < 1$ and $\alpha_2 > 0$, it can be shown that

$x_{1,t}$ approaches $\dfrac{1}{1-\alpha_1}$ asymptotically if $\alpha_1\alpha_2 < 1$ and $\alpha_1 > \dfrac{4\alpha_2}{(1+\alpha_2)^2}$;

$x_{1,t}$ oscillates and converges to $\dfrac{1}{1-\alpha_1}$ if $\alpha_1\alpha_2 < 1$ and $\alpha_1 < \dfrac{4\alpha_2}{(1+\alpha_2)^2}$;

$x_{1,t}$ oscillates around $\dfrac{1}{1-\alpha_1}$ and diverges if $\alpha_1\alpha_2 > 1$ and $\alpha_1 < \dfrac{4\alpha_2}{(1+\alpha_2)^2}$;

and

$x_{1,t}$ increases almost geometrically if $\alpha_1\alpha_2 > 1$ and $\alpha_1 > \dfrac{4\alpha_2}{(1+\alpha_2)^2}$.

These results are independent of the magnitudes of $x_{1,0}$ and $x_{1,1}$. If the magnitudes of $x_{1,0}$, $x_{1,1}$, α_1 and α_2 are specified, the solution can be used to calculate the magnitude of $x_{1,t}$ at any time t. Such solutions, however, become increasingly difficult to find as the number of variables and relationships increases, other things being equal. In short, mathematical techniques are applicable only to relatively small systems.

For larger systems it becomes necessary at some point to abandon mathematical techniques and to deduce the behavior of the system numerically by performing a sequence of arithmetic calculations for each set of data inputs. Whether the calculations are performed by hand or by computer, it is appropriate to call this simulation. Briefly, the procedure is to specify quantitative values for each of the initial conditions and parameters, and then calculate the values of the variables at the next and all suceeding time periods. The procedure for the small system (1.4) is presented as a flow chart in Figure 1.2. Arrows between boxes indicate the sequence of steps. Arrows within boxes indicate that the quantity on the right is to be assigned to the variable on the left. The particular data inputs given in Figure 1.2 produce the time series presented in case *b* of Table 1.1. To determine the possible qualitative types of behavior of a system through simulation, it is necessary to perform calculations for each unique set of inputs and then examine the results. One never knows whether enough sets of inputs have been tried to produce all of the qualitative possibilities. In this sense, simulation is a less powerful method than mathematical methods, but it can be used to explore much larger systems.

The behavioral properties of very large models containing hundreds of variables and relationships have been studied for specific sets of inputs through the use of computer simulation.[29] However, the utility of simulation

Figure 1.2—A Flow Chart to Determine the Behavior
of a Small Illustrative Model

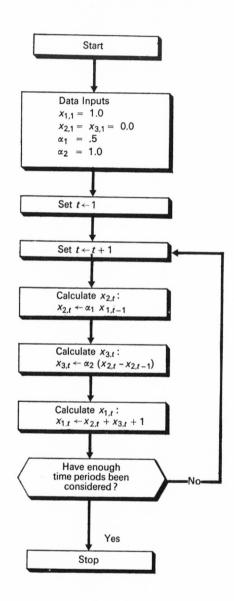

for theory-building drops off sharply as the size of a model increases, because it becomes increasingly difficult for the investigator to understand the complicated patterns of direct and indirect cause and effect in the model. Although it is still possible to compare simulated and historical time series to find out whether the behavior of the model is unrealistic, it is more difficult to use the comparisons to propose meaningful revisions of the model. The investigator loses control. In short, although it is possible to deduce the behavior of very large models through computer simulation, the limited capacity of the investigator to understand this behavior and to infer productive revisions in very large models is the critical barrier to theory-building.

How complex should a model be? Simple enough to be useful theoretically, but complex enough to be realistic.

> The dilemma of the scientist is to select models that are at the same time simple enough to permit him to think with the aid of the model but also sufficiently realistic that the simplifications do not lead to [highly inaccurate] predictions. . . . The more complex the model, the more difficult it becomes to decide exactly which modifications to make and which new variables to introduce. Put simply, the basic dilemma faced in all sciences is that of how much to oversimplify reality.[30]

Models of political systems that are simple enough for mathematical techniques are not likely to be sufficiently realistic. Experience will determine whether computer simulation models that are simple enough to suggest productive revisions can be at the same time sufficiently complex to be realistic.

A MODEL OF MODERNIZATION AND MASS POLITICS

With these reflections on systems, complexity, and simulation in mind, let us introduce the model of a political system developed in the first essay. The model is designed to study the processes of modernization and mass politics in the less developed countries, in particular Turkey and the Philippines. By modernization we mean primarily demographic and economic changes and changes in communications and transportation networks. By mass politics we mean political interactions among large aggregates of the population, not individual political actors. The aggregates defined in the model are the rural population, the urban population, the government, and (implicitly) the political opposition.

Table 1.2—The Model's State Vector:
Variables and Parameters

a. Demographic Subsystem

U_t = the number of migrants from rural to urban areas at time t.

$N_{i,t}$ = the population of sector i at time t.

s = the proportion of the participant rural population that would urbanize when economic performance in the two sectors is the same.

a_i = the rate of natural increase in sector i.

b. Economic Subsystem

$Y_{i,t}$ = gross product in constant currency for sector i at time t. Gross national product is the sum of gross product in the rural and urban sectors.

GR_t = total government revenue from all revenue-generating schemes in constant currency.

$C_{i,t}$ = consumption in constant currency in sector i at time t.

$I_{i,t}$ = private investment in constant currency for sector i at time t.

$F_{i,t}$ = net foreign contribution to sector i at time t, aggregating the value in constant currency of both commodity trade and monetary transfers.

τ_i = the effective tax rate in sector i.

m_i = the proportion of per capita gross disposable income consumed in sector i. Gross disposable income in sector i is $(1-\tau_i)Y_{i,t}$.

r_i = the proportion of the change in per capita consumption that induces additions to (or deletions from) the previous level of investment.

c. Political Subsystem

$V_{i,t}$ = the proportion of sector i supporting the government at time t.

$G_{i,t}$ = government expenditures in constant currency in sector i at time t.

$D_{i,t}$ = government communications and transportation expenditures in constant currency in sector i at time t.

$P_{i,t}$ = the proportion of the people in sector i at time t that are participant.

$E_{i,t}$ = the expected rate of change in economic performance.

σ = the scale of fluctuations in support.

α_i = political penetration, or the proportional extent to which responses to economic performance in sector i are channeled through the government.

β_i = the relative preference of the government for sector i.

γ_i = the ratio of government communications and transportation expenditures to total government expenditures in sector i.

δ_i = the communications and transportation expenditure in constant currency in sector i at which the communications and transportation system can be maintained with no appreciable effect on participation.

ϵ = the ratio of the change in the expected rate of economic performance to the difference between the actual and expected rates.

WINVOT = the proportion of aggregate support below which the government loses the election.

The state vector consists of the set of variables and parameters listed and defined in Table 1.2. These components are grouped into three subsystems: The demographic subsystem, which is relatively specialized to the increase and distribution of the population $N_{i,t}$; the economic subsystem, which is relatively specialized to the production and distribution of economic goods $Y_{i,t}$; and the political subsystem, which is relatively specialized to the production of changes in the size and distribution of mass support for the government $V_{i,t}$ and the determination of the size and distribution of government expenditures $G_{i,t}$. The variables in each subsystem are denoted by upper case letters and have time subscripts; the parameters are denoted by lower case Roman and Greek letters. Any component with an i subscript is disaggregated into rural ($i = 1$), urban ($i = 2$) subcomponents, and has a rural and urban aggregate ($i = 3$). Variables and parameters without i subscripts are defined only for the system as a whole, not the individual sectors.

All of the components can be expressed in two and only two dimensions or units of measurement: The number of people and the value of economic goods in constant local currency. Variables measured in terms of the number of people are U_t (the number of migrants) and $N_{i,t}$ (the population of the ith sector). Variables measured in terms of constant local currency are $Y_{i,t}$ (gross product), GR_t (government revenue), $C_{i,t}$ (consumption), $I_{i,t}$ (investment), $F_{i,t}$ (net foreign contribution to the economy), $G_{i,t}$ (government expenditures), and $D_{i,t}$ (government communications and transportation expenditures). The remaining variables are pure or dimensionless numbers. $V_{i,t}$ and $P_{i,t}$ are *proportions* of the population supporting the government and participating in processes of political and social change. $E_{i,t}$ is based on the *ratio* of economic performance (consumption per capita) in $t + 1$ to economic performance in t. Similarly, all of the parameters are pure or dimensionless numbers. As such, their values can be compared from one application of the model to the next, whereas some quantities measured in specific units cannot. For example, m_i, the proportion of disposable income consumed, can be directly compared in the applications of the structure to Turkey and the Philippines, whereas economic variables measured in Turkish liras and Philippine pesos cannot.

The relationships are grouped according to subsystems and presented in Table 1.3. (Here the relationships are given the same numbers assigned in the first essay.) As in the case of the relationships in the three-variable system considered above, the relationships in this system are hypotheses about the way in which each variable changes as a function of the others, with the magnitude of the change being in part determined by the parameters. These relationships are derived in section 3 of the first essay from an examination of some general theoretical work and case study material from Turkey and the Philippines.[31]

Table 1.3—The Model's Set of Relationships

a. Demographic Subsystem

$$U_t = s\left(\frac{C_{2,t}}{N_{2,t}}\frac{N_{1,t}}{C_{1,t}}\right)P_{1,t}N_{1,t} \tag{3.1}$$

$$N_{1,t} = (1 + a_1)N_{1,t-1} - U_{t-1} \tag{3.2a}$$

$$N_{2,t} = (1 + a_2)N_{2,t-1} + U_{t-1} \tag{3.2b}$$

b. Economic Subsystem

$$Y_{i,t} = C_{i,t} + I_{i,t} + G_{i,t} + F_{i,t} \tag{3.3}$$

$$GR_t = \tau_1 Y_{1,t-1} + \tau_2 Y_{2,t-1} \tag{3.4}$$

$$C_{i,t} = m_i(1 - \tau_i)Y_{i,t-1}\frac{N_{i,t}}{N_{i,t-1}} \tag{3.5b}$$

$$I_{i,t} = I_{i,t-1}\frac{N_{i,t}}{N_{i,t-1}} + r_i\left(C_{i,t} - C_{i,t-1}\frac{N_{i,t}}{N_{i,t-1}}\right) \tag{3.6b}$$

c. Political Subsystem

$$V_{i,t} = V_{i,t-1} + \alpha_i \sigma P_{i,t-1}[(1 - V_{i,t-1})V_{i,t-1}]^3\left[\frac{C_{i,t}}{N_{i,t}}\frac{N_{i,t-1}}{C_{i,t-1}} - E_{i,t-1}\right] \tag{3.7}$$

$$G_{i,t} = \beta_i\left[\frac{N_{i,t-1}V_{i,t-1} - \Delta(N_iV_i)}{N_{1,t-1}V_{1,t-1} + N_{2,t-1}V_{2,t-1} - \Delta(N_1V_1) - \Delta(N_2V_2)}\right]GR_{t-1}$$

where $$\Delta N_iV_i = N_{i,t}V_{i,t} - N_{i,t-1}V_{i,t-1} \tag{3.8}$$

$$D_{i,t} = \gamma_i G_{i,t} \tag{3.9}$$

$$P_{i,t} = 1 - \left(\frac{\delta_i}{D_{i,t-1}}\right), P_{i,t} \geq P_{i,t-1} \tag{3.10}$$

$$E_{i,t} = E_{i,t-1} + \epsilon\left(\frac{C_{i,t}}{N_{i,t}}\frac{N_{i,t-1}}{C_{i,t-1}} - E_{i,t-1}\right)P_{i,t-1} \tag{3.11}$$

$$V_{i,t} = (1 - V_{i,t})\text{ If }t\text{ is an election year and }V_{3,t} < \text{WINVOT} \tag{3.12}$$

Having introduced the system we can ask, How large is it? A partial answer is that its state vector at any time t consists of twenty-two variables (twenty of which are disaggregated according to rural or urban sector) and twenty parameters (sixteen of which are disaggregated). Another partial answer is that—as a consequence of structural relationships rather than particular context—there is no completely decomposable subset of variables and relationships. This can be seen in Figure 1.3 where the variables are

Figure 1.3—Structural Connectedness

a. By Functional Subsystems

INPUTS

		Demographic Subsystem			Economic Subsystem							Political Subsystem									
		U	N_1	N_2	Y_1	C_1	I_1	Y_2	C_2	I_2	GR	V_1	G_1	D_1	P_1	E_1	V_2	G_2	D_2	P_2	E_2
Demographic Subsystem	U	0	1	1	0	1	0	0	1	0	0	0	0	0	1	0	0	0	0	0	0
	N_1	1	1	0	0	0	0	0	0	0	0	0	0	0	0	0	0	0	0	0	0
	N_2	1	0	1	0	0	0	0	0	0	0	0	0	0	0	0	0	0	0	0	0
Economic Subsystem	Y_1	0	0	0	0	1	1	0	0	0	0	0	1	0	0	0	0	0	0	0	0
	C_1	0	1	0	1	0	0	0	0	0	0	0	0	0	0	0	0	0	0	0	0
	I_1	0	1	0	0	1	1	0	0	0	0	0	0	0	0	0	0	0	0	0	0
	Y_2	0	0	0	0	0	0	0	1	1	0	0	0	0	0	0	0	1	0	0	0
	C_2	0	0	1	0	0	0	1	0	0	0	0	0	0	0	0	0	0	0	0	0
	I_2	0	0	1	0	0	0	0	1	1	0	0	0	0	0	0	0	0	0	0	0
OUTPUTS	GR	0	0	0	1	0	0	1	0	0	0	0	0	0	0	0	0	0	0	0	0
Political Subsystem	V_1	0	1	0	0	1	0	0	0	0	0	1	0	0	1	1	0	0	0	0	0
	G_1	0	1	1	0	0	0	0	0	0	1	1	0	0	0	0	1	0	0	0	0
	D_1	0	0	0	0	0	0	0	0	0	0	0	1	0	0	0	0	0	0	0	0
	P_1	0	0	0	0	0	0	0	0	0	0	0	0	1	0	0	0	0	0	0	0
	E_1	0	1	0	0	1	0	0	0	0	0	0	0	1	1	0	0	0	0	0	0
	V_2	0	0	1	0	0	0	0	1	0	0	0	0	0	0	0	1	0	0	1	1
	G_2	0	1	1	0	0	0	0	0	0	1	1	0	0	0	0	1	0	0	0	0
	D_2	0	0	0	0	0	0	0	0	0	0	0	0	0	0	0	0	1	0	0	0
	P_2	0	0	0	0	0	0	0	0	0	0	0	0	0	0	0	0	0	1	0	0
	E_2	0	0	1	0	0	0	0	1	0	0	0	0	0	0	0	0	0	0	1	1

$F_{i,t}$, the net exogenous contribution to the economy of sector i at time t appears in (3.3) but has been deleted from this figure.

b. By Geographic Subsystems

INPUTS

		Societal Subsystem		Rural Subsystem									Urban Subsystem								
		U	GR	N_1	Y_1	C_1	I_1	V_1	G_1	D_1	P_1	E_1	N_2	Y_2	C_2	I_2	V_2	G_2	D_2	P_2	E_2
Societal Subsystem	U	0	0	1	0	1	0	0	0	0	1	0	1	0	1	0	0	0	0	0	0
	GR	0	0	0	1	0	0	0	0	0	0	0	0	1	0	0	0	0	0	0	0
Rural Subsystem	N_1	1	0	1	0	0	0	0	0	0	0	0	0	0	0	0	0	0	0	0	0
	Y_1	0	0	0	0	1	1	0	1	0	0	0	0	0	0	0	0	0	0	0	0
	C_1	0	0	1	1	0	0	0	0	0	0	0	0	0	0	0	0	0	0	0	0
	I_1	0	0	1	0	1	1	0	0	0	0	0	0	0	0	0	0	0	0	0	0
	V_1	0	0	1	0	1	0	1	0	0	1	1	0	0	0	0	0	0	0	0	0
	G_1	0	1	1	0	0	0	1	0	0	0	0	1	0	0	0	1	0	0	0	0
	D_1	0	0	0	0	0	0	1	0	0	0	0	0	0	0	0	0	0	0	0	0
OUTPUTS	P_1	0	0	0	0	0	0	0	0	1	0	0	0	0	0	0	0	0	0	0	0
	E_1	0	0	1	0	1	0	0	0	0	1	1	0	0	0	0	0	0	0	0	0
Urban Subsystem	N_2	1	0	0	0	0	0	0	0	0	0	0	1	0	0	0	0	0	0	0	0
	Y_2	0	0	0	0	0	0	0	0	0	0	0	0	0	1	1	0	1	0	0	0
	C_2	0	0	0	0	0	0	0	0	0	0	0	1	1	0	0	0	0	0	0	0
	I_2	0	0	0	0	0	0	0	0	0	0	0	1	0	1	1	0	0	0	0	0
	V_2	0	0	0	0	0	0	0	0	0	0	0	1	0	1	0	1	0	0	1	1
	G_2	0	1	1	0	0	0	1	0	0	0	0	1	0	0	0	1	0	0	0	0
	D_2	0	0	0	0	0	0	0	0	0	0	0	0	0	0	0	0	1	0	0	0
	P_2	0	0	0	0	0	0	0	0	0	0	0	0	0	0	0	0	0	1	0	0
	E_2	0	0	0	0	0	0	0	0	0	0	0	1	0	1	0	0	0	0	1	1

$F_{i,t}$, the net exogenous contribution to the economy of sector i at time t appears in (3.3) but has been deleted from this figure.

grouped according to functional and geographic subsystems. (Time subscripts have been ignored.) The numerical entries in the cells of each matrix denote the presence (1) or absence (0) of a direct structural link between the output (or row) variable and the input (or column) variable. In each grouping, each subsystem has at least one input from each of the other subsystems. Every subsystem, in short, is influenced by every other. A third partial answer is that this system is very small compared to the real-world systems it purports to represent. Our verbal, non-formalized understanding of the important variables and processes in the less developed countries goes considerably beyond the structure of the small system introduced here.

How complex is this system? It is much too complex for verbal forms of analysis. It is too complex to yield to mathematical techniques, although if *ceteris paribus* assumptions are made its subsystems can be isolated from the rest of the system for independent mathematical analysis. Finally, it is a trivial matter to express the system as a computer program,[32] to deduce its behavior in specific contexts, and to infer meaningful changes in its structure as a result of a comparison of its behavior with historical time series. While too complex for other forms of analysis, the system is sufficiently simple to yield to the technique of computer simulation.

2. Purposes

Scientific, historical, projective, normative, and policy studies tend to have not only relatively distinct purposes but also relatively distinct research problems. However, to the extent that these studies deal with political systems, each confronts the problem of complexity in some form. In this section we attempt to demonstrate how at least one important problem in each of these fields of specialization is basically a problem of complexity and how computer simulation can be adapted to it. To the extent that we are convincing, some conventional assumptions about the nature of political systems may be modified, and computer simulation may supplement other techniques as a form of analysis within each field and as a means of integrating their relatively specialized results.

SCIENTIFIC ORIENTATION

Science and Complexity. In 1948 Warren Weaver contended that scientists had not yet learned the techniques necessary to cope successfully with complex systems, which he called problems of organized complexity. Weaver's contention is based on a distinction among three types of problems.

Problems of *simplicity*, characterized by a few variables with fixed relationships, are the problems that yielded to mathematical analysis in the nineteenth century. For example, the pressure, temperature, and volume of a small physical system can be related to each other by a simple equation. Problems of *disorganized complexity* yielded to statistical analysis in this century. A problem of disorganized complexity

> is a problem in which the number of variables is very large, and one in which each of the many variables has a behavior which is individually erratic, or perhaps totally unknown. However, in spite of this helterskelter, or unknown, behavior of all the individual variables, the system as a whole possesses certain orderly and analyzable average properties.[33]

An insurance company, to use one of Weaver's examples, has no knowledge of the approaching death of one of its policy-holders, but it has dependable statistical knowledge of the average frequency of deaths. Another class of problems,

> as contrasted with the disorganized situations with which statistics can cope, show the essential feature of *organization*. In fact, one can refer to this group of problems as those of *organized complexity*. . . . They are all problems which involve dealing simultaneously with a *sizable number of factors which are interrelated into an organic whole*. . . . A very substantial number of relevant variables are involved here, and they are all interrelated in a complicated, but nevertheless not in a helter-skelter, fashion.[34]

Political systems conceived as systems and not merely collections of citizens are problems of this kind. According to Weaver, problems of organized complexity

> are just too complicated to yield to the old nineteenth-century techniques which were so dramatically successful on two-, three-, or four-variable problems of simplicity. These new problems, moreover, cannot be handled with the statistical techniques so effective in describing the average behavior in problems of disorganized complexity.[35]

If our interpretation of Weaver is correct, the contention is that statistical techniques underestimate the degree of order and organization in the diverse behavior of individual members of a class of systems.

To our knowledge there is still no well-defined scientific procedure developed specifically for the clarification of the structure of complex systems. In the scientific study of political systems in particular, the most prevalent practice is to assume the relevance of descriptive and inductive statistics. Thus Daniel Lerner, in the example considered in our first essay, used multiple correlation coefficients in an attempt to document the existence of systemic relationships among indicators of urbanization, literacy, media participation and political participation.[36] We shall consider in some detail the scientific role of statistical techniques in the study of complex systems in a subsequent section. At this point it is appropriate to consider an alternative to statistical procedures, the procedure used to develop the small model of modernization and mass politics. With further experience, perhaps it can be shown to be a worthwhile step in the development of scientific procedures specifically designed for the study of complex systems.

Clarification of Structure. The procedure, which we considered in the abstract in section 1, is summarized crudely in Figure 2.1. The multiple

Figure 2.1—On Clarifying the Structure of a System

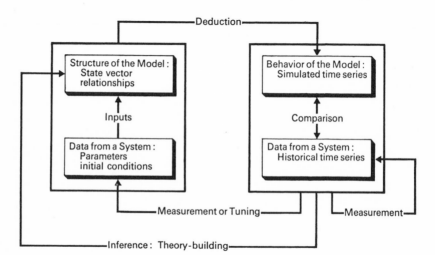

responses to the comparison between historical and simulated time series—theory-building, measurement, and tuning—suggest that the procedure takes somewhat different form depending on the degree of development of the model and the degree of confidence in the data. After the initial translation of our understanding of theoretical and case studies of social and political processes into mathematical relationships, the first stage in the development of the model focused primarily on assessing its plausibility. Round figures approximating the Turkish situation in 1950 were used as inputs, and intuitions about what constitutes plausible behavior were used to assess the outputs. A number of alternative relationships were rejected in this stage. For example, we found that if the increase through time in per capita consumption is assumed to determine the *level* of per capita investment, the behavior of the economic subsystem and the whole model is extremely unstable. However, if the same stimulus is assumed to determine the *change* in per capita investment, the behavior of the model is more plausible. A number of variables and relationships were also added to the system to make it more consistent with our understanding of the available theoretical and case materials. About ten major revisions of the model were produced in this stage.

After developing some confidence in the plausibility of the model, we concentrated in the second stage on "tuning" it. Here the quantitative and qualitative data readily available from primary and secondary sources were used to constrain the inputs to the model and to evaluate its outputs. Since the data were not complete enough to specify all the inputs with confidence, estimates of the missing items were used to generate the behavior of the model. Discrepancies between generated and historical time series were attributed to these estimates, the estimates were revised, and the revised estimates were used to generate a new set of time series. In short, *we attempted to adjust the inputs within the constraints of the available data in order to make the model's behavior fit the historical time series data.* As we shall see below, what appears to be an heretical departure from scientific method is in fact a weak test of the model made possible by the assumption that we are dealing with a system and not merely a set of unrelated or statistically related components.

After each cycle of trial and error, a judgment is made about the overall degree of fit. If the fit is not sufficiently close there are in principle three things that can be done: Continue tuning on the assumption that untried combinations of inputs exist that would produce a better fit; attempt to reassess the accuracy of the historical time series data on the assumption that the lack of fit can be attributed to measurement error in these time series; or reassess the structure of the model on the assumption that some feature of the real-world system is inappropriately represented in the model or omitted altogether.

In this case we found that it was possible to tune the model so that it would reproduce the major trends in the data with maximum errors of about 17% and much smaller average errors. However, certain errors in the *form* of the time series generated by the model remained and could not be completely eliminated through further tuning. In the Turkish experiment, economic growth that was initially too slow and then too rapid seemed to account for the errors in the demographic and political time series. The rapid growth of the economy in the experiment seemed to result from levels of government expenditures that were much higher than the historical data indicated. Reconsideration of the historical data revealed that different sources give different estimates of government expenditures, and we had used the higher estimates. Reconsideration of Turkish case studies suggested that resource constraints imposed upon the tendency of the Menderes

Administration to pour increasing amounts of government funds into the economy for political purposes. No such resource constraints exist in the model. The Turkish experiment, in short, revealed the need for further consideration of government expenditure data and an important omission in the model.

In the Philippine experiment, the historical and simulated time series for non-agricultural product $Y_{2,t}$ were found to be out of phase. Reconsideration of the Philippine national accounts revealed considerable doubt about the accuracy of the historical time series, and, as an unintended consequence, suggested that the implausible negative rate of induced investment may be an artifact of the underestimation of private investment by official Philippine sources. Reconsideration of the structure of the model suggested that an increase in the time lag between political stimulus and government allocation of funds might eliminate the phase problem. However, we have no information that such long time lags have been observed in the Philippines. The Philippine experiment, in short, revealed the need for further work on the national accounts data and the possibility of an inappropriate time lag in the model.

As we suggested, after each cycle of trial and error in the tuning process a judgment is made about the over-all degree of fit. What happens if the fit is so close that the errors are insignificant? In this case no further progress can be made until some or all of the missing inputs and time series are measured more accurately. This requires a third stage in the development of the model, field work. Consultation with officials of central statistical offices might be helpful, but the most promising possibility is to use the model to construct a survey research instrument that can be applied and reapplied at appropriate time intervals. For example, for any sector the results of individual responses to questions could be aggregated to estimate the average propensity to reproduce and to consume as well as levels of participation, support for the government, income, and other quantities defined in the model. The first survey could be used to set initial conditions and parameters; subsequent surveys could be used to evaluate the behavior of the model. Survey results have the advantage that the entire sample can readily be disaggregated according to any shared characteristic ascertained in the survey. To the extent that a high degree of confidence in the accuracy of all quantitative data in the analysis is justified, lack of fit between historical and generated time series can be attributed to the structure of the model alone. Furthermore, to the extent that lack of fit can be attributed to structure alone, the structure can be improved rapidly.

There are several important observations to be made about the procedure as a whole. First, each change in the structure of the model or its inputs is evaluated in terms of its contribution to the behavior of the model as a whole, and this contribution depends on the configuration of other components. Consequently, the process assumes that the system under consideration is in fact a system and not merely a collection of unrelated or statistically related components. Second, this systemic assumption severely constrains the range of permissible structural formulations and estimates of unmeasured inputs. For example, structural choices that seem plausible in the initial specification of the model can often be shown to be implausible when allowed to operate as a part of the model in the generation of simulated time series. Similarly, the range of plausible estimates of any unmeasured parameter or initial condition is much broader than the range of estimates that prove to be consistent with the operation of the model as a whole. Consequently, if attempts to achieve a good fit through the adjustment of unmeasured inputs are unsuccessful, the remaining errors can be attributed to structural specifications. Third, because of the previous points, progress in proposing and rejecting structural alternatives can be made without complete data. However, the more complete and accurate the data, the more efficient is the process of theory-building.

Some Qualifications. The procedure we have outlined shares some inherent limitations with other scientific procedures. Historical data contain both systematic and random components, the latter being most easily interpreted as the result of stochastic factors or measurement errors. Since these components cannot be distinguished in practice, the comparison between historical and simulated time series may produce invalid inferences based on the random components.[37] Although they cannot be eliminated entirely, the effects of the random components can be controlled through aggregation of units of analysis. As units are aggregated from individuals to increasingly larger groups, the systematic effects tend to be cumulative while the random effects tend to cancel out: ". . . the larger the number of units we group, the less, relatively speaking, will their total be affected by erratic fluctuations."[38] The cost of aggregation is loss of information, which may mean an inability to distinguish among structural alternatives.[39] Another limitation is that a structure may be invalid even if its behavior fits the historical pattern very well. A structure is, after all, only an abstraction inferred from "hard" and "soft" observations of systems' behavior and more or less capable of reproducing that behavior given appropriate inputs. Alternatives just as capable of reproducing the same behavior may exist. One consequence is that we cannot validate a model even though we can invalidate it. From this perspective the thrust of some of the growing literature on the *validation* of simulation models seems misdirected.[40] Another consequence is that quantitative fit alone is not a sufficient criterion for evaluating a model. Attention should be given also to the adequacy of the verbal formulations on which the model is based, the fidelity with which these verbal formulations are translated into mathematical relationships, and qualitative aspects of the model's behavior. Finally, even if a model fits and is essentially correct, it may still be irrelevant. This is particularly true if the scientific need for precision and rigor leads to the omission of normatively interesting but difficult-to-quantify aspects of the systems under consideration.

HISTORICAL AND PROJECTIVE ORIENTATIONS

History and Complexity. While the purpose of much scientific study is the clarification of the underlying order in systems, the purpose of much historical work is the clarification of the behavior of systems, in particular specific, concrete events. In historical research, the ambiguity of the relationship between generalizations, in the form of theories, hypotheses, or processes, and specific historical events is primarily a reaction to the complexity of the subject matter. This ambiguity seems to generate a good deal of tension about the essential differences and similarities among historical events, conceptions of history as an art or a science, and the compatibility of aims and methods in historical research.

The tension is apparent in Meyerhoff's survey of historiography:

> The *facts* of history are peculiar, as historicism has insisted all along. They are individual, concrete, unrepeatable events and entities. . . . The *primary aim* of a historical narrative is to reconstruct these events in their unique individuality, not to formulate general laws, to bring out the particular differences rather than the common properties of the events included in the historical portrait. In this respect, a historical work seems to resemble a literary work much more than a scientific treatise.[41]

But

> *Fact, theory, and interpretation* form a closely knit complex in a historical narrative. . . . The facts of history invariably appear in a context of interpretation; and there is no interpretation without theory. How, then, do we disentagle this complex web of facts and theory, narration, and interpretation?[42]

Stuart Bruchey, another historian, confronts the same tension in his book on the causes of economic development in the United States:

> To apply formal economic analysis to the complexities of long-run change is to invite the rigor of *rigor mortis.*
>
> On the other hand, to proceed without the guidance of any hypothesis at all is impossible. A leading historiographical tradition, it is true, would deny this statement of necessity and place its emphasis

upon the uniqueness of particular events. Admittedly, there is a fundamental sense in which the emphasis is not mistaken. To every event
there belongs a temporal singularity, a contextual particularity, and it
is because of this that all historical being possesses a quality of never-
quite-the-sameness. But it is equally true that the essence of a thing is
not altogether its separateness. There is essential sharedness as well as
essential singularity, and if this were not so, all experience were a
succession of differentiated particulars, without meaning because nothing would be recognizable.[43]

Similarly, Henri Pirenne speculates that

Past societies would remain unintelligible to us if the natural needs
which they experienced and the psychical forces which stimulated them
were qualitatively different from ours. How are the innumerable differences that humanity presents in time and space to be explained if one
does not consider them as changing nuances of a reality which is in its
essence always and everywhere the same?[44]

In short, there is tremendous diversity in social affairs as suggested by such
phrases as the "unrepeatable" historical events, and the "temporal singularity" and "contextual particularity" of events. But there is also order and
organization in the form of "general laws," "theory," and "hypothesis."
The relationship between the two is not spelled out.

The theories, laws, principles and other abstractions used to render
historical events intelligible may be incorrect. What is more, they may be
too general to accommodate the distinctiveness, concreteness, and diversity
of historical events. How, then, is the historian to reconstruct accurately the
events of history? The answer is commonly a form of the comparative method.
Pirenne, for example, writes that

The comparative method alone can diminish racial, political, and
national prejudices among historians. These prejudices inevitably en-
snare him who, confined within the narrow limits of national history,
is condemned to understand it badly because he is incapable of compre-
hending the bonds attaching it to the histories of other nations. . . . The
comparative method permits history to appear in its true perspective.
. . . Therefore to the degree in which history is viewed in the totality
of its development, and in which one accustoms himself to study
particular or national histories in the functioning of general evolution,
will the weaknesses inherent in historical method be diminished.[45]

Bruchey, with less emphasis on permitting history to appear in its true
perspective than in discovering causes, relies on the same method.

The method of comparison ... makes it possible to conduct a causal inquiry by affording a means of coping with what would otherwise be the nearly illimitable tyranny of conditions necessary to economic growth.[46]

After consideration of the projective orientation, we shall investigate the utility of the method of comparison as well as the relationship between specific events and general order in society.

The Future and Complexity. Like historians, those who study the future have considered the relationship between specific trends and local contexts on the one hand and general processes that might shape them on the other. Unlike the historians, however, students of the future seem to have a more precise understanding of the relationship. For example, Lawrence Frank, in a symposium on "The Nature and Limitations of Forecasting" notes that

> For our consideration of human and social events, we are beginning to utilize a conception of process, recognizing that the same process can produce different products depending upon where, when and how it operates. The process of organic fertilization and gestation, for example, produces many different offspring.[47]

Frank's reconciliation of diversity and order in social events reflects an understanding of the nature of complex systems.

For students of the future a degree of tension often appears not in the relationship between trends or contexts and processes but in the choice between the analysis of trends or the construction of models to study the future. According to Wassily Leontieff, policy-relevant predictions require more than trend analysis.

> There are predictions by models and predictions by trends. Predictions by models are based on the belief that it is possible to view the world as one whole with separate parts that are in some way interrelated. Prediction by trends gives us a view of the world as if it were a handful of sand, each particle distinct from the others. These are not symmetrical things. ... To discuss policies not in a deterministic way, but as a problem of choice, I think you must work with models. To build policies into trends is difficult.[48]

According to Martin Shubik, the "chartists" who extrapolate trends cannot be so easily dismissed. Using the example of stock-market forecasting, Shubik contends that

> There are the chartists and the fundamentalists. The fundamentalists want to discover as much as they can about the firm—where its technology is going and so forth—while the chartists draw some linear extrapolations of what is going on and invent such phrases as "when

the thing has heads and shoulders." You cannot idly dismiss the chartists, because in one sense a key to forecasting is the amount of time one has available in the decision process to make a statement about the future. A chartist can come up with some sort of fairy tale in ten or fifteen minutes. If you do not have more time, perhaps that is the best you can get.[49]

Shubik goes on to advocate the construction of

an incremental systematic process that involves, among other things, linking large data-processing procedures with models or conceptual frameworks. This would give an opportunity to link the fundamentalist and chartist approaches.[50]

We shall consider this and similar proposals at the end of this section.

Diversity, Order, and Decomposability. The model of modernization and mass politics can be used to suggest a basis for the partial reconciliation of diversity and order. In the model, the potential for diversity can be found in the size of the state vector and the degree of connectedness in the set of relationships governing changes in the state vector. In principle the degree of contextual particularity of an individual event or variable increases with the number of variables that shape and determine it. Order can of course be found in the set of relationships that limit and constrain the behavior of the model.

The static description of the structural connectedness of the model (see Figure 1.3) underestimates the potential for diversity or contextual particularity in individual variables. For example, as shown in relationship (3.4), since government revenue GR_t is merely a function of gross product in the rural and urban sectors, $Y_{1,t-1}$ and $Y_{2,t-1}$, variation in GR_t within one yearly cycle is limited to variation in these two variables. However, if the model is operated through time, the number of variables causally connected to GR_t increases. Thus while GR_t is a direct function of $Y_{1,t-1}$ and $Y_{2,t-1}$, as we have seen, it is also through these two variables an indirect function of $C_{1,t-1}$, $I_{1,t-1}$, $G_{1,t-1}$, $C_{2,t-1}$, $I_{2,t-1}$, and $G_{2,t-1}$; and through these variables, GR_t is an indirect function of several other variables, and so on. The causal chains of one, two, and three links connecting GR_t and these variables are diagrammed in Figure 2.2.

More generally, it can be shown that as the model is operated through time, the potential contextual particularity of any individual variable or event increases. On the one hand, each yearly cycle of the model expands the temporal context. That is to say, if the initial state vector X_1 contains k quantities describing the initial values of the variables, then the first yearly cycle of the model produces the state vector X_2, and this adds k *more*

Figure 2.2—Causal Chains of One, Two, and Three Links
Affecting Government Revenue GR_t

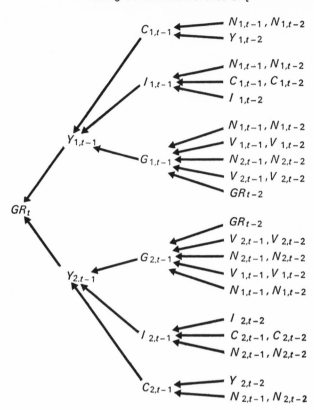

quantities to the analysis. These are merely the later values of the variables stated in the initial condition. Each subsequent cycle, by expanding the temporal context, adds k more quantities and thereby increases the potential for the variety in the system.

On the other hand, since each additional yearly cycle of the model corresponds to one additional power of the connectedness matrix in Figure 1.3,[51] it can be shown that the operation of the model through time *extends the length* of indirect causal chains. Stated differently, not only does the number of quantities expand with time, so does the number of indirect causal chains linking these quantities. In precise terms the entry in the i-th row and j-th column of the n-th power of the connectedness matrix gives the number of causal chains of n links by which variable i is indirectly connected to variable j. For this particular model, the increases are dramatic as shown in Figure 2.3. (Notice that the twenty causal chains of three links diagrammed

Figure 2.3—Indirect Structural Connectedness by Functional Subsystems

a. Causal Chains of 2 Links: Connectedness Matrix Squared

INPUTS

			Demographic Subsystem			Economic Subsystem							Political Subsystem									
		U	N_1	N_2	Y_1	C_1	I_1	Y_2	C_2	I_2	GR	V_1	G_1	D_1	P_1	E_1	V_2	G_2	D_2	P_2	E_2
Demographic Subsystem	U	2	2	2	1	0	0	1	0	0	0	0	0	1	0	0	0	0	0	0	0
	N_1	1	2	1	0	1	0	0	1	0	0	0	0	0	1	0	0	0	0	0	0
	N_2	1	1	2	0	1	0	0	1	0	0	0	0	0	1	0	0	0	0	0	0
Economic Subsystem	Y_1	0	3	1	1	1	1	0	0	0	1	1	0	0	0	0	1	0	0	0	0
	C_1	1	1	0	0	1	1	0	0	0	0	0	1	0	0	0	0	0	0	0	0
	I_1	1	3	0	1	1	1	0	0	0	0	0	0	0	0	0	0	0	0	0	0
	Y_2	0	1	3	0	0	0	1	1	1	1	1	0	0	0	0	1	0	0	0	0
	C_2	1	0	1	0	0	0	0	1	1	0	0	0	0	0	0	0	1	0	0	0
	I_2	1	0	3	0	0	0	1	1	1	0	0	0	0	0	0	0	0	0	0	0
OUTPUTS	GR	0	0	0	0	1	1	0	1	1	0	0	1	0	0	0	0	1	0	0	0
Political Subsystem	V_1	1	4	0	1	2	0	0	0	0	0	1	0	1	2	2	0	0	0	0	0
	G_1	2	2	2	1	1	0	1	1	0	0	1	0	0	1	1	0	0	0	1	1
	D_1	0	1	1	0	0	0	0	0	0	1	1	0	0	0	1	0	0	0	0	0
	P_1	0	0	0	0	0	0	0	0	0	0	0	1	0	0	0	0	0	0	0	0
	E_1	1	3	0	1	1	0	0	0	0	0	0	0	1	1	0	0	0	0	0	0
	V_2	1	0	4	0	0	0	1	2	0	0	0	0	0	0	0	1	0	1	2	2
	G_2	2	2	2	1	1	0	1	1	0	0	1	0	0	1	1	1	0	0	1	1
	D_2	0	1	1	0	0	0	0	0	0	1	1	0	0	0	1	0	0	0	0	0
	P_2	0	0	0	0	0	0	0	0	0	0	0	0	0	0	0	0	1	0	0	0
	E_2	1	0	3	0	0	0	1	1	0	0	0	0	0	0	0	0	0	1	1	1

b. Causal Chains of 3 Links: Connectedness Matrix Cubed

INPUTS

			Demographic Subsystem			Economic Subsystem							Political Subsystem									
		U	N_1	N_2	Y_1	C_1	I_1	Y_2	C_2	I_2	GR	V_1	G_1	D_1	P_1	E_1	V_2	G_2	D_2	P_2	E_2
Demographic Subsystem	U	4	4	4	0	3	1	0	3	1	0	0	2	0	2	0	0	1	0	0	0
	N_1	3	4	3	1	1	0	1	1	0	0	0	0	1	1	0	0	0	0	0	0
	N_2	3	3	4	1	1	0	1	1	0	0	0	0	1	1	0	0	0	0	0	0
Economic Subsystem	Y_1	4	6	2	2	3	2	1	1	0	0	1	1	0	1	1	1	0	0	1	1
	C_1	1	5	2	1	2	1	0	1	0	1	1	0	0	1	0	1	0	0	0	0
	I_1	3	6	1	1	3	2	0	1	0	0	0	1	0	1	0	0	0	0	0	0
	Y_2	4	2	6	1	1	0	2	3	2	0	1	0	0	1	1	1	1	0	1	1
	C_2	1	2	5	0	1	0	1	2	1	1	1	0	0	1	0	1	0	0	0	0
	I_2	3	1	6	0	1	0	1	3	2	0	0	0	0	1	0	0	1	0	0	0
OUTPUTS	GR	0	4	4	1	1	1	1	1	1	2	2	0	0	0	0	2	0	0	0	0
Political Subsystem	V_1	4	10	1	2	5	1	0	1	0	0	1	2	2	4	3	0	0	0	0	0
	G_1	4	7	7	1	5	1	1	5	1	0	1	1	1	4	2	1	1	1	2	2
	D_1	2	2	2	1	1	0	1	1	0	0	1	0	0	1	1	0	0	0	1	1
	P_1	0	1	1	0	0	0	0	0	0	1	1	0	0	0	0	1	0	0	0	0
	E_1	3	6	1	1	3	1	0	1	0	0	0	2	1	2	1	0	0	0	0	0
	V_2	4	1	10	0	1	0	2	5	1	0	0	0	0	1	0	1	2	2	3	3
	G_2	4	7	7	1	5	1	1	5	1	0	1	1	1	4	2	1	1	1	2	2
	D_2	2	2	2	1	1	0	1	1	0	0	1	0	0	1	1	1	0	0	1	1
	P_2	0	1	1	0	0	0	0	0	0	1	1	0	0	0	0	1	0	0	0	0
	E_2	3	1	6	0	1	0	1	3	1	0	0	0	0	1	0	0	2	1	1	1

c. Causal Chains of 4 Links:
Connectedness Matrix to the Fourth Power

INPUTS

		Demographic Subsystem			Economic Subsystem							Political Subsystem									
		U	N_1	N_2	Y_1	C_1	I_1	Y_2	C_2	I_2	GR	V_1	G_1	D_1	P_1	E_1	V_2	G_2	D_2	P_2	E_2
Demographic Subsystem	U	8	15	15	3	5	1	3	5	1	3	3	0	2	4	0	3	0	0	0	0
	N_1	7	8	7	1	4	1	1	4	1	0	0	2	1	3	0	0	1	0	0	0
	N_2	7	7	8	1	4	1	1	4	1	0	0	2	1	3	0	0	1	0	0	0
Economic Subsystem	Y_1	8	18	10	3	10	4	1	7	1	1	2	2	1	6	2	2	1	1	2	2
	C_1	7	10	5	3	4	2	2	2	0	0	1	1	1	2	1	1	0	0	1	1
	I_1	7	15	6	3	6	3	1	3	0	1	1	1	1	3	0	1	0	0	0	0
	Y_2	8	10	18	1	7	1	3	10	4	1	2	1	1	6	2	2	2	1	2	2
	C_2	7	5	10	2	2	0	3	4	2	0	1	0	1	2	1	1	1	0	1	1
	I_2	7	6	15	1	3	0	3	6	3	1	1	0	1	3	0	1	1	0	0	0
OUTPUTS	GR	8	8	8	3	4	2	3	4	2	0	2	1	0	2	2	2	1	0	2	2
	V_1	11	26	8	5	11	3	1	4	0	2	3	4	4	8	4	2	0	0	0	0
	G_1	14	22	22	5	9	2	5	9	2	2	3	2	4	7	3	3	2	2	3	3
	D_1	4	7	7	1	5	1	1	5	1	0	1	1	1	4	2	1	1	1	2	2
	P_1	2	2	2	1	1	0	1	1	0	0	1	0	0	1	1	1	0	0	1	1
Political Subsystem	E_1	7	16	7	3	6	2	1	3	0	2	2	2	2	4	1	2	0	0	0	0
	V_2	11	8	26	1	4	0	5	11	3	2	2	0	1	4	0	3	4	3	4	4
	G_2	14	22	22	5	9	2	5	9	2	2	3	2	4	7	3	3	2	2	3	3
	D_2	4	7	7	1	5	1	1	5	1	0	1	1	1	4	2	1	1	1	2	2
	P_2	2	2	2	1	1	0	1	1	0	0	1	0	0	1	1	1	0	0	1	1
	E_2	7	7	16	1	3	0	3	6	2	2	2	0	1	3	0	2	2	1	1	1

in Figure 2.2 are summarized in Figure 2.3b in the row labeled GR.) While there are only 59 direct causal chains, there are 163, 459, and 1,257 indirect causal chains of 2, 3, and 4 links, respectively. Furthermore, there are 3,382, 9,172, and 24,708 indirect causal chains of 5, 6, and 7 links, respectively. Of the 400 possible connections between pairs of variables, only 16 pairs remain unconnected in the fifth power of the matrix, 2 in the sixth power, and none in the seventh power. In short, there is at least one indirect causal chain of seven links through which each variable as an output is affected by each variable as an input. In the model as in Bruchey's characterization of history, "The conditions of any event . . . must beat their way back into the past via a process of 'infinite' regression until they disappear in the mists of the unknowable . . . ."[52]

Because this analysis has shown that ultimately every outcome or event in the model depends upon every other, it has several implications for the comparative method that historians and others use to deal with the complexity of society. In one sense, the comparative method is indispensable. If any event is the cumulative result of a large number of causal chains, then there are in principle an equally large number of explanations for the event. However, if the weight of any chain in determining the event varies with the context (that is to say, parameter settings and the magnitudes of prior variables), then the best explanations of similar outcomes in different contexts may be different even for structurally identical systems. Thus, for example, economic growth and political stability may be primarily the result of economic resources in one country and the result of governmental skill in another. In short, only one of the many behavioral patterns inherent in a structure is realized in a particular context. Consequently, to paraphrase Pirenne, we must examine many similar systems before we can understand any one of them.

In another sense, the comparative method is inherently limited as a means of discovering causes in complex systems, even though Bruchey, among others, contends this is an important use of the method. To be sure, by comparing cases it is possible in an approximate sense to eliminate cross-national similarities as causes of cross-national differences. But for such complex systems each event has a large number of possible causal explanations, and it is very unlikely that there are enough systems and enough similarities in the behavior of the systems to eliminate more than a few causal explanations. In simulation, in contrast to the comparative method, the possible causal explanations and conditions in a particular country are not controlled through matching but allowed to combine, interact, and flow through the operation of the model.

This analysis of structural connectedness has obvious implications for the chartist approach to projection. Leaving aside the issues of time constraints and policy purposes raised above, our analysis suggests that even in a system that is loosely connected in its static description, every variable in the system may ultimately depend upon every other variable as the system operates through time. A simple extrapolation of trends that ignores these dependencies may indeed be highly misleading. However, there is the possibility that in a particular system or in a particular application of a model, certain of these causal dependencies may be sufficiently weak to be safely ignored. If this were the case, the projections of the chartist who ignores these dependencies and of the fundamentalist who takes them more fully into account may be approximately the same. To consider this possibility, we must turn from the general structure of the model to its behavior in particular contexts, and to the results of the Ando-Fisher theorem on the decomposability of systems.

As suggested in section 1, the Ando-Fisher theorem and related efforts deal with the general problem of determining the circumstances under which a system can be decomposed into its component subsystems for purposes of analysis. More precisely, consider a *nearly decomposable system S'* in which one subsystem P is causally dependent on the rest of the system, but the rest of the system is only weakly dependent on the subsystem P. Consider also a *decomposable system S* identical to S' except that the weak casual dependencies from the subsystem P to the rest of the system are assumed to be absent. The nearly decomposable and decomposable versions of S are diagrammed in Figure 2.4, with the weak causal links indicated by the dotted line. Finally, let us define the *relative behavior* of the variables in P as their ratios. The result of the Ando-Fisher theorem is that for linear systems, the long-run relative behavior of the variables in *P* in the nearly decomposable system *S'* and the decomposable system *S* is approximately the same, even though their behavior in terms of absolute levels and rates of change may be very different. The weaker the weak dependency in *S'*, the better the approximation. In short, to the extent that the chartist is dealing with a system that approximates the nearly decomposable system *S'*, he may extrapolate relative trends in *P* and safely ignore the rest of the system.[53]

Figure 2.4—A Comparison of a Nearly Decomposable System *S'*
and a Decomposable System *S*

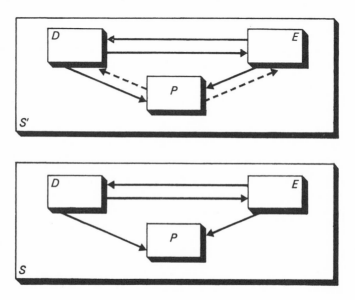

Let us conjecture that the model of modernization and mass politics in the Turkish and Philippine contexts is a nearly decomposable system in which relative behavior in the political subsystems can be explored independently of the rest of the system. Let us also conjecture that the result of the Ando-Fisher theorem holds for this model even though it is non-linear. If the model is nearly decomposable as applied to the Turkish case, the Philippine case, or both, the ratios of the political variables over time generated by the complete version of the model should approximate the ratios generated by the decomposable version. To specify a decomposable version, we need only replace the variable $P_{1,t}$ in relationship (3.1) and the variables $G_{i,t}$ in (3.3) by constants equal to their initial values. These are, respectively,

$P_{1,1}$ and $G_{i,1}$. With these modifications the urbanization and income relationships become

$$U_t = s\left(\frac{C_{2,t}}{N_{2,t}}\frac{N_{1,t}}{C_{1,t}}\right)P_{1,1}\,N_{1,t}$$

$$Y_{i,t} = C_{i,t} + I_{i,t} + G_{i,1} + F_{i,t}$$

The results are presented in Table 2.1, where the degree of approximation is calculated as the difference between the relative behavior of the

Table 2.1—The Long-run Relative Behavior of a Model: Complete Version (S') and Decomposable Version (S)

a. Turkey

	$V_{1,t}/V_{2,t}$				$G_{1,t}/G_{2,t}$			
	S'	S	Diff.	% Diff.	S'	S	Diff.	% Diff.
1950	1.000	1.000	.000	0.0	.509	.509	.000	0.0
1951	1.007	1.007	.000	0.0	.614	.614	.000	0.0
1952	1.063	1.023	.040	3.8	.575	.599	−.024	− 4.2
1953	1.096	1.048	.048	4.4	.609	.591	.018	3.0
1954	1.142	1.081	.061	5.3	.609	.589	.020	3.3
1955	.956	.885	.071	7.4	.759	.725	.034	4.5
1956	1.048	.925	.123	11.7	.488	.477	.011	2.3
1957	1.040	.972	.068	6.5	.582	.482	.100	17.2
1958	1.079	1.029	.050	4.6	.539	.490	.049	9.1
1959	1.090	1.096	−.006	− 0.6	.564	.504	.060	10.6
1960	1.106	1.175	−.069	− 6.2	.555	.521	.034	6.1
1961	1.110	1.267	−.157	−14.1	.561	.544	.017	3.0
1962	1.110	1.373	−.263	−23.7	.556	.573	−.017	− 3.1
1963	1.102	1.494	−.392	−35.6	.552	.607	−.055	−10.0
1964	1.090	1.632	−.542	−49.7	.543	.647	−.104	−19.2
1965	1.072	1.789	−.717	−66.9	.531	.693	−.162	−30.5

	$G_{1,t}/V_{1,t}$				$G_{2,t}/V_{2,t}$			
	S'	S	Diff.	% Diff.	S'	S	Diff.	% Diff.
1950	1,047	1,047	0	0.0	2,056	2,056	0	0.0
1951	1,052	1,052	0	0.0	1,725	1,725	0	0.0
1952	1,155	1,165	− 10	− 0.9	2,136	1,992	144	6.7
1953	1,197	1,236	− 39	− 3.3	2,155	2,192	− 37	− 1.7
1954	1,250	1,304	− 54	− 4.3	2,346	2,395	− 49	− 2.1
1955	1,662	1,800	−138	− 8.3	2,094	2,197	−103	− 4.9
1956	1,524	1,698	−174	−11.4	3,271	3,293	− 22	− 0.7
1957	1,583	1,765	−182	−11.5	2,827	3,560	−733	−25.9
1958	1,652	1,838	−186	−11.3	3,309	3,855	−546	−16.5
1959	1,720	1,905	−185	−10.8	3,326	4,146	−820	−24.7
1960	1,803	1,965	−162	− 9.0	3,591	4,428	−837	−23.3
1961	1,898	2,016	−118	− 6.2	3,755	4,691	−936	−24.9
1962	2,009	2,055	− 46	− 2.3	4,009	4,925	−916	−22.8
1963	2,141	2,079	62	2.9	4,276	5,120	−844	−19.7
1964	2,305	2,086	219	9.5	4,623	5,263	−640	−13.8
1965	2,508	2,072	436	17.4	5,059	5,346	−287	− 5.7

b. Philippines

		$V_{1,t}/V_{2,t}$				$G_{1,t}/G_{2,t}$		
	S'	S	Diff.	% Diff.	S'	S	Diff.	% Diff.
1951	1.021	1.021	.000	0.0	.292	.292	.000	0.0
1952	.996	.996	.000	0.0	.369	.369	.000	0.0
1953	.940	.975	−.035	− 3.7	.303	.318	−.015	− 5.0
1954	.905	.991	−.086	− 9.5	.306	.299	.007	2.3
1955	.931	1.008	−.076	− 8.2	.259	.286	−.027	−10.4
1956	.912	1.024	−.112	−12.3	.266	.276	−.010	− 3.8
1957	.948	.970	−.022	− 2.3	.232	.267	−.035	−15.1
1958	.939	.973	−.034	− 3.6	.241	.242	−.001	− 0.4
1959	.990	.973	.017	1.7	.212	.232	−.020	− 9.4
1960	.983	.969	.014	1.4	.227	.222	.005	2.2
1961	1.055	1.033	.022	2.1	.197	.212	−.015	− 7.6
1962	1.042	1.026	.016	1.5	.220	.217	.003	1.4
1963	1.146	1.017	.129	11.3	.184	.207	−.023	−12.5
1964	1.109	1.004	.105	9.5	.222	.197	.025	11.3
1965	1.268	1.011	.257	20.3	.172	.187	−.015	− 8.7
1966	1.177	.995	.182	15.5	.237	.181	.056	23.6

		$G_{1,t}/V_{1,t}$				$G_{2,t}/V_{2,t}$		
	S'	S	Diff.	% Diff.	S'	S	Diff.	% Diff.
1951	335	335	0	0.0	1,171	1,171	0	0.0
1952	375	375	0	0.0	1,011	1,011	0	0.0
1953	355	357	− 2	− 0.6	1,101	1,095	6	0.5
1954	379	388	− 9	− 2.4	1,121	1,287	−166	−14.8
1955	412	423	−11	− 2.7	1,480	1,492	− 12	− 0.8
1956	447	462	−15	− 3.4	1,535	1,714	−179	−11.7
1957	478	461	17	3.6	1,948	1,675	273	14.0
1958	515	493	22	4.3	2,002	1,978	24	1.2
1959	542	534	8	1.5	2,524	2,232	292	11.6
1960	582	576	6	1.0	2,524	2,513	11	0.4
1961	602	512	90	15.0	3,228	2,490	738	22.9
1962	647	558	89	13.8	3,065	2,642	423	13.8
1963	657	597	60	9.1	4,088	2,931	1,157	28.3
1964	711	637	74	10.4	3,552	3,243	309	8.7
1965	703	644	59	8.4	5,179	3,476	703	13.6
1966	778	689	89	11.4	3,869	3,779	90	2.3

complete and decomposed versions expressed as a percentage of the relative behavior of the complete version. Perhaps the best approximation is in the behavior of $G_{1,t}/V_{1,t}$ in the Philippine application. The maximum error is 15% (1961), and the errors are all less than 5% over the first ten years. The worst approximations are in $V_{1,t}/V_{2,t}$ and $G_{2,t}/V_{2,t}$ in the Turkish application. Maximum errors are, respectively, 66.9% (1965) and 25.9% (1957); the approximations are particularly poor after the eleventh year in the former and the eighth year in the latter. In general, for each comparison of relative behavior there is a tendency for the approximation to be better in the short run than in the long run.

In terms of the choice between the chartist and fundamentalist approaches, is the complete model a nearly decomposable system in which the political subsystem can be isolated from the rest of the system for purposes of studying political trends? Lacking mathematical proof that the result of the Ando-Fisher theorem holds for this nonlinear system, the answer is not clear. If the result of the theorem does not hold, the errors may not be evidence of near decomposability or the lack of it, but irrelevant to the issue. If the result of the theorem does hold, then we have gained some information on its degree of near decomposability in the Turkish and Philippine cases; whether the degree of near decomposability is sufficient depends on one's purposes. If the errors are within the limits of tolerable error for given purposes, the *ceteris paribus* assumption is appropriate and the political system's behavior can be studied apart from the rest of the system. If these errors are not within acceptable limits, the *ceteris paribus* assumption is inappropriate and the functional boundaries of the analysis must be expanded beyond the political subsystem to take into account demographic and economic factors. For most purposes, the errors seem to be rather large.

Some Qualifications. In order to highlight both the major advantages and limitations of computer simulation in the understanding of past and future events, it is worthwhile to consider a statement by Henri Pirenne on the limitations imposed on the historian by his subject matter.

> To achieve certainty about a subject as flowing, diverse, and complex as social behavior is impossible. Each kind of activity reacts upon all others. How, then, distinguish in the ensemble the part taken by each? How evaluate exactly the role which, for example, the economic or the religious factor has played in a given evolution? The conditions indispensable to all really scientific knowledge—calculation and measurement—are completely lacking in this field. And the interference of chance and individuals increases still more the difficulty of the historian's task by constantly confronting him with the unforseen, by changing at every moment the direction which events seemed to take.[54]

Perhaps the most important advantage of simulation relative to other methodologies is that in principle a good deal of the flowing, diverse, and complex behavior that Pirenne discerns in history can be replicated in a simulation model, as our consideration of diversity and order suggests. Furthermore, in a simulation experiment it is possible to "distinguish in the ensemble the part taken by each" factor. For example, the relative weight of alternative causal chains in producing an outcome can be assessed by varying one factor at a time and noting its impact. To be sure, the reconstruction of events through simulation depends on the degree of empirical validity of the model employed, and Pirenne is correct in saying that it is impossible to achieve certainty. However, as we noted in the preceding section, it is possible to reduce uncertainty through the use of scientific procedures.

The role of chance and individuals in changing the course of events and in introducing another source of diversity in the behavior of systems has not been explored here. However, stochastic factors could be introduced in various ways and at various points. Similarly, relationships attempting to account for the role of individual behavior in an otherwise aggregated system could be proposed and evaluated. These possibilities notwithstanding, it is inconceivable that many historical events of importance can be adequately incorporated into abstract systems and reproduced in their application to specific cases. For example, in February of 1959 an airplane carrying Prime Minister Menderes and fifteen other members of a Turkish delegation to London to sign the Cyprus agreement crashed. The fifteen were killed, but Menderes walked away from the crash. According to Walter Weiker, "As a result of this escape, he was viewed as almost superhuman by many superstitious Turkish peasants. This considerably reinforced his already large peasant support. . . ." [55] Similarly, President Magsaysay of the Philippines was killed in a plane crash shortly before the election of 1957. His death drastically changed the national political situation and, among other things, reduced the level of popular support for his Nacionalista party. In each case an accident affected popular support, a variable defined in the model.

Finally, Pirenne in our opinion overstates the degree to which calculation and measurement are lacking in matters of concern to historians, as the accelerating activity of quantitatively oriented historians suggests.[56] However, his point is useful if it serves to remind us that for many problems we are not now in a position to perform calculations or to measure. Consequently, our range of concerns should not be limited to those problems which we can presently explore through simulation or quantitative techniques.

NORMATIVE AND POLICY ORIENTATIONS

Values and Contexts. Among specialists in social ethics, the assumption that norms and values are absolute, *a priori*, and transcendental has been under attack. According to Abraham Kaplan

> The absence of . . . a determinate connection [between moral values and concrete policy] is the most pressing objection to moral absolutism from the stand point of its bearing on policy formation. I am directing attention to the futility of the belief that all moral problems have been essentially solved, and that the task for policy is only to translate these solutions into action. Where is the dictionary for such a translation? Just this is the problem. . . .[57]

For example,

> The maxim of the greatest good for the greatest number . . . is useless as a basis of choice when, as is almost always the case, one alternative provides a greater good for some while the other benefits more people

though to a lesser extent; what, on this basis, is an equitable distribution of the tax burden?[58]

In Kaplan's view values are *contextual*, not absolute. That is to say, on the one hand, values can be appraised only in a concrete setting. "The lessons of operationism are as important for policy as for science: to be able to guide practice, [ethical] theory must be formulated in terms that connect it with determinate behavior."[59] And to connect ethical theory with determinate behavior, one must refer to specific, concrete contexts. On the other hand, in any concrete setting there is always an appraisal to be made, because there is a potential for both gains and losses and because there is uncertainty about the consequences of policy.

> Sound policy minimizes [losses and risks] but cannot eliminate them; simple prudence demands that they be carefully taken into account beforehand. This means a contextual appraisal, not a reliance on general and abstract principles.[60]

In short,

> Morality is rarely a matter simply of applying an unquestioned principle to a case that indubitably falls under its scope. The moral problem is to weigh conflicting principles and to act on a balance of probabilities on behalf of the preponderant values.[61]

Among specialists in the normative aspects of political development, the same problems are important. For example, Roland Pennock, who adopts the contextual approach in a well-known article on political goods, focuses on several kinds of value trade-offs and uncertainty about consequences in his analysis of a hypothetical situation.

> *If* it is clear . . . that in a given situation a second political party can be permitted only at the price of such governmental instability as will discourage the entrance of much needed foreign capital, *and if* it seems reasonable to suppose that denial of a second party now will probably not foreclose the opportunity a few years hence, then most people would be likely to agree that freedom of association should be to this extent limited. The difficulties about this choice reside in the "if" clauses. But these are matters of calculating probable consequences, not of weighing one value against another.[62]

In this example the normative dimension of choice at the simplest level is at least twofold. There is a choice between governmental stability, foreign capital, and implicitly the possibility of increased welfare on the one hand, and freedom of association on the other. There is also a choice between foregoing freedom of association in the present and the possibility of realizing freedom of association in the future.

Both the need to deal with uncertainties—such as those implicit in Pennock's "if" clauses—and the need to tie ethical theory to determinate behavior reflect a sensitivity to the diversity of behavior inherent in complex systems. The state of a system at any point in time, including the normatively important trade-offs realized, may differ from the state of other, structurally similar systems as well as the state of the same system at different points in time. If the order underlying this diversity can be taken into account, then in principle uncertainties about consequences can be reduced.

Policy and Complexity. The contextual nature of value judgments and the resulting conflicts and trade-offs among goods are also familiar problems for policy analysts. For example, one policy analyst has written that

> Government involves constant adjustment both of the way things are going, to bring them more into line with the relevant standards, and of the standards, either to accommodate them more nearly to what is attainable or to bring them more into line with new levels of aspiration.[63]

If the standards which reflect our aspirations are subject to appraisal and modification through experience, they are not absolute, *a priori*, or transcendental. Sensitivity to the complexity of normative choice in concrete settings is found in statements that "every choice is in some measure multi-valued"[64] and that

> men have a multiplicity of goals ... the maximization of one goal frequently conflicts with the maximization of another or even numerous ones. Hence, ... rational appraisal is usually a matter of calculating how much one is prepared to sacrifice some attainment of certain goals in order to attain other goals somewhat more fully.[65]

The focus of the policy analysts, however, is on the solution of social problems through rational social action. In Dahl and Lindblom's important study, *Politics, Economics and Welfare*, the possibilities for rational social action by an individual or group depend upon both rational calculation of the ways in which goals can be achieved, and control over those whose responses are needed to fulfill goals.[66] Here we are concerned only with the former, the making of rational calculations.

In their analysis, rational calculation is limited by the nature of man as a thinking animal. In addition to the irrational aspects of human personality discovered by Freud and his successors, "The number of alternatives man would need to consider in order to act rationally is very often far beyond his limited mental capacity."[67] Furthermore,

> it is difficult to use such foresight as feeble brain and personality might otherwise permit because often one cannot judge between present goal achievement and future—partly because one cannot always know what

he wants until he has tested the goal; experience often is the only adequate test.[68]

Rational calculation is also limited by the level of knowledge applicable to a policy problem, and limited knowledge gives rise to unforeseen consequences. Dahl and Lindblom consider the paradox of specialization to be one aspect of the problem.

> When one specializes he focuses his attention on certain categories of repetitive events; by decreasing the number of variables at the focus of attention, specialization enables one to increase his capacity for rational calculation about these particular categories. This increased capacity for rational calculation enables men to undertake social action hitherto impossible. But these social actions have unforeseen consequences—unforeseen in part because men can become specialists only by ignoring some of the variables. Hence a calculation that is rational in the short run or with respect to certain limited goals may prove to be irrational in the long run or with respect to different goals.[69]

In short, knowledge of consequences is necessary for rational social action, but the limited mental capacity of human beings and the *ceteris paribus* assumption implicit in specialization are barriers to such knowledge.

Some Possibilities for Simulation. In order to illustrate the relevance of simulation to these problems, we propose to elaborate a part of the sensitivity analysis presented in the first essay. In particular we shall investigate the joint impact of changes in β_1 and β_2, the government propensities to distribute funds to the rural and urban sectors, on the level of consumption per capita (a measure of the standard of living) and support for the government. We are interested in how the system responds to these parameter changes, which can be interpreted as policy changes in the model, and the relationship between this analysis and the problems of normative and policy analyses outlined above.

For both the Turkish and Philippine contexts, we define a parameter space of various combinations of β_1 and β_2. The range of variation for each parameter is $\beta_i \pm .10\bar{\beta}$ where β_i is the setting used in the reference runs of the first essay and where $\bar{\beta} = (\beta_1 + \beta_2)/2$, the simple mean. The range for each parameter is divided into twenty equal intervals, each of which is $.01\bar{\beta}$ in width. Consequently, for each country there are 21 different settings of β_1, 21 different settings of β_2 and $21 \times 21 = 441$ *combinations* of different settings. Each combination was used for one run of the model. From each run we selected eight outcomes: the standard of living and support for the government for both the rural and urban sectors and for both the fifth and tenth yearly cycles of the model.

Figure 2.5—Contour Maps: Response of the Standard of Living and
Support for the Government to Joint Variation in β_1 and β_2

a. Turkey

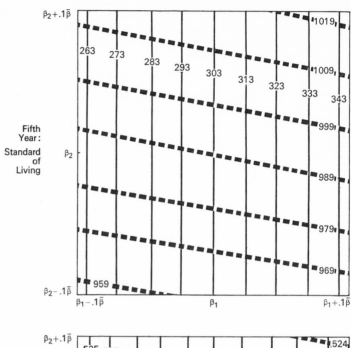

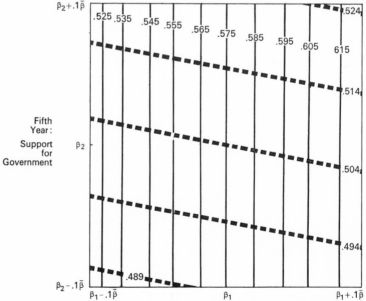

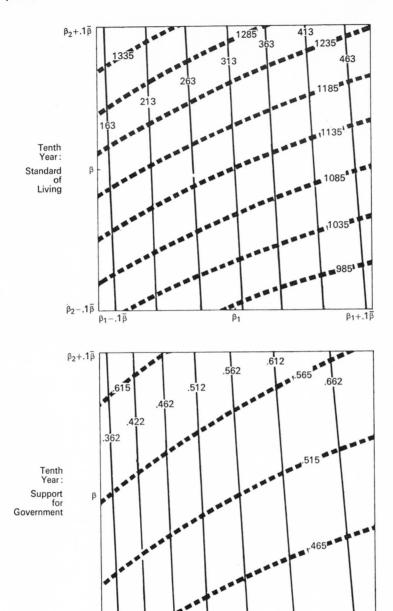

b. Philippines

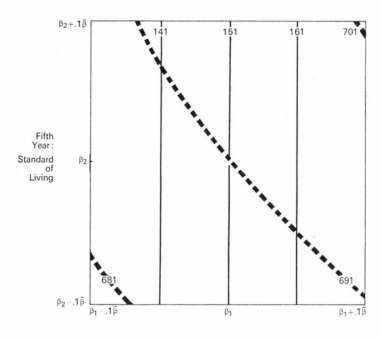

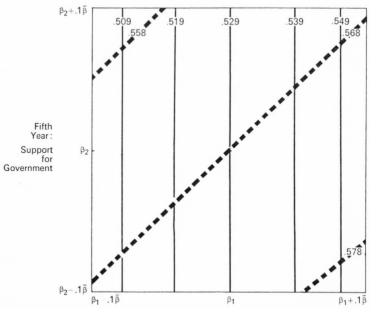

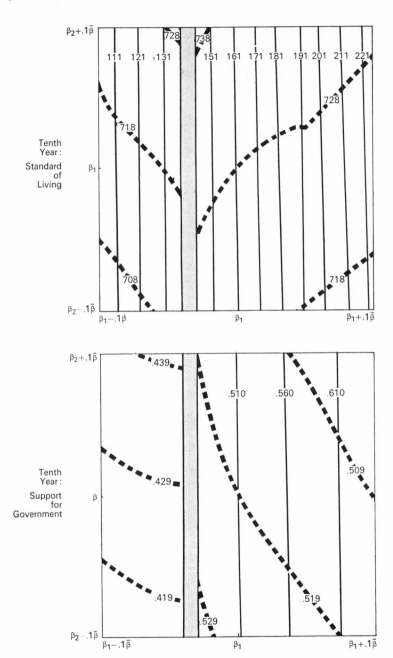

The results are presented graphically as contour maps in Figure 2.5. Each of the 441 points defining the surface for each country represents one unique run of the model. The outputs of the reference runs are located at the center of each map at the point (β_1, β_2). Solid lines connect runs with equal levels of output in the rural sector, and dashed lines connect runs of equal output in the urban sector. These lines are called *isoquants.*[70] The *slope* of the lines reflects the relative sensitivity of the output to variation in β_1 and β_2. For example, vertical isoquants are solely a function of variation in β_1: To get from one such isoquant to another requires a change in β_1, but a change in β_2 has no effect. The *sign of the slope* reflects the relative direction of the impact of β_1 and β_2. If the slope is negative (that is, from upper left to lower right), increases in β_1 and β_2 work in the same direction to either increase or decrease the output. If the slope is positive (that is, from lower left to upper right), increases in β_1 and β_2 work in the opposite direction: One tends to increase the output, the other to decrease it. The *distance* between isoquants of the same output reflects the magnitude of the sensitivity to changes in β_i. The closer the isoquants, the greater is the sensitivity per unit change in β_i.

Even to those familiar with the structure and behavior of the model, several consequences of these parameter changes were unforseen. The most striking example is the effect of the electoral subsystem in the Philippine experiment. In the reference run as in all runs where the setting of β_1 is less than the reference run value minus $.03\bar\beta$, the government won the election of 1957. In all the other runs in this experiment, the government lost the election. The difference in electoral outcomes creates a discontinuity (represented by a vertical shaded bar) in the tenth year results in Figure 2.5b. To the right of the discontinuity, the urban standard of living and urban support for the government decrease as β_1 increases; to the left they increase as β_1 increases. This example is sufficient to illustrate the point that even for a system of such modest size, a determinate connection between knowledge of structure and context on the one hand and knowledge of behavior on the other requires the specification and operation of a formal model. To the extent that such a connection is a problem in normative and policy analyses, simulation models can be useful as supplements to existing methods of analyses.

The contour maps also highlight several kinds of trade-offs in each context. One kind of trade-off, the distribution of a single good across sectors, is illustrated in the tenth-year levels of the standard of living in Figure 2.5a. If β_2 is increased by $.03\bar\beta$ over the reference run setting, consumption per capita in the urban sector increases about 50 T.L., but consumption per capita in the rural sector hardly increases at all. However, if β_1 is increased by $.03\bar\beta$ over the reference run setting, the standard of living improves in the rural sector but declines in the urban. Another kind of trade-off, the distribution of a single good across time, is illustrated in the comparison of fifth- and tenth-year levels of the standard of living in Figure 2.5a. If β_1 is increased by $.03\bar{\beta}$ over the reference run setting, the standard of living in the urban sector increases slightly by the fifth year, but, as we have seen above, decreases slightly under the same conditions by the tenth year. A third type of trade-off, the trade-off between gains in one value and losses in another is illustrated in the fifth-year results in Figure 2.5b. An increase of $.10\bar{\beta}$ in the reference run setting of β_2 increases the urban standard of living by about 5 pesos per capita and decreases urban support for the government by about two-thirds of one per cent. To say that the policies implicit in the changes in β_i are good or bad depends at the very least upon normative judgments about inequalities in the standard of living between sectors, the relative value of short-run gains in the standard of living as against long-run losses, and about improvements in the standard of living relative to losses in support. What this type of analysis can do in principle is to clarify the empirical basis of the judgments by elaborating the consequences of potential policies.

In a somewhat broader perspective, these examples suggest that experience in the testing of policies and the clarification of goals through simulation experiments can supplement experience in the real world but at much less cost. While experience gained in simulation experiments involves research and computer time primarily, experience gained in the real world often involves the well-being of human beings. Furthermore, since computer simulation models require a distinction between structural similarities and contextual differences, they may help to suggest whether and how experience gained in one real world situation can be used in another. For example, consideration of the relevance, if any, of Munich to Vietnam is a difficult problem that might benefit from such a distinction. Finally, if we can understand the processes operating in a class of systems and represent them formally in computer simulation models, then uncertainty regarding consequences that arises from the complex nature of systems can be reduced. We need not treat organized complexity as disorganized complexity.

Some Limitations. At any given point in time, the most that can be done through simulation analysis is to simplify and aggregate the knowledge and information relevant to a policy problem and formalize it in a computer simulation model. The payoff from simplification, aggregation, and formalization is an increased capacity to cope with organized complexity, and we have tried to suggest that these payoffs are considerable. At the same time the limitations cannot be ignored.

From the viewpoint of normative analysis, the most serious limitation is that the components of a model will never correspond precisely to any comprehensive normative conception of society. The values at stake in social and political processes are numerous and include not only power and wealth in their various forms but also respect, rectitude, affection, well-being, skill, and enlightenment.[71] However, because we must simplify, those values considered less important in themselves, less important in explaining the behavior of a system, or most difficult to formalize may be eliminated from a model. Moreover, because we must aggregate to some level, important questions about the distribution of values included in the analysis may be ignored. For example, aggregation to the level of mass political groups glosses over the existence of inequality *within* these groups and directs attention toward inequality *between* them. But to what extent are we justified in ignoring inequality between, say, the peasantry and the small minority of wealthy landowners in the rural sector? Some but not all such distinctions necessary for the investigation of distributive questions can be included in any single model. In this sense, aggregate models tend to underestimate the degree of inequality in society.

From the viewpoint of policy analysis, the most serious limitation is that models will never produce entirely accurate results. Whether the results will be sufficiently accurate depends on the quality of our limited knowledge and information, the skill with which it is simplified and formalized into models, and the skill with which the models are tested. Moreover, at any given level of aggregation, chance and key individuals may still account for important aspects of a system's behavior. Even in well-designed and skillfully tested models with stochastic factors, these aspects of a system's behavior cannot be anticipated or reproduced adequately. A significant part, but only a part, of the diverse behavior of large systems can be attributed to the orderly interaction of a large number of components and processes.

Consequently, computer simulation models can be utilized most effectively for normative and policy purposes within an institutional framework that compensates for these limitations. Shubik's proposal to link large data-processing procedures with models is well-suited to improving the quality of both models and the data they require. Harold Lasswell's proposal to develop institutions called decision seminars is similar but much more elaborate.[72] A central function of the decision seminar is to monitor the course of social and political events as they unfold and to relate these data quickly and systematically to current verbal and formal models. The agenda of the decision seminar includes not only the use of the models to project the future course of events, to clarify the values implicated, and to invent and evaluate policy alternatives; it also includes the revision of normative judgments and empirical formulations emphasized in the models as they are challenged by experience. If we cannot consider all our normative concerns or evaluate policies with completely accurate results at any given time through the use of simulation models, we can at least recognize our errors quickly and attempt to rectify them through the development of simulation models within the framework of decision seminars.

3. Empirical Approaches

As suggested in the Introduction, the major empirical approaches—cybernetics, structural-functionalism, and political culture—each propose basic concepts as means of studying political systems as wholes. Yet the connection between these abstractions and the behavior of political systems is not sufficiently close for significant scientific progress or for more than heuristic explanations of the systems' behavior. After summarizing the basic concepts in each approach, we propose to show how some of these concepts are represented in both the structure and behavior of the model of modernization and mass politics and how they can be used to suggest revisions of the model.

CYBERNETICS

Basic Concepts. Perhaps the most basic concept in the cybernetic approach is the concept of feedback. In Deutsch's analysis

> . . . by feedback—or, as it is often called, a servo-mechanism—is meant a communications network that produces action in response to an input of information, and *includes the results of its own action in the new information by which it modifies its subsequent behavior.*[73]

Every feedback mechanism is sensitive to some kind of stress, tension, or disequilibrium. The stress is a function of a comparison between a goal or (more generally) a criterion on the one hand and information about an aspect of the system's behavior on the other. Stress produces a response that either decreases the discrepancy between criterion and information about behavior (the case of negative feedback) or increases the discrepancy (the case of positive feedback). Thus a thermostat is a feedback mechanism sensitive to the difference between a temperature setting and actual room temperature. When this difference becomes sufficiently large, the mechanism switches on a furnace, which raises actual room temperature. When this difference is sufficiently small, the mechanism switches off the furnace.[74]

The thermostat is a very simple feedback mechanism: It merely seeks to maintain a given temperature setting in a room. More complex feedback systems are capable of goal-changing as well as goal-seeking. Both types of feedback are related to what we conventionally call learning, but the distinction between the two is important.

Simple learning is goal-seeking feedback. . . . It consists in adjusting repsonses, so as to reach a goal situation of a type that is given once for all by certain internal arrangements of the net; these arrangements are fixed throughout its life. A more complex type of learning is the self-modifying or *goal-changing* feedback. It allows for feedback adjustments of those internal arrangements that implied its original goal, so that the net will change its goal, or set for itself new goals that it will now have to reach if its internal disequilibrium is to be lessened.[75]

In the case of goal-seeking or first-order feedback, the internal arrangements of the system and the values implied by it are fixed. In the case of goal-changing or second-order feedback, they are modified. The setting of a new goal in this formulation is analogous to, say, a peasantry's decreased sensitivity to religious issues or to an aggregate increase or decrease in a political party's sensitivity to economic issues among one or more groups in a society.

The concept of feedback appears at least implicitly in many generalizations about the behavior of social and political systems. Consider Wilbur Schramm's analysis:

> In very general terms all behavioral systems, of whatever complexity, appear to behave in the same way. That is, they try to maximize their level of desired functioning and minimize the associated stress and strain. Their desired functioning reflects needs, goals, values. Their levels of stress and strain reflect the difficulties, the frustrations, the effort associated with behaving in a particular way. . . . Just as the healthy body maintains its temperature within the limits of a degree or two, so does the healthy social system appear to try to keep strain within certain limits, satisfying as many of its needs and goals as possible, varying strain up and down, but trying to keep the peaks of variation within tolerable extremes.[76]

Schramm does not consider the mechanisms by which stress is controlled.

In the more historical tradition of social and political analysis, many observers have characterized particular events or patterns of behavior as means of reducing tension and strain in societies. Bernard Lewis conceived of the formation of the Democratic Party in Turkey in 1946 as a means of alleviating political conflicts that could no longer be contained within the framework of the Republican People's Party: "The Democrats claim that by 1945 the strains of discontent had become so serious in Turkey that the C.H.P. [*Cumhuriyet Halk Partisi* or Republican People's Party] was forced to open a safety-valve to prevent a general upheaval."[77] Similarly, mass rebellions may be thought of as mechanisms to alleviate stress through system change when the more conventional mechanisms have been ineffective. A case in point might be the Huk movement in the Philippines and the resulting attempts at resettlement, reform and land colonization instigated by Magsaysay.[78]

The performance of a feedback mechanism can be analyzed in terms of its load, lag, gain, and lead. *Load* is the degree of stress, tension, or disequilibrium. *Lag* is the time that elapses between the moment a sufficiently large load is sensed and the moment the system completes action in response to the load. "The greater its lag in relation to its load, the less likely is a system to reach a changing goal or moving target."[79] *Gain* is the magnitude of the corrective action taken by the system expressed as the ratio of output to input. *Lead* is the time between the present and the point in the future at which the state of the system can still be predicted with sufficient accuracy.

According to Deutsch,

> The overall performance of political decision systems will depend upon the interplay of all these factors. Since gain is related to power, governments or organizations with little power may have to try to compensate for their low rates of gain by trying to increase their foresight and the speed of their response, that is to say, to cut down their lag and to increase their lead. Great powers, on the other hand, may often succeed in coping with a situation by the sheer size of their response, even though their reactions may be slow and their predictions poor. Again governments or political organizations, whose rates of lag, gain, and lead were sufficiently adjusted to each other for dealing with moderate rates of change in their environment, may find themselves unable to control their behavior effectively in times of rapid change that may put an excessive load upon their decision-making system.[80]

In general, the probability of controlling the stresses and strains in the system varies inversely with the degree of load and lag, directly with the amount of lead, and, up to a point, directly with the amount of gain. At high rates of gain a system may over-respond and thereby increase rather than reduce the load on the system.

Power, in one relatively narrow sense, is closely related to gain in feedback systems involving contending political actors.

> In simple language, to have power means not to give in, and to force the environment or the other person to do so. Power in this narrow sense is the priority of output over intake, the ability to talk instead of listen. In a sense, it is the ability to afford not to learn.[81]
>
> A concept of net power might define it as a difference—the difference between the amount of changes imposed and changes accepted by the actor.[82]

If the changes in behavior imposed on actor A by actor B are greater than the changes imposed on B by A, B enjoys a net power advantage. The changes can be represented as gains, and net power as the difference between gains. This analysis of power in a system depends not only on power resources such as votes or dollars, but on how these resources are utilized as well. In short, the application of power in the specific case depends not only on the muscles of government but on the nerves of government as well.

Feedback in the Model. The model of modernization and mass politics can be interpreted as a multiple feedback system composed of ten inter-dependent feedback mechanisms. These mechanisms are listed in Table 3.1 together with specifications of loads and lags and definitions of gains. The investment, support, government expenditure, and expectation mechanisms are defined for both the rural and urban sectors, while the urbanization and electoral mechanisms are defined for the system as a whole. These mechanisms account for much of the interesting behavior of the model.

Table 3.1—Feedback Mechanisms: Load, Lag, and Gain

Relationship		Specification of Load	Specification of Lag	Definition of Gain
(3.1)	Urbanization	$\left[\dfrac{C_{2,t}}{N_{2,t}}\dfrac{N_{1,t}}{C_{1,t}}\right]P_{1,t}$	Less than one year	$\dfrac{U_t}{U_{t-1}}$
(3.6b)	Investment	$\left[\dfrac{C_{i,t}}{N_{i,t}}-\dfrac{C_{i,t-1}}{N_{i,t-1}}\right]$	One year	$\dfrac{I_{i,t}}{I_{i,t-1}}$
(3.7)	Support	$\left[\dfrac{C_{i,t}}{N_{i,t}}\dfrac{N_{i,t-1}}{C_{i,t-1}}-E_{i,t-1}\right]P_{i,t-1}$	One year	$\dfrac{V_{i,t}}{V_{i,t-1}}$
(3.8)	Expenditures	$\left[\dfrac{N_{i,t-1}V_{i,t-1}-\Delta N_i V_i}{N_{1,t-1}V_{1,t-1}+N_{2,t-1}V_{2,t-1}-\Delta N_1 V_1-\Delta N_2 V_2}\right]$	One year	$\dfrac{G_{i,t}}{G_{i,t-1}}$
(3.11)	Expectations	$\left[\dfrac{C_{i,t}}{N_{i,t}}\dfrac{N_{i,t-1}}{C_{i,t-1}}-E_{i,t-1}\right]P_{i,t-1}$	One year	$\dfrac{E_{i,t}}{E_{i,t-1}}$
(3.12)	Elections	$V_{3,t}<\text{WINVOT}$	Less than one year	$\dfrac{V_{i,t}}{V_{i,t-1}}$

The urbanization relationship determines the number of persons who migrate from rural to urban areas in a year. This mechanism is sensitive to inequality between the urban and rural standards of living. Mathematically, this load is represented as the ratio of consumption per capita in the urban area $C_{2,t}/N_{2,t}$ to consumption per capita in the rural area $C_{1,t}/N_{1,t}$. The gain is represented as the ratio of the number of migrants in t to the number of migrants in $t - 1$. A load greater than one produces migration in excess of the minimum level. This migration reduces the size of the rural population [through relationship (3.2a)], increases the size of the urban population [through (3.2b)], and, other things being equal, thereby reduces the load. Thus over time there is a tendency toward equality in the standards of living, but in general the gain is not large enough to achieve it.

The investment relationship determines the change in the amount of investment from one time period to the next in each sector independently. The load that controls investment behavior in a sector is the difference between the standard of living at t and the standard of living at $t - 1$. The gain is defined as the ratio of the investment at t to investment at $t - 1$. Depending upon the context, this mechanism can produce the explosive behavior characteristic of positive feedback. A sufficiently large increase in investment increases the subsequent standard of living, which in turn increases investment. On the other hand, a sufficiently large decrease in investment decreases the subsequent standard of living, which in turn decreases investment. In short, this mechanism tends to amplify rather than reduce a given positive or negative load, although other feedback mechanisms may compensate for its outputs and reduce its explosive tendencies.

The support relationship, which also operates independently in each sector, determines the level of support for the government in response to a comparison between the actual increase through time in the standard of living and the expected increase. The actual increase is presented as the ratio of the standard of living in t to the standard of living in $t - 1$. The expected increase is represented by the variable $E_{i,t-1}$. The difference between the actual and expected increase is the load to which this mechanism responds. The gain in support is the ratio of support in t to support in $t - 1$. In contrast to the other relationships, the gain in this relationship varies not only with the load but also with the absolute level of support, as seen in the term $[(1 - V_{i,t-1})\ V_{i,t-1}]^3$. The loads being equal, this term produces larger gains when support for the government is about 50% in a sector, and smaller gains when support is less evenly distributed between government and opposition. Under the latter condition, the assumption is that both government and opposition have a firmly committed core of supporters who are less likely to respond by withdrawing support given the same economic stimulus. Under the former condition, there is a swing vote that is more susceptible to giving and withholding support. The effects of this term are shown graphically in Figure 3.1. The efficiency of this mechanism in reducing the stress is hard to assess in general terms, since either an increase or a decrease in support can produce a government response that increases or decreases the load. However, at high levels of support or non-support for the government, the mechanism becomes less effective as a control mechanism because the magnitude of the gains decreases: Regardless of the stress, gains tend to converge toward 1.0.

The expenditure relationship determines government expenditures in each sector as a result of changes in the levels of support for the government. The load which stimulates changes in government expenditures in a sector through time is the ratio of the number of supporters in the sector $N_{i,t-1}$ $V_{i,t-1}$ less the change in the number of supporters $\Delta N_i V_i$ to the total number of supporters minus the total change in the number of supporters. The gain

Figure 3.1—Support Relationship: Gains in Support
Are in Part a Function of the Level of Support

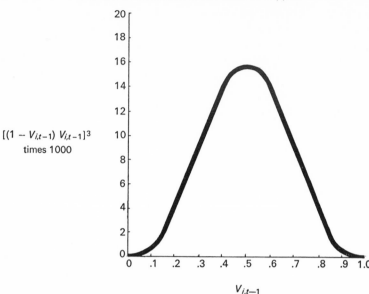

$[(1 - V_{i,t-1})\, V_{i,t-1}]^3$
times 1000

$V_{i,t-1}$

in government expenditures is defined as the ratio of current expenditures $G_{i,t}$ to previous expenditures $G_{i,t-1}$. As shown in relationship (3.8), the gain varies with this load and with government revenues GR_{t-1}. As in the case of the support relationship, it is difficult to assess the general efficiency of this relationship in reducing the load generated by the amount and change of support in each sector. If support levels in the two sectors are approximately equal, a withdrawal of support by a sector generates a gain in expenditures that may be sufficiently large to increase support. If support levels in the two sectors in the model are very different, the sector giving the more support to the government receives a larger share of expenditures regardless of changes in support. Other things being equal, the expenditures increase support in this sector and further reduce it in the other.

The expectation relationship adjusts expectations about the rate of increase in the standard of living in the direction of recent experience. The load in this mechanism is exactly the same as the load in the support relationship: The difference between the rate of increase in the standard of living and the expected rate of increase. The gain is expressed as the ratio of current expectations $E_{i,t}$ to previous expectations $E_{i,t-1}$. Other things being equal, this mechanism tends to reduce the load.

The electoral mechanism changes the governing group in power if their popular support falls to sufficiently low levels in an election year. The result is that support previously withheld from the old government $(1 - V_{i,t})$ now becomes the support for the new government $V_{i,t}$. The load in this mechanism is a comparison between the government's aggregate support and the level of support needed to win the election. The gain, as in the support relationship, is the ratio of support in t (after the election) to support in $t - 1$. In the other mechanisms, the relationship between load and gain is a continuous one; in this mechanism, the relationship is discrete. That is to say, the load either stimulates a change or it does not, the government either loses or wins. It is not the magnitude of the difference between aggregate support and the winning threshold, but the arithmetic sign of the difference that matters. The electoral'mechanism enters into the control of support for the government only in election years; but in an election year the time lag is less than one year.

In three of the feedback mechanisms—urbanization, support, and expectations—the load is moderated or "filtered" by a participation factor $P_{i,t}$. Only a proportion $P_{1,t}$ of the rural population responds to the inequality in the standard of living by migrating to urban areas. Similarly, only a proportion $P_{i,t-1}$ of the population in sector i responds to differences between the actual and expected rate of increase in the standard of living by giving or withholding support for the government or revising its economic expectations in the light of actual experience. Consequently, an increase in the proportion of persons behaving in a participant manner increases the amount of effective stress or load in the system and the magnitude of the responses to these loads.

An analysis of the structure of each individual feedback mechanism says little about its behavior in the context of the system as a whole. Consequently, the behavior of each mechanism in the applications of the model to Turkey and the Philippines is summarized in Table 3.2. The loads are given in the upper half of the table for each country; the corresponding gains are given in the lower half. A few examples from Table 3.2 are sufficient to illustrate the feedback behavior of the model.

Table 3.2—Feedback Behavior

a. Turkish Application

LOADS IN THE SYSTEM

t	Urban-ization	Investment		Support		Expenditures		Expectations	
		Rural	Urban	Rural	Urban	Rural	Urban	Rural	Urban
1951	2.27	12.2	33.1	.012	.005	.816	.184	.012	.005
1952	2.16	13.3	— .7	.013	—.028	.805	.195	.013	—.028
1953	2.07	17.2	19.8	.019	—.006	.814	.186	.019	—.006
1954	1.96	20.0	13.5	.022	—.012	.814	.186	.022	—.012
1955	2.64	—74.3	18.2	—.169	—.007	.845	.155	—.169	—.007
1956	2.43	18.6	— 6.2	.037	—.028	.779	.221	.037	—.028
1957	2.38	18 2	53.6	.030	.028	.807	.193	.030	.028
1958	2.26	21.8	28.9	.033	.002	.795	.205	.033	.002
1959	2.17	26.2	51.9	.037	.021	.802	.198	.037	.021
1960	2.07	31.2	53.3	.040	.018	.800	.200	.040	.018

Table 3.2—Feedback Behavior (Cont.)

a. Turkish Application

GAINS IN THE SYSTEM

t	Urban-ization	Investment		Support		Expenditures		Expectations	
		Rural	Urban	Rural	Urban	Rural	Urban	Rural	Urban
1951	1.01	2.09	1.13	1.01	1.01	1.02	.85	1.00	1.00
1952	.97	1.59	1.04	1.01	.96	1.11	1.19	1.00	1.00
1953	.98	1.50	1.09	1.02	.99	1.06	1.00	1.00	1.00
1954	.97	1.40	1.07	1.02	.98	1.07	1.07	1.00	1.00
1955	1.38	.00	1.08	.83	.99	1.10	.88	.98	1.00
1956	.94	359.07	1.03	1.05	.96	.96	1.49	1.00	1.00
1957	1.01	2.02	1.16	1.04	1.05	1.08	.90	1.00	1.00
1958	.97	1.63	1.10	1.04	1.00	1.09	1.17	1.00	1.00
1959	.98	1.48	1.14	1.04	1.03	1.09	1.04	1.00	1.00
1960	.98	1.40	1.13	1.04	1.03	1.09	1.11	1.00	1.00

b. Philippine Application

LOADS IN THE SYSTEM

t	Urban-ization	Investment		Support		Expenditures		Expectations	
		Rural	Urban	Rural	Urban	Rural	Urban	Rural	Urban
1952	2.63	−1.10	13.73	−.021	−.010	.819	.181	−.021	−.010
1953	2.55	− .68	−24.47	−.018	−.047	.788	.212	−.018	−.047
1954	2.54	.35	24.44	−.012	.007	.790	.210	−.012	.007
1955	2.63	.58	− 6.01	−.010	−.026	.761	.239	−.010	−.026
1956	2.80	1.08	17.70	−.008	.002	.765	.235	−.008	.002
1957	2.87	1.60	− 4.66	−.005	−.024	.741	.259	−.005	−.024
1958	2.98	2.04	14.94	−.003	.001	.748	.252	−.003	.001
1959	3.01	2.66	− 5.89	−.001	−.024	.723	.277	−.001	−.024
1960	3.09	3.08	15.07	.001	.004	.736	.264	.001	.004
1961	3.08	3.85	− 8.72	.004	−.025	.707	.293	.004	−.025

GAINS IN THE SYSTEM

t	Urban-ization	Investment		Support		Expenditures		Expectations	
		Rural	Urban	Rural	Urban	Rural	Urban	Rural	Urban
1952	1.05	.97	.85	.95	.97	1.06	.84	1.00	1.00
1953	.99	.99	1.61	.96	.88	1.13	1.37	1.00	.99
1954	1.05	1.03	.72	.98	1.01	1.04	1.03	1.00	1.00
1955	1.01	1.04	1.20	.98	.95	1.07	1.26	1.00	1.00
1956	1.08	1.06	.73	.98	1.00	1.07	1.04	1.00	1.00
1957	1.04	1.08	1.20	.99	.95	1.06	1.21	1.00	1.00
1958	1.06	1.09	.69	.99	1.00	1.07	1.03	1.00	1.00
1959	1.03	1.11	1.30	1.00	.95	1.05	1.19	1.00	1.00
1960	1.04	1.11	.58	1.00	1.01	1.08	1.01	1.00	1.00
1961	1.01	1.13	1.58	1.01	.94	1.04	1.20	1.00	1.00

The most interesting behavior in the Turkish application occurred as a result of an exogenous drop in agricultural income in 1954, which was intended to reflect the consequences of drought and some of the government's agricultural policies. This drop generates very high loads in the urbanization relationship, the rural investment relationship, and the rural support relationship in 1955. These loads reflect, respectively, a sharp increase in rural–urban inequality, a sharp decline in rural demand, and a sharp decline in the rural standard of living relative to expectations. These loads, in turn, generate a gain of 138% in migration to urban areas, a decline in rural investment to less than 1 % of the previous level, and a withdrawal of support for the government to 83% of the previous level. In response to the latter, the government diverts funds from the urban to the rural sector in 1955. The decline in rural investment tends to amplify rather than moderate the loads, but the other responses are sufficient to counteract its effects and to begin to dissipate the loads in the rural sector in 1956. In the meantime, however, the diversion of government funds to the rural sector cut demand in the urban sector and reduced the urban standard of living relative to expectations by 1956. This new set of loads, together with those generated directly by the exogenous drop in agricultural income, are nearly stabilized by 1960.

The cyclical pattern of loads and gains in the urban sector is the most interesting aspect of the behavior of the model in the Philippine context. A positive load in the investment relationship tends to generate a gain of less than one in investment in even numbered years. This decreases the standard of living, generates a negative load in the support relationship, and causes a gain of less than one in support in the following odd-numbered year. Consequently the gain in government expenditures in the urban sector increases; this in turn generates another positive load in the investment relationship. The cycle is then repeated. Over the ten-year period, loads in the urbanization relationship, the rural investment relationship, and the urban expenditure relationship tend to increase. The other loads are relatively stable or decline. In both applications, over-all performance in controlling the loads depends upon the net effect of several partially reinforcing and partially conflicting tendencies toward adjustment. Thus in an important sense each outcome has multiple causes and is overdetermined.

As noted above, gain is closely related to political power where political interactions are concerned. In the structure of this small model the major political interaction can be interpreted as the attempt of each sector to obtain government funds (as a factor in maintaining an acceptable rate of growth of the standard of living) by giving or withholding support for the government, and the government's attempt to maintain an acceptable level of support by giving or withholding expenditures from the sectors. Using this interpretation and the relationship between gain and power, the change in behavior imposed on the government by a sector can be represented as $G_{i,t}/G_{i,t-1}$, and the change accepted by the sector as $V_{i,t}/V_{i,t-1}$. The difference is the net power of the sector *vis-à-vis* the government. Because the impact of expenditures on support is time-lagged by one year in the model, the change in behavior imposed on a sector by the government is $V_{i,t+1}/V_{i,t}$, and the change accepted by the government is $G_{i,t}/G_{i,t-1}$. The difference is the net power of the government *vis-à-vis* the sector. It should be pointed out that these net power indices are not measured in votes or lira or pesos but are dimensionless, as are the gains from which they are calculated; that they are conditioned by other aspects of the demographic, economic, and political environment; and that they refer to power actually exercised in the operation of the model rather than latent or potential power.

A reconstruction of the model's behavior in terms of power exercised is given in Table 3.3. With some exceptions, in both applications of the model

Table 3.3—Net Power in the Behavior of the Model

a. Turkish Application

t	$\dfrac{G_{1,t}}{G_{1,t-1}}$	$\dfrac{V_{1,t}}{V_{1,t-1}}$	Rural Net Power	$\dfrac{V_{1,t+1}}{V_{1,t}}$	$\dfrac{G_{1,t}}{G_{1,t-1}}$	Gov't Net Power	Rural + Gov't Net Power
1951	1.02	1.01	.01	1.01	1.02	—.01	.00
1952	1.11	1.01	.10	1.02	1.11	—.09	.01
1953	1.06	1.02	.04	1.02	1.06	—.04	.00
1954	1.07	1.02	.05	.83	1.07	—.24	—.19
1955	1.10	.83	.27	1.05	1.10	—.05	.22
1956	.96	1.05	—.09	1.04	.96	.08	—.01
1957	1.08	1.04	.04	1.04	1.08	—.04	.00
1958	1.09	1.04	.05	1.04	1.09	—.05	.00
1959	1.09	1.04	.05	1.04	1.09	—.05	.00
1960	1.09	1.04	.05	1.04	1.09	—.05	.00

t	$\dfrac{G_{2,t}}{G_{2,t-1}}$	$\dfrac{V_{2,t}}{V_{2,t-1}}$	Urban Net Power	$\dfrac{V_{2,t+1}}{V_{2,t}}$	$\dfrac{G_{2,t}}{G_{2,t-1}}$	Gov't Net Power	Urban + Gov't Net Power
1951	.85	1.01	—.16	.96	.85	.11	—.05
1952	1.19	.96	.23	.99	1.19	—.20	.03
1953	1.00	.99	.01	.98	1.00	—.02	—.01
1954	1.07	.98	.09	.99	1.07	—.08	.01
1955	.88	.99	—.11	.96	.88	.08	—.03
1956	1.49	.96	.53	1.05	1.49	—.44	.09
1957	.90	1.05	—.15	1.00	.90	.10	—.05
1958	1.17	1.00	.17	1.03	1.17	—.14	.03
1959	1.04	1.03	.01	1.03	1.04	—.01	.00
1960	1.11	1.03	.08	1.04	1.11	—.07	.01

b. Philippine Application

t	$\dfrac{G_{1,t}}{G_{1,t-1}}$	$\dfrac{V_{1,t}}{V_{1,t-1}}$	Rural Net Power	$\dfrac{V_{1,t+1}}{V_{1,t}}$	$\dfrac{G_{1,t}}{G_{1,t-1}}$	Gov't Net Power	Rural + Gov't Net Power
1952	1.06	.95	.11	.96	1.06	—.10	.01
1953	1.13	.96	.17	.98	1.13	—.15	.02
1954	1.04	.98	.06	.98	1.04	—.06	.00
1955	1.07	.98	.09	.98	1.07	—.09	.00
1956	1.07	.98	.09	.99	1.07	—.08	.01
1957	1.06	.99	.07	.99	1.06	—.07	.00
1958	1.07	.99	.08	1.00	1.07	—.07	.01
1959	1.05	1.00	.05	1.00	1.05	—.05	.00
1960	1.08	1.00	.08	1.01	1.08	—.07	.01
1961	1.04	1.01	.03	1.09	1.04	.05	.08

t	$\dfrac{G_{2,t}}{G_{2,t-1}}$	$\dfrac{V_{2,t}}{V_{2,t-1}}$	Urban Net Power	$\dfrac{V_{2,t+1}}{V_{2,t}}$	$\dfrac{G_{2,t}}{G_{2,t-1}}$	Gov't Net Power	Urban + Gov't Net Power
1952	.84	.97	—.13	.88	.84	.04	—.09
1953	1.37	.88	.49	1.01	1.37	—.36	.13
1954	1.03	1.01	.02	.95	1.03	—.08	.06
1955	1.26	.95	.31	1.00	1.26	—.26	.05
1956	1.04	1.00	.04	.95	1.04	—.09	—.05
1957	1.21	.95	.26	1.00	1.21	—.21	.05
1958	1.03	1.00	.03	.95	1.03	—.08	—.05
1959	1.19	.95	.24	1.01	1.19	—.18	.06
1960	1.01	1.01	.00	.94	1.01	—.07	—.07
1961	1.20	.94	.26	1.02	1.20	—.18	.08

the rural and urban sectors enjoy net power advantages over the government, and the government suffers net power disadvantages with respect to the individual sectors. This is primarily a result of the lack of an effective resource constraint on $G_{i,t}$. Regardless of the level of $G_{i,t}$, $G_{i,t}/G_{i,t-1}$ responds to the political situation even if total government expenditures exceed revenues by a large amount over long periods of time. In contrast, at sufficiently high (or low) levels of $V_{i,t}$, $V_{i,t}/V_{i,t-1}$ tends to converge toward 1.00 even if the load in the support relationship remains constant (see Figure 3.1). In short, the lack of a resource constraint on government spending in response to political pressures has the effect of giving the sectors net power advantages. The temporary net power advantages of the government in the Turkish application are a result of the concentration of funds in individual sectors after the exogenous drop in agricultural product in 1954. The government achieves a power advantage over a sector by withdrawing funds from it and allocating them to the other sector. Finally, net power in the interaction between a sector and the government is not zero sum—what the sector gains the government does not necessarily lose—but may be negative or positive.[83] Thus the agricultural crisis in the Turkish application creates a deficit of — .19 in the interaction between the rural sector and the government in 1954, and the resulting concentration of government funds creates a surplus of .22 in 1955. In this model as in Deutsch's communication and control model, the amount and distribution of power exercised depends not only on resources but on how these resources are utilized as well.

Directions for Further Development. Several aspects of the cybernetics approach to the study of political systems are not represented in this small model of modernization and mass politics. These aspects suggest directions for further development of the model.

Those who use the cybernetics approach, including Karl Deutsch, make a distinction between the state of a system and *information* about the state of the system. Deutsch, as we have seen, describes a feedback mechanism as one that produces action in response to an input of *information* and includes the results of its own action in the new *information* by which it modifies its subsequent behavior. However, the model we have been considering makes no distinction between the state of the system and information about the state of the system. According to the model, the masses do in fact know how their average standard of living in the current year compares with their standard of living in the previous year, and the government does in fact know both the magnitude of its support and recent changes in that support. In political systems there are a number of means by which, for example, the government tries to obtain accurate information about the current level of popular support. In Turkey since the onset of the multi-party era in 1946, the major parties have constructed huge organizations reaching down to the village level in order to provide party leaders with information about the sentiments of the people. In many countries elections are used to gauge the degree of support for the contending political organizations. In many Western nations, public opinion surveys are used for similar purposes. These and other means of obtaining accurate information will vary in efficiency from one context to the next and the costs of inaccurate information tend to be large, but in no case is the information obtained likely to be perfectly accurate. To the extent that information about an element of the system differs from the actual state of the system and thereby influences behavior in the system, the model should incorporate the flow of information and symbols as well as the flow of people, goods, and support.

The concept of lead time, the time into the future at which events in the system can still be accurately forecast, is an important concept in the cybernetic approach but is not incorporated in the model. Few would under-estimate the potential for increasing control of a system if the means for making accurate forecasts were available and utilized. Many however, would argue that most aggregate political and social behavior is undertaken in response to past or present events rather than forecasts of possible future events. For example, governments' detailed plans to facilitate an economically productive allocation of national resources over a period of five or ten years often become quite flexible in their implementation owing to the pressure of developing political circumstances. While it might not be worthwhile to incorporate forecasting relationships into the model for empirical purposes, it might be very worthwhile to do so for purposes of exploring the behavior of the system *if* accurate plans and forecasts could be made and implemented.

Second-order feedback is a third interesting idea in the cybernetic approach having implications for further development of the model. As suggested above, first-order mechanisms such as those in Table 3.1 adjust to stress by modifying the behavior of a variable. In contrast, second-order mechanisms adjust to stress by modifying the internal arrangements of the system itself. Crudely put, the distinction is between goal-seeking and goal-changing behavior. In order to suggest how goal-changing behavior might be included in a later version of the model, suppose that the rural and urban sectors of the population give or withhold support for the government on the basis of government performance with respect to the largely symbolic issue of nationalism, the maintenance of democratic procedures, and trends in the standard of living. A set of parameters $\mu_{i,j}$ can be defined to represent the relative weight of each issue j in determining support for the government in sector i. Suppose further that the government responds to the giving or withholding of support by manipulation of the salience of the nationalism issue through the creation or cultivation of a foreign enemy, by the main-tenance or destruction of democratic procedures, and by the allocation of pork barrel funds. A set of parameters $\beta_{i,j}$ can be defined to represent the relative preference of the government in the utilization of option j to maintain an acceptable level of support in sector i. Mechanisms producing changes in the $\mu_{i,j}$ reflecting changes in the relative salience of the issues, and mechanisms producing changes in the $\beta_{i,j}$ reflecting changes in the prominence of policy options as a result of the behavior of the system, would be second-order feedback mechanisms in Deutsch's sense. $\mu_{i,j}$ and $\beta_{i,j}$ might still be considered parameters whose changes in the short run are negligible, but they would have to be considered slowly changing variables in the long run. In form these second-order feedback mechanisms might be similar to those listed in Table 3.1, but in function they would affect support and expenditure levels independently of current loads in the support and expenditure mechanisms.

Second-order changes of this sort seem to have occurred in Turkey and the Philippines in the last two decades. The Menderes government in Turkey developed an increasing preference for political repression as a means of dealing with the opposition through the 1950's. By pressing its claim on the Malaysian state of Sabah (formerly North Borneo), the Philippine government at least in part seems to have attempted to divert attention from domestic political problems in recent years. Furthermore, second-order changes of this type also appear in theories of political change in the less developed countries. In John Kautsky's theory, for example, totalitarianism as a set of repressive policies and nationalism as a policy to increase the domestic political salience of a foreign enemy are typical responses of the ruling nationalist intellectuals to the breakdown of domestic political unity resulting from modernization. Totalitarianism replaces nationalism as the latter becomes increasingly ineffective in maintaining the nationalist coalition.[84]

Through the detailed analysis of theories and case studies it should be possible to locate the relevant second-order feedback mechanisms, to refine our understanding of them, and to represent them formally in computer simulation models.

STRUCTURAL-FUNCTIONAL

Basic Concepts. There are several structural-functional approaches to the study of political systems,[85] but we shall concentrate in particular on the approach of Almond and Powell. In this approach three levels of functioning play a key role in the comparative study of political systems:

> When we compare classes of political systems with one another, or individual political systems with one another, we need to compare *capabilities, conversion functions*, and *system maintenance and adaptation functions*, and the interrelations among these three kinds, or levels, of functions. When we talk about political development, it will also be in these same terms. A change in capability will be associated with changes in the performance of the conversion functions, and these changes in turn will be related to changes in political socialization and recruitment.[86]

The *capability* functions focus on the way a system performs in its environment, and in particular on its inputs and outputs or interchanges with the environment.[87] Almond and Powell consider five capability functions: the extractive, distributive, regulative, symbolic, and responsive. "The extractive capability of a political system refers to the range of system performance in drawing material and human resources from the domestic and international environments."[88] The extractive and distributive capabilities are closely related. "The distributive capability refers to the allocation of goods, services, honors, statuses, and opportunities of various kinds from the political system to individuals and groups in the society."[89] This capability varies with the amount of government expenditures and the range of individuals and groups who are benefited. "However, it is important to remember that the expenditures of a political system represent only a part, although perhaps a major part, of its distribution."[90] Tax rates, which determine in part the extractive capability of the government, affect the distribution of wealth in a society. In addition to wealth, the political system may also distribute educational opportunities, honors, statuses, and the like. "The regulative capability refers to the political system's exercise of control over behavior of individual groups."[91] The types of control include censorship, restrictions on the right to assemble, and the like. "The symbolic capability is the rate of effective symbol flow from the political system into the society and the international environment."[92] "While the extractive, regulative, distributive, and symbolic capabilities are ways of describing the pattern of outputs of the political system into the internal and external environments, the responsive capability is a relationship between inputs and outputs."[93] All political systems respond to internal or external pressures and demands, but the salient questions are: "To whom is the system responsive? In what policy areas is it responsive? How does it manage to sustain a pattern of responsive behavior?"[94]

"The second level of functioning is internal to the system. Here we refer to *conversion processes*. . . . In the political system this involves the ways in which demands and supports are transformed into authoritative decisions and are implemented."[95] Demands and supports mark the beginning of the conversion process, and the implementation of decisions mark the end; in between the conversion process can be disaggregated into a number of separate functions: interest articulation, interest aggregation, rule making, rule application, rule adjudication and communication. "Every political system has some way of processing demands. . . . The process by which individuals and groups make demands upon the political decision makers we call interest articulation. It is the first functional step on the political conversion process."[96] Channels and means of access for interest articulation include personal connection, elite representation, the mass media, and legislatures, bureaucracies, and cabinets. More latent and diffuse demands on the part of the masses may be communicated through physical demonstrations and violence. "The function of converting demands into general policy alternatives is called interest aggregation."[97] Presumably aggregation occurs across various issues and across the partially competing groups whose interests are affected by the policy alternatives. For example, in a two-party system, "The desire to seek widespread electoral support will require both parties to include in their policy 'package' those demands which have very broad popular support and to attempt to avoid alienating the most prominent interest groups."[98] The rule-making function includes legislation but is broader. "We refer to 'rule making' rather than 'legislation' for the simple reason that the term 'legislation' seems to connote some specialized structure and explicit process, whereas in many political systems the rule-making function is a diffuse process, difficult to untangle and specify."[99] The rule-application function involves the enforcement of rules and the rule adjudication function involves the ". . . process of making the authoritative decision as to whether or not a rule has been transgressed in a given case."[100] The communication function focuses on the most significant flows of information in the political system and the structures involved. "The performance of the communication function does not include all the other political functions, but it constitutes instead a necessary prerequisite for performance of other functions."[101]

The *system maintenance and adaptation functions* provide for changes in the system itself. "They do not directly enter into the conversion processes of the system, but they affect the internal efficiency and propensities of the system, and hence condition its performance."[102] The processes relatively specialized to the maintenance and adaptation function are socialization and recruitment. Socialization is closely related to political culture.

In studying any political system . . . we need to know its underlying propensities as well as its actual performance over a given period of time. We refer to these propensities, or this psychological dimension of the political system, as the *political culture*. . . . The propensities, attitudes, beliefs, and values to which we have referred are the consequences of *political socialization*.[103]

Recruitment processes determine who occupies political roles.

In a political system the incumbents of the various roles (diplomats, military officers, tax officials) must be recruited to these roles and learn how to perform in them. New roles are created and new personnel "broken in."[104]

Table 3.4 summarizes all the various functions.

Table 3.4—A Summary of Functions in Almond and Powell's Structural-Functional Approach

Capability Functions

Extractive
Distributive
Regulative
Symbolic
Responsive

Conversion Functions

Interest articulation
Interest aggregation
Rule making
Rule application
Rule adjudication
Communication

System Maintenance and Adaptation Functions

Socialization
Recruitment

In order to help "compare, classify, and characterize"[105] political systems, Almond and Powell introduce two characteristics common to all political systems. One is that

All political systems can be compared in terms of the relationship between functions and structures. That is, in a particular political system at a particular interval of time, there is a given probability that function *A* will be performed by structure *X*. . . . This proposition assumes that all the political functions can, *in some sense*, be found in all political systems, and that all political systems, including the simplest ones, have political structure.[106]

The proposition also assumes that "Any particular structure may perform more than one function."[107] A second common characteristic is that "All political systems have mixed political cultures . . ."[108] in the sense that they contain both traditional and more modern secular and rational components. These generalizations are essentially pre-theoretical. The most basic generalization intended to be of a predictive and explanatory nature is that ". . . . the development of higher levels of system capabilities is dependent upon the development of greater structural differentiation and cultural secularization."[109] In short, when the existing structure and culture of a political system become overloaded, survival of the crisis requires new structures (or more specialization among the older ones) and a more modern political culture.

Structural-Functional Interpretation of the Model. We shall postpone our discussion of political culture and focus here on the performance of functions in the model. Given our exploration of structural connectedness (see the discussion of Figure 2.3), it should be apparent that each of the structural relationships in the model is ultimately involved in the performance of each of the functions represented in the model. Thus from one point of view, the model as a representation of a political system has both structure and multifunctional structures as the approach asserts it should. From another point of view, these assertions of the structural-functional approach are approximately equivalent to the assertion that political systems are in fact systems.

Of the functions represented in the model, the most obvious are the extractive and distributive functions. The extractive function, as we have seen, is concerned with drawing material and human resources from the environment, and the distributive function is concerned with the allocation of goods, services, honors, and the like by the political system. In this simple model, the political system extracts $\tau_i Y_{i,t}$ in taxation and distributes government expenditure $G_{i,t}$. The government revenue relationship (3.4) and the expenditure relationship (3.8) are the structures relatively specialized to the performance of these functions.

The performance of the extractive and distributive functions in the Turkish and Philippine applications is summarized in Table 3.5. In the Turkish case, the level of government transactions with the urban sector exceeds those with the rural sector: The government put more resources into the urban sector and took more resources out of it. However, the rural sector enjoyed net gains in its transactions with the government in every simulated year from 1950 to 1960, while the urban sector suffered net losses in every year. More was put into the rural sector than was taken out, and more was taken out of the urban sector than was put in. The over-all effect is to redistribute income to the rural sector. The behavior of the model in this respect is at least qualitatively realistic. In the 1950's in Turkey there was "a shift in income distribution through increasing state support of com-

Table 3.5—Performance of the Extractive and Distributive Functions in the Model

a. Turkish Application *

	RURAL			URBAN		
t	$G_{1,t}$	$\tau_1 Y_{1,t}$	Difference	$G_{2,t}$	$\tau_2 Y_{2,t}$	Difference
1950	560	94	466	1,100	1,485	— 385
1951	571	101	470	930	1,552	— 622
1952	636	110	525	1,106	1,656	— 550
1953	673	121	552	1,105	1,753	— 648
1954	719	94	625	1,181	1,861	— 680
1955	792	104	688	1,043	1,927	— 884
1956	761	114	647	1,559	2,126	— 567
1957	820	126	694	1,408	2,282	— 874
1958	890	141	749	1,653	2,497	— 844
1959	966	159	807	1,714	2,726	—1,012
1960	1,055	181	875	1,900	3,004	—1,104

*In millions of Turkish lira at 1948 market prices.

b. Philippine Application†

	RURAL			URBAN		
t	$G_{1,t}$	$\tau_1 Y_{1,t}$	Difference	$G_{2,t}$	$\tau_2 Y_{2,t}$	Difference
1951	164	78	86	562	523	39
1952	174	79	96	473	545	— 72
1953	197	80	117	649	609	40
1954	205	82	123	670	648	22
1955	218	84	134	842	713	129
1956	232	86	146	875	758	118
1957	246	89	157	1,056	828	228
1958	263	92	171	1,088	878	210
1959	276	95	181	1,299	958	340
1960	297	99	198	1,310	1,010	300
1961	310	103	207	1,574	1,102	472

†In millions of Philippine pesos at 1951 market prices.

modity prices, continued tax exemption of agriculture, and a variety of other programs, all of which channeled income out of the city and into the village."[110]

In the Philippine case, the level of government transactions with the urban sector is again greater than the level of transactions with the rural sector. However, in all except one year (1952) both the urban and rural sectors received more than they paid in taxes, with the government using non-tax sources of revenue and incurring budgetary deficits. In terms of redistribution, the net result of transactions with the government is to redistribute income slightly in favor of the urban sector. These comparisons are of course made in terms of pesos, not pesos per capita.

Responsiveness, one of the capability functions, is also represented in the model. As we have seen, the responsive function deals with the relationship between the inputs to the political system and its outputs. To what pressures does the political system respond, and how does it respond? In this simple model, the government responds to change in popular support by giving or withholding government funds. The government response can be represented as ΔG_i or, equivalently, as $G_{i,t} - G_{i,t-1}$. If this number is positive, the government is increasing expenditures in sector i; if negative, the government is withdrawing expenditures. Popular demands and supports can be represented as $\Delta N_i V_i$ or, equivalently, $N_{i,t}V_{i,t} - N_{i,t-1}V_{i,t-1}$, the change in the number of people supporting the government. If this number is negative, the number of supporters in sector i is decreasing and a diffuse demand is being placed on the government; if positive, the number of supporters is increasing and pressure is being taken off the government. The structures relatively specialized to the responsive function are of course the support relationship (3.7) and the expenditure relationship (3.8).

The performance of the responsive function is summarized in Table 3.6.

Table 3.6—Performance of the Responsive Function in the Model*

a. Turkish Application

t	$\Delta N_1 V_1$	ΔG_1	$\Delta N_2 V_2$	ΔG_2	$\Delta N_3 V_3$	ΔG_3
1951	356	10.9	113	—170.3	469	—159.4
1952	371	64.8	9	175.9	379	240.7
1953	457	37.4	76	— .6	532	36.8
1954	510	46.0	55	76.2	554	122.6
1955	—1,628	72.9	73	—137.7	—1,556	— 64.9
1956	670	—30.8	3	515.1	672	484.3
1957	616	58.9	223	—150.8	839	— 91.9
1958	683	70.3	125	245.3	809	315.6
1959	752	75.8	210	61.3	962	137.1
1960	805	89.1	208	186.0	1,013	275.0

b. Philippine Application

t	$\Delta N_1 V_1$	ΔG_1	$\Delta N_2 V_2$	ΔG_2	$\Delta N_3 V_3$	ΔG_3
1952	—280	10.5	104	— 89.3	—175	— 78.8
1953	—222	22.4	—113	176.6	—335	199.0
1954	— 79	7.9	251	20.6	172	28.5
1955	— 54	13.3	65	171.6	11	184.9
1956	— 3	14.3	233	33.8	230	48.1
1957	35	13.1	61	180.8	96	193.9
1958	75	17.0	247	31.7	322	48.7
1959	128	13.2	44	210.9	172	224.1
1960	165	21.0	287	11.4	451	32.4
1961	230	13.1	5	264.3	236	277.4

*$\Delta N_i V_i$ is in thousands of persons. ΔG_i is in millions of Turkish lira at 1948 market prices or millions of Philippine pesos at 1951 market prices.

The only clear case of non-responsiveness occurs in the Philippine application. Even though there is considerable variation in demands and supports in the rural sector, there is almost no variation in government responses. In the rural sector in the Turkish application, particularly after 1956, increases in the number of supporters tend to elicit increases in government expenditures. In the urban sectors in both applications, relatively large increases in the number of supporters tend to generate relatively small increases or even decreases in government expenditures in the same time period. But an increase in support over one time interval tends to be followed by an increase in expenditures in the next interval.

In this small model, which telescopes many structures into one or a few, the responsive function overlaps to a considerable extent with the interest articulation and aggregation functions. As a first step in the political conversion process, interest aggregation is the function performed by individuals and groups in making demands on the political system. In the model this function is performed primarily by relationship (3.7), which generates changes in support. However, the giving or withholding of support as a means of articulating diffuse interests is not mentioned by Almond and Powell. Aside from mass demonstrations and violence, the means and channels of interest articulation considered by Almond and Powell are available primarily to elites, not to the masses.

Interest aggregation is the function of converting demands into general policy alternatives. This function is performed by the government expenditure relationship (3.8) in the comparison of the political situation in sector i (numerator) with the over-all political situation (denominator). Interest aggregation is apparent in the time series of demands, supports, and government responses in Table 3.6. If no interest aggregation occurred and consequently the interests of each sector were considered independently, there would be an almost perfect correlation between a sector's interest articulation (in terms of demands and supports) and the government's response in that sector, and almost no correlation between interest articulation in one sector and the government's response in another.

The degree of interest aggregation in the behavior of the model in each application can be estimated from Table 3.7. On the left side of the table $N_{i,t}V_{i,t} - N_{i,t-1}V_{i,t-1}$ is correlated with $G_{i,t} - G_{i,t-1}$ and on the right side with $G_{i,t+1} - G_{i,t}$, the government response in the next time interval. The correlations from the Turkish application should be interpreted with caution since the extreme values of the variables at $t = 1955$ and $t = 1956$ have a disproportionate effect on the correlation. For example, the correlation of $-.16$ between $\Delta N_1 V_1$ and $G_{1,t} - G_{1,t-1}$ would be positive and larger in absolute value if the observation for $t = 1955$ were removed from the sample. In any case, it is apparent that the correlations of demands and supports with government responses within sectors are never perfect and the correlations

Table 3.7—Interest Aggregation in the Model: Product Moment Correlations of Demands and Supports with Government Responses

a. Turkish Application

	$\Delta t = t - (t - 1)$			$\Delta t = (t + 1) - t$		
	ΔG_1	ΔG_2	ΔG_3	ΔG_1	ΔG_2	ΔG_3
$\Delta N_1 V_1$	—.16	.44	.43	.93	—.68	—.55
$\Delta N_2 V_2$	.55	—.39	—.31	.52	.47	.61
$\Delta N_3 V_3$	—.09	.38	.38	.95	—.61	—.46

<table>
<tr><td>(N = 10 time intervals)</td><td>(N = 10 time intervals)</td></tr>
</table>

b. Philippine Application

	$\Delta t = t - (t - 1)$			$\Delta t = (t + 1) - t$		
	ΔG_1	ΔG_2	$G\Delta_3$	ΔG_1	ΔG_2	ΔG_3
$\Delta N_1 V_1$	.13	.44	.44	.35	—.12	—.10
$\Delta N_2 V_2$	—.14	—.69	—.69	—.22	.87	.88
$\Delta N_3 V_3$	.01	—.08	—.08	.13	.41	.42

<table>
<tr><td>(N = 10 time intervals)</td><td>(N = 10 time intervals)</td></tr>
</table>

across sectors are never zero. To the extent that these extreme values of the correlation coefficient are not obtained, the behavior of the model reflects interest aggregation.

Directions for Further Development. The symbolic capability function and the communication function are not incorporated in the present version but suggest some interesting directions for further development. If the people give or withhold support for the government in response to the difference between an actual and expected level of government performance with respect to such issues as nationalism, the maintenance of democratic procedures, and the standard of living, then the government can attempt to control its popular support by manipulating these expectations through use of the mass media. The symbolic capability and the performance of the communication function depend upon the receptivity of the people to the issues, to biases in being influenced by one group as opposed to another, and to the degree of development of the communication system and control over its use. Receptivity might be represented by the $\mu_{i,j}$ discussed in the cybernetic section. These weights might govern both the relative degree to which a sector responds to an issue and the relative degree to which it is receptive to influence on it. For example, in Turkey in the late 1950s, public criticism of actions by the government of Menderes to restrict the political activity of the opposition had little influence on the rural masses, and the issue did little to change their support for the government. This situation might be reflected in a relatively low value of $\mu_{i,j}$. Biases in communication among actors could be represented by another set of parameters linking each actor to every other actor. In Lipset's theory of political development, for example, intolerance among pairs of actors serves in part as a barrier to effective communication between them. Patterns of intolerance both reflect and maintain patterns of political cleavage.[111]

The rule-making, rule-application, and rule-adjudication functions suggest the possibility of incorporating legislative, executive and judicial phenomena into the model. The aspects of the present version of the model most obviously susceptible to rule-making procedures are a_i, the rate of natural increase; m_i, the rate at which income is consumed; τ_i, the effective tax rate; and β_i, the relative preference of the government for one sector or another in the allocation of government funds. The rate of natural increase can be influenced by legislation providing for public birth control programs, tax exemptions for children, and the like. Tax rates are of course changed through legislation. The rate of consumption can be influenced by legislation providing for rationing, import quotas, and the like. Finally, the relative preference of the government for a sector can be influenced by less formal procedures perhaps located within political parties rather than at the governmental level. The implications of changes in these parameters in the Turkish and Philippine contexts have been traced in the first essay. The processes that would produce these changes depend in part on formal arrangements of government: a parliamentary vs. presidential form of democracy; an authoritarian form of government where the style of legislation is more arbitrary; and the like. The essential structural problem is to locate the sources of pressure to change these rules, and to specify processes determining which of these pressures can be brought to bear on rule changes.

Structures performing the rule application function could be based on the distinction between formal and effective rules. For example, let us define $\hat{\tau}_i$ as the formal (or legal) tax rate in sector i and τ_i as the effective tax rate. The quantity $(\hat{\tau}_i - \tau_i)/\tau_i$ could then be defined to indicate the extent to which the formal rate is applied in practice. If $\hat{\tau}_i = .25$ and $\tau_i = .20$ then the quantity is .25, indicating that revenue from sector i could be increased by 25% through more efficient application of the legal rate. Case studies might reveal that above some threshold of inefficiency, resources are diverted to tax collection in order to reduce the difference between formal and effective rates.

The system maintenance and adaptation functions, as we have seen, are primarily socialization and recruitment functions. Socialization processes in general produce changes in aspects of culture such as those reflected in a_i and m_i. Political socialization and recruitment processes produce changes in more directly political aspects of culture such as reflected in β_i through the inculcation of new operating norms and the recruitment of new incumbents into the relevant roles. To the extent that these functions are performed in response to the need to control an aspect of system's behavior, the processes performing the functions can be represented as second-order feedback mechanisms.

Finally, let us consider structural differentiation, the form of system behavior which Almond and Powell call development.[112] As the increasing *specialization* of existing multi-functional structures, structural differentiation may be produced in the operation of a model if it contains second-order feedback mechanisms. For example, in a larger model than the one considered here, the government expenditure process might depend on both political pressures of a pork barrel nature and on technical criteria for efficient economic growth. Second-order feedback processes could be incorporated to decrease the impact of political pressure on the allocation of funds (a decrease of $\beta_{i,j}$ to use our earlier example) and to increase the weight of the technical criteria. (Political pressures might be dealt with through the manipulation of symbols or through repression.) In this manner, the allocation processes would become increasingly specialized to the function of achieving economic growth. As the *creation of new structures* in response to crises in the system, structural differentiation cannot be represented in a computer simulation model in the present state of the art. This would be equivalent to producing a new statement in a computer program as a result of the execution of the others.[113] In short, while the barriers to specifying models that perform all of the functions listed by Almond and Powell are primarily theoretical, the barrier to specifying models that produce the second form of structural differentiation is a technical limitation of the methodology.

POLITICAL CULTURE

Basic Ideas. Definitions of political culture often identify political culture as the subjective dimension of politics. According to Verba

> The political culture of a society consists of the system of empirical beliefs, expressive symbols, and values which defines the situation in which political action takes place. It provides the subjective orientation to politics.[114]

Similarly, in Pye's analysis, "Political culture is . . . the manifestation in aggregate form of the psychological and subjective dimension of politics."[115]

While political culture is the subjective dimension of politics, it is intimately connected with political behavior. On the one hand, political

culture regulates and controls political behavior; on the other, political
culture is in part a result of political behavior. Verba explores the first
connection in the following terms:

> . . . political culture represents a system of control *vis-à-vis* the system
> of political interactions. Political culture regulates who talks to whom
> and who influences whom. It also regulates what is said in political
> contacts and the effects of these contacts. It regulates the ways in which
> formal institutions operate as well. A new constitution, for instance,
> will be perceived and evaluated in terms of the political culture of a
> people. When put into practice in one society it may look quite different
> from the same constitution instituted in another nation with another
> political culture.[116]

Pye is referring to essentially the same role of political culture when he
conceives of political culture as a

> . . . set of attitudes, beliefs, and sentiments that give order and meaning
> to the political process and that provide the underlying assumptions
> and rules that govern behavior in the political system. It encompasses
> both the political ideals and the operating norms of a polity.[117]

Viewed as a set of operating norms, the role of political culture is similar
to the role of values in the approach emphasizing communication and control.
For Deutsch, ". . . in its crudest and simplest form, a 'value' is a repetitive
preference for a particular class of messages or data that is to be received,
transmitted, or acted upon in preference to others."[118] Easton apparently
has essentially the same idea in mind when he writes that "The typical
demands that will find their way into the political process will concern the
matters in conflict that are labelled important by the culture."[119]

While political culture regulates and controls behavior, it is also in part
determined by political behavior. To be sure, changes in political culture
may be the result of incompatibilities within the culture itself: "Not all
political cultures are well integrated and consistent."[120] But

> The political culture of a nation . . . derives from, among other things,
> the experiences that individuals have with the political process. One
> way to learn about political beliefs is to observe the ways in which
> political structures operate.[121]
>
> *   *   *
>
> The study of political culture leads invariably to the study of
> political socialization, to the learning experiences by which a political
> culture is passed on from generation to generation and to the situations
> under which political cultures change.[122]
>
> *   *   *
>
> The basic political values of a group may not be easily changed,
> yet under certain types of pressure and over time they can change
> rather drastically.[123]

Verba's analysis of change in political culture is very similar to Deutsch's analysis of second-order feedback, which we considered above. The operation or behavior of a system generates pressures or loads which feed back to change the norms or values on which the behavior was based.

Several aspects of the political culture approach, as we have seen, are expressed in somewhat different terms in the other approaches as well. However, while the cybernetic approach emphasizes the feedback processes that are common to all systems, and the structural-functional approach emphasizes structures and the functions they perform in all societies, the political culture approach emphasizes the *differences* in operating norms both between and within polities. This distinction is of course relative rather than absolute. Nevertheless, consider how one scholar sums up the results of several studies of political culture:

> Possibly the most striking conclusion which emerges from bringing together these studies of ten countries is an appreciation of the diversity of man's experiences in creating and ordering his political life. Differences abound; and even with respect to certain common broad themes, such as democracy and authoritarianism, there is remarkably little similarity.[124]

Pye goes on to note that the authors in this volume felt compelled to stress several common themes.

> In spite of the great diversity among countries, we find certain common generalizations about the structure of political cultures. The first of these is the observation that in no society is there a single uniform political culture . . .[125]

Every polity, it turns out, is similar in the sense that there are important internal differences in the political culture of each. "[I]n all polities there is a fundamental distinction between the culture of the rulers or power holders and that of the masses, whether they are merely parochial subjects or participating citizens."[126]

> In addition to the division between elite and mass political cultures the process of political development tends to create a second division in all political cultures. This is the division which separates those more acculturated to modern ways from the people who are still closer to the traditional patterns of life.[127]

Pye believes that change in political culture is the key to nation-building. Nation-building depends "upon changes in the basic values and attitudes of the people, even to the point of changes in personality and culture;" . . . "there must be a change in the outlook and sentiments of people before it is even possible to have economic, to say nothing of political, change."[128]

For our purposes, then, the relatively distinctive contribution of the political culture approach is this emphasis on the fundamental, underlying, relatively stable differences in operating norms or behavioral propensities both between and within polities.

Culture in the Model. Aspects of political as well as demographic and economic culture are represented in the model in the set of parameters. The connection between parameters and culture is not a simple one. As slowly changing dependent variables in the long run, parameters can be interpreted as the cumulative quantitative results of cultural norms, institutional factors, and physical environment on the relatively stable, underlying bases of aggregate behavior. The parameter β_i, for example, can be influenced in principle not only by ideological and cultural preferences in the allocation of government funds, but also by formal and informal rule-making procedures within the governing party and by geographical and technical barriers to channeling funds into distant or remote areas. In this case culture in the model can be construed narrowly as the normative component of the parameters. As approximately constant factors in the short run, the parameters can be treated as the aspects of the system which govern and regulate political behavior. In this case culture can be interpreted broadly as the parameter itself. In either case, the cultural component of behavior reflected in parameters can be distinguished from the more immediate, the more variable, and the more conscious component of aggregate behavior reflected in variables such as consumption and support for the government. Furthermore, it is important to note that the parameters do not encompass the total demographic, economic, or political culture. Rather they summarize the effect of various aspects of culture on selected types of aggregate behavior. The types of behavior are implicit in the relationships in the model: For example, (3.5) deals with consumer behavior and (3.8) deals with the distributive behavior of the government.

Given the complicated nature of the relationship between culture and parameters, the most we can do at this point is to offer some tentative and incomplete culture interpretations of those parameters in the model which appear to have a significant political cultural component.[129] We have already discussed the government's propensity to allocate funds β_1 at several points, but the scale of fluctuations in support σ, the degree of penetration of the government α_i, and the rate of change in expected economic performance ε require further elaboration.

At least for Turkey and the Philippines, the relative strength of kinship systems seems to make a difference in σ. In the Philippines, party politics, as a result of behavioral patterns rooted in the kinship system, are structured around dyadic ties between prosperous patrons and their relatively poor and dependent clients rather than classes, occupations, regions, or the like.[130] One consequence is that intra-party solidarity is weak and interparty switching is common, producing relatively large net changes in support for the governing party and even larger gross changes. In Turkey these dyadic ties are less important, and fluctuations in support tend to be moderated by occupational, regional, and policy differences among parties.

In both Turkey and the Philippines mass political activity tends to be channeled through the party system, and consequently α_i for these countries tends to be close to one. In other political cultures extra-governmental or even non-political responses to similar problems may be more prominent. For example, violence and revolt are relatively salient options in the Mexican political culture, as suggested by the admonition among Mexican politicians that "the Mexicans are a violent people."[131] In some historical circumstances religion and religious organizations have deflected social discontent from the political arena.

> The various orders, sects, sometimes also the churches, could in periods of political adversity and decline or through alliance with aristocratic forces promote a distinctly apolitical attitude which severed, as it were, the relation between the religious and the secular-political images of man, emphasizing the inherent wickedness of the political order. In this way they might deflect much social fervor from active participation in the political process.[132]

To the extent that these influences encroach upon the channeling of social problems through governmental procedures, α_i is close to zero.

The rate of change of expected economic performance ε may reflect in part the "Image of the Limited Good" proposed by the anthropologist George Foster. The basic tenants of this image are that all things of value in life are scarce; that the peasant is not capable of increasing the available quantities directly; and that "an individual or a family can improve a position only at the expense of others. Hence an apparent improvement in someone's position with respect to any 'Good' is viewed as a threat to the entire community."[133] In a closed peasant economy where this concept is most applicable to the explanation of behavior, "to accept and be satisfied with the social role and traditional material rewards given by the society is essential."[134] Complete satisfaction with the material situation can be represented statically in the model as equality between expected performance and actual performance, and dynamically as $\varepsilon = 1$, which implies that expected performance tends to adjust completely to actual performance. $\varepsilon < 1$, however, implies in the model that the adjustment is incomplete, giving rise to the possibility of dissatisfaction and political action to improve the material situation. Such behavior might occur where the closure of peasant economies has been eroded.

While the cultural interpretations of these parameters are tentative and incomplete, the over-all role of these parameters in governing the aggregate behavior of the model can be explored with some confidence. For this purpose we have used the model to create a sample of twenty-five hypothetical "Turkeys" and twenty-five hypothetical "Philippines." Specifically, for each of the parameters α_1, α_2, β_1, β_2, σ and ε we used a random number table to generate a distribution of twenty-five settings with the mean of each distribution equal to the reference run setting and the standard deviation equal to 5% of the reference run setting. For example, the mean of the distribution of twenty-five settings of β_2 in the sample of hypothetical "Turkeys" is 3.60 and the standard deviation is (.05) (3.60) = .18. Within each sample, only these culturally significant parameters in the political subsystem differ from one case to the next; all other inputs are identical to those used in reference runs. Consequently, differences in behavior among the countries in each sample can be attributed to minor differences in political cultural parameters alone.

Table 3.8 indicates the degree of cross-system variability in the behavior of selected political outputs that can be attributed to cross-system variation in these inputs. In order to compare the variability among outputs, the

Table 3.8—Culture and Behavior: Variability in Culture Generates Variability in Behavior

	a. Turkish Sample				b. Philippine Sample			
	Ref. Run Value	Mean of Sample	Standard Dev. of Sample	Coeff. of Variab.	Ref. Run Value	Mean of Sample	Standard Dev. of Sample	Coeff. of Variab.
$V_{1,5}$	.575	.575	.007	.01	.529	.529	.002	.00
$V_{1,10}$	.562	.561	.022	.04	.510	.510	.012	.02
$V_{1,15}$	.683	.681	.034	.05	.551	.548	.028	.05
$V_{2,5}$	.504	.504	.016	.03	.568	.568	.007	.01
$V_{2,10}$	.515	.515	.072	.14	.519	.520	.006	.01
$V_{2,15}$	.627	.595	.170	.29	.434	.450	.044	.10
$G_{1,5}$	719	719	38	.05	218	218	12	.06
$G_{1,10}$	966	967	90	.09	297	297	18	.06
$G_{1,15}$	1,575	1,597	387	.24	387	386	25	.06
$G_{2,5}$	1,181	1,182	84	.07	841	841	45	.05
$G_{2,10}$	1,714	1,743	353	.20	1,310	1,308	55	.04
$G_{2,15}$	2,899	3,133	1,450	.46	2,250	2,299	243	.11
$E_{1,5}$	1.037	1.037	.001	.00	1.021	1.021	.001	.00
$E_{1,10}$	1.033	1.033	.004	.00	1.018	1.018	.002	.00
$E_{1,15}$	1.057	1.057	.008	.01	1.024	1.024	.003	.00
$E_{2,5}$	1.026	1.026	.002	.00	1.024	1.024	.001	.00
$E_{2,10}$	1.027	1.027	.009	.01	1.017	1.017	.001	.00
$E_{2,15}$	1.043	1.041	.027	.03	1.007	1.007	.002	.00

coefficient of variability is calculated by dividing the standard deviation of each output by its mean. In both samples government spending $G_{i,t}$ exhibits the most variability and the expected economic performance $E_{i,t}$ exhibits the least. Furthermore, in both samples there is a tendency for the variability of each output to increase with time. Finally, it should be noted that the over-all variability of the outputs in the Turkish sample is greater than their over-all variability in the Philippine sample. In short, initial cross-system differences in political culture generate diverging patterns of system behavior. As Verba observed in the real world and we observe in the model, identical or at least similar structures behave differently in different political cultures.

Table 3.9—Culture and Behavior: Product Moment Correlations Among Selected Inputs and Outputs

	a. Turkish Sample						b. Philippine Sample					
	α_1	α_2	β_1	β_2	σ	ε	α_1	α_2	β_1	β_2	σ	ε
$V_{1,5}$	.42	.54	.88	—.01	.26	.21	.52	.40	.74	.16	.46	.36
$V_{1,10}$	.04	.54	.91	.33	.11	.34	.03	.49	.95	.22	—.04	.46
$V_{1,15}$	—.01	.28	.43	.82	.46	.34	.14	.24	.65	.09	—.12	.25
$V_{2,5}$	—.34	—.07	—.08	.99	.23	.30	.41	.47	.31	—.79	.10	—.08
$V_{2,10}$	—.32	—.06	—.14	.99	.31	.29	.51	.25	.06	—.73	.16	.22
$V_{2,15}$	—.31	—.06	—.17	.98	.37	.28	—.01	—.25	—.55	—.13	.16	—.21
$G_{1,5}$	.00	.59	.97	.19	—.02	.29	.06	.52	.99	.10	—.08	.29
$G_{1,10}$	—.21	.54	.37	.80	.20	.39	.03	.55	.97	.23	.00	.33
$G_{1,15}$	—.29	.08	.07	.99	.28	.34	.03	.44	.98	.05	—.20	.27
$G_{2,5}$	—.33	.00	—.08	1.00	.31	.30	—.28	.17	.11	.98	.40	.34
$G_{2,10}$	—.32	—.11	—.23	.98	.30	.26	—.38	—.17	—.19	.97	.21	.26
$G_{2,15}$	—.33	—.11	—.26	.97	.30	.24	—.18	.12	—.19	.90	.58	.23
$E_{1,5}$	.04	.59	.93	.09	—.07	.46	.10	.44	.85	—.10	—.10	—.22
$E_{1,10}$	—.06	.57	.90	.37	.03	.37	.06	.52	.97	.10	—.06	.13
$E_{1,15}$	—.22	.34	.48	.84	.21	.49	.02	.55	.97	.20	—.03	.34
$E_{2,5}$	—.30	.02	—.05	.98	.33	.21	—.31	—.03	—.05	.59	.11	—.52
$E_{2,10}$	—.31	—.04	—.13	.99	.32	.28	—.07	.00	—.28	.59	.50	—.43
$E_{2,15}$	—.33	—.08	—.19	.99	.32	.29	—.04	—.61	—.60	—.43	—.33	—.64

Table 3.9 gives us some indication of the degree of variation in the same selected political outputs that can be accounted for by variation in each of the individual inputs. A few observations on the role of β_1 and β_2, the parameters with the strongest influence, are sufficient to illustrate the complicated way in which parameters govern the behavior of the systems. First, the impact of β_1 and β_2 on an output often varies through time. For example, the correlations between β_1 and $V_{1,t}$ at successive five-year intervals are .88, .91, and .43 in the Turkish sample, and the correlations between β_2 and $G_{2,t}$ are .19, .80, and .99 in the Philippine sample. Second, the impact of β_1 and β_2 varies from one set of relative homogeneous contexts to the next. In the Turkish sample β_2 has a very strong *positive* impact on $V_{2,t}$ but in the Philippine sample it has a moderately strong *negative* impact. Finally, as a result of structural connectedness, the *indirect* impact of β_1 and β_2 is often greater than or equal to the *direct* impact of other parameters. Although ε

has a direct impact on $E_{2,t}$, β_2 explains virtually all the variance in these outputs, and ε explains only a fraction in the Turkish sample. In the model as in the real world, the relationships between political culture and political behavior are complicated and depend on the unique configuration of other components in each system.

Further Development. As we have already suggested, the relatively distinctive contribution of the political cultural approach is its emphasis on differences in behavioral propensities and operating norms both within and between systems. Consequently, suggestions for further development of the model do not focus on the incorporation of new process relationships but on the elaboration of the components of the state vector to reflect culturally important distinctions.

One kind of elaboration has already been considered in the discussion of second-order feedback mechanisms. There we defined a set of parameters $\mu_{i,j}$ to represent the relative salience of issue j in determining support for the government in sector i, and a set of parameters $\beta_{i,j}$ to represent the relative salience to the government of policy option j to maintain an acceptable level of support in sector i. In general, both the *identification* of the issues and options and the relative *salience* of the particular issues and options within each set are aspects of political culture. Political culture, according to conventional understanding, governs political behavior both by defining the prominent aspects of the political environment and by defining the prominent means of altering that environment. There is no reason to believe that they will be the same from one country to the next. As we have seen, violence as a political but extra-governmental means of redressing political grievances is more prominent in the Mexican than the Turkish or Philippine political cultures. In short, the political cultural approach suggests the elaboration of issues and options defined in the state vector.

Another kind of modification suggested by the political cultural approach is the disaggregation of mass and elite groups that differ significantly in behavior and behavioral propensities. The relevant distinctions may be regional, tribal, religious, or the like, depending on the context. For example, Frederick Frey has employed survey data from a large sample of Turkish peasants to assess the relative significance of several analytical distinctions such as region, literacy, formal educational levels, mass media exposure, travel experience, level of village development, and various attitudinal characteristics as predictors of many aspects of peasant behavior. He concludes that "regions predicted peasant behavior more effectively than any other indicator employed except for peasant mass media exposure, which was nearly equal to region in predictive power. No other factors came near these two."[135] To incorporate a distinction between the relatively modern western region and the relatively traditional eastern region, it would be necessary to increase the size of the state vector and to redefine the sector subscripts. That is to say, each variable and parameter in the present version that has values defined for $i = 1$ (rural) and $i = 2$ (urban) would have values defined for $i = 1$ (rural-west), $i = 2$ (rural-east), $i = 3$ (urban-west), and $i = 4$ (urban-east). A factor such as media exposure might be represented as a variable defined on groups rather than as a basis for defining the groups themselves.

Cultural or at least ideological distinctions within the elite might be represented somewhat differently. In the case of Turkey for example, intra-elite conflict became increasingly apparent after about 1935. Partly as a result of the success of the R.P.P.'s development policies, a locally oriented elite with primarily commercial occupations and interests rose to challenge the nationally oriented elite which had dominated the R.P.P. Organized as the leadership of the Democratic Party in 1946, this opposition won the election of 1950 and directed government policy away from selective development projects toward relatively large-scale efforts to develop the whole country, including the rural areas.[136] To incorporate an opposition and policy changes such as those resulting from the election of 1950, one might define a set of parameters $\beta_{i,j,k}$ where i and j refer, respectively, to mass groups and government options, and k refers to the alternative political parties. Compared to the R.P.P., the β-propensities of the D.P. would tend to be both higher and relatively biased toward the rural sector. In this formulation, a change from opposition to government would change not only levels of support for the government, but also the policies employed by the government. In the Philippines, where the parties tend to be homogeneous with respect to these propensities, such a distinction is much less important.

With a close examination of individual countries and some theoretical choices, these modifications of the state vector can be incorporated into a model rather easily. However, they cannot be generated or produced through the operation of the model itself. For example, to simulate adequately the formation of the Democratic Party from the Republican People's Party in Turkey in 1946 would require the creation of new parameters for the D.P. and values of those parameters during the execution of the computer simulation program. The most we can do in any single computer simulation run is to modify the values of existing parameters and variables within a fixed, given structure. Consequently, our present inability to define new structural relationships and new state vectors *during the execution* of a computer simulation program precludes the generation or replication of several fundamental types of change that occur in the course of political development.

4. Methods

Up to this point the role of various methodological approaches in the study of complex systems has been largely implicit. In this section we shall summarize the roles of the theoretical and case study approaches, since these are relatively well-understood and familiar, and probe more deeply into the role of statistical methods for quantitative data analysis.

THE NEED FOR MULTIPLE METHODS: A SUMMARY

Theoretical and Pre-theoretical Approaches. The concepts and hypotheses produced by theoretical approaches are a temporary commitment on the part of the investigator about the phenomena of importance and the nature of the underlying order and organization to be found in a class of systems. They are inferred but not rigorously derived from observations of events in order to render those events more intelligible. To the extent that we wish to develop knowledge that is transferable from one context to the next, these abstractions are essential: Observations of behavior differ from one context to the next, but knowledge of structure, to the extent that it is accurate, does not.

The typologies and analytical frameworks produced by theoretical and pre-theoretical approaches serve the function of guiding the course of inquiry, and in particular of reinforcing an image of the whole enterprise that is more comprehensive than any of its parts. For example, in this study Harold Lasswell's classification of intellectual tasks is a reminder that scientific objectives and techniques of analysis constitute only a part of the scope and methods of political science. Similarly, the cybernetic, structural-functional, and political cultural approaches suggest further developments in the direction of including a broader range of phenomena in the model. As these examples suggest, a comprehensive image of the whole enterprise not only helps to define the limits of the current formulation, it also indicates the range of options for further development.

Case Study Method. The rich, detailed, contextually specific information produced by case studies plays an equally important and complementary role in the study of complex systems, particularly as an essential element in the development and appraisal of tentative statements of structure. In this study, information from case studies was used to select those phenomena which seemed to be important enough to include in a simple formal model. For example, in both the Turkish and Philippine contexts the amount and distribution of economic goods clearly accounts for more political activity than questions concerning the practice of religion. Case study information is also useful in evaluating the quantitative data used to specify the inputs and to test the outputs of the model. We found, for example, that those qualities of urbanism associated with settlements of 10,000 or more in Turkey are found only in much larger settlements in the Philippines. We also found that there was good reason to doubt the reliability of Philippine census and national accounts data. Finally, information from case studies along with structural and quantitative information was used in the appraisal of the model's outputs. Thus of all the possible explanations for the unrealistically rapid economic growth produced in the Turkish reference run, case studies suggested that by far the most persuasive explanation was the omission in the model of fiscal constraints on government expenditures.

Statistical Methods. In this study statistical methods have been used to condense and to summarize the behavior of the model. Product-moment correlations, for example, were used to investigate the degree of interest aggregation in the model, and standard deviations and correlations were used to explore the role of political culture in the model. We have not however, used quantitative methods to verify and discover theories of political development or to test individual hypotheses, as others have done. Furthermore, we have noted Warren Weaver's reservations about the use of statistical techniques in the scientific study of complex, organized systems, which he characterized as problems of organized rather than disorganized complexity. Given the importance of these methods in the scientific study of political development, their somewhat different role in this study, and Warren Weaver's reservations, the role of statistical methods needs to be explored in some detail.

We shall limit our comments to multiple regression analysis, one of the more powerful and theoretically relevant statistical techniques. What is lost in generality is, we hope, more than recovered in concreteness. Those interested in the assumptions of regression analysis may refer to statistical textbooks.[137] In its simplest form, however, regression analysis is a means of determining for a given set of data the parameters a and b of an equation

$$\hat{Y}_i = a + b X_i \quad \text{or} \quad Y_i = a + bX_i + u_i$$

such that the least-squares criterion denoted by the expression

$$\sum_{i=1}^{n} (Y_i - \hat{Y}_i)^2$$

is minimized. The subscript i refers to individual observations in the sample of n observations, Y_i is the actual value of the dependent variable for the i-th observation, $\hat{Y}_i$ is the corresponding predicted value, and X_i is the value of the independent variable for the i-th observation. u_i is the error term, the difference $(Y_i - \hat{Y}_i)$, reflecting errors in specifying the form of the regression equation, errors attributable to stochastic factors, and observation errors.[138]

According to one text on applied social statistics, regression equations are the "laws" of science.[139]

AN EXPERIMENT WITH REGRESSION ANALYSIS

A Question. The question at hand is this: In what respects and to what extent is regression analysis useful in clarifying the structure of a class of systems given quantitative data on their behavior and some theoretical hunches about their structure? With respect to real-world systems, this question is unanswerable because our knowledge of their structure is always tentative: We cannot know with certainty that the variables we have included are the appropriate ones, nor can we know that the processes we have inferred from observations are correct. Moreover, our observations are incomplete and in various degrees inaccurate. However, with respect to the model of modernization and mass politics as a simple representation of a complex real-world system, the question can be answered with some confidence, since our knowledge of the structure of the model and its behavior in any previous application is complete and accurate. Consequently, we shall use the model to generate data on the behavior of hypothetical systems and to specify regression equations that can be applied to these data in an attempt to rediscover the systems' common structure.

A First Approximation. To create the necessary data we followed a procedure similar to that used in the consideration of political culture. We used a random number table to generate a distribution of twenty-five settings for each input in the Turkish and Philippine reference runs. The mean of the distribution for each input is equal to the reference run setting, and the standard deviation of each distribution is equal to 5% of the mean for parameters and 10% of the mean for initial conditions. Given these inputs the model was used to generate data on the behavior of twenty-five hypothetical systems based on the Turkish reference run and twenty-five hypothetical systems based on the Philippine reference run. In crude terms, the hypothetical countries within the samples differ only marginally from each other in cultural and other behavioral propensities (as reflected in the random differences among parameters) and in past history up to the point at which the analysis begins (as reflected in random differences among the initial conditions). It should be emphasized that each system has an identical structure; that in the operation of each system the structure and parameter settings do not change over time; and that we have complete data on the behavior of each system, uncontaminated by measurement error or the influence of stochastic factors. Consequently, the error term u can be attributed only to errors in the specification of regression equations, and these data are a much less formidable challenge to regression analysis than data from real-world systems.

To specify regression equations based on the model's structure we selected the five continuous feedback mechanisms in the model and applied a simple transformation rule to each of them. The output of the mechanism became the dependent variable, the inputs became the independent variables, and no distinction was made between variables at different points in time. The resulting regression equations, which are listed in Table 4.1, are formally quite similar to those which have appeared in cross-national data analytic studies of political development. In terms of the structure of the model,

Table 4.1—Multiple Regression Versions of the Five Continuous Feedback Mechanisms in the Model

$$U_t = a + b_1\left(\frac{C_{1,t}}{N_{1,t}}\right) + b_2\left(\frac{C_{2,t}}{N_{2,t}}\right) + b_3 N_{1,t} + b_4 P_{1,t} + u \qquad (3.1\mathrm{r})$$

$$I_{i,t} = a + b_1\left(\frac{C_{i,t}}{N_{i,t}}\right) + u \qquad (3.6\mathrm{r})$$

$$V_{i,t} = a + b_1\left(\frac{C_{i,t}}{N_{i,t}}\right) + b_2 E_{i,t} + b_3 P_{i,t} + u \qquad (3.7\mathrm{r})$$

$$G_{i,t} = a + b_1(N_{1,t}V_{1,t}) + b_2(N_{2,t}V_{2,t}) + b_3 GR_t + u \qquad (3.8\mathrm{r})$$

$$E_{i,t} = a + b_1\left(\frac{C_{i,t}}{N_{i,t}}\right) + b_2 P_{i,t} + u \qquad (3.11\mathrm{r})$$

the forms of these equations are accurate with respect to the variables included, the variables tagged as dependent and independent, and the rural–urban disaggregation. Other aspects of the structure of the model are not included. These equations will be applied to a number of different situations in each of the two samples: The rural and urban sectors (except the first equation) and the 5th and 10th cycles of the model.

Aside from the structural information already incorporated into the equations, their application to sets of data produces additional information in the form of several coefficients and statistics. One is the coefficient of determination R^2 (the multiple correlation coefficient squared), which can be interpreted as the proportion of variance explained in the dependent variable by the independent variables. Another statistic is the F-ratio, the ratio of explained to unexplained estimates of variance, which can be compared with a known sampling distribution to determine the probability that an R of a given value or larger for a particular sample could have been obtained if the actual linear association in the population were in fact zero.

If this probability is sufficiently low, the multiple correlation coefficient is said to be statistically significant. Finally, fitting of the equations to a set of data produces numerical estimates of the intercept a and the partial regression coefficients b_i. A t-test can be applied to each regression coefficient to estimate the probability that it is significantly different from zero.

The results are presented in Table 4.2. It should be immediately apparent

Table 4.2—Results of the Experiment with Regression Analysis

a. Turkish Sample

Relationship and Context		a	b_1	b_2	b_3	b_4	R^2
Urbanization (3.1r)							
	$t = 5$	—.130	—.0002 *	.0001 *	.0056 *	.1529 *	.971 *
	$t = 10$	.316	—.0003 *	.0001 *	.0108	—.740 *	.929 *
Investment (3.6r)							
$i = 1$	$t = 5$	— 529	2.67 *	—	—	—	.665 *
$i = 1$	$t = 10$	— 906	4.08 *	—	—	—	.940 *
$i = 2$	$t = 5$	—1,443	2.84 *	—	—	—	.790 *
$i = 2$	$t = 10$	—2,257	4.16 *	—	—	—	.971 *
Support (3.7r)							
$i = 1$	$t = 5$	1.84	.0006 *	—1.280 *	—.225	—	.678 *
$i = 1$	$t = 10$	2.26	.0009 *	—2.189 *	.270	—	.601 *
$i = 2$	$t = 5$	2.50	.0006 *	—2.387 *	—.224	—	.882 *
$i = 2$	$t = 10$	.02	.0002 *	.099	.088	—	.681 *
Expenditure (3.8r)							
$i = 1$	$t = 5$	231	13.3 *	—41.1 *	.233 *	—	.622 *
$i = 1$	$t = 10$	— 81	37.7 *	18.7	.165 *	—	.862 *
$i = 2$	$t = 5$	340	— 62.8 *	231.1 *	.553 *	—	.947 *
$i = 2$	$t = 10$	1,387	—175.2 *	51.6	1.049 *	—	.932 *
Expectation (3.11r)							
$i = 1$	$t = 5$	.705	.0003	.412	—	—	.141
$i = 1$	$t = 10$	.890	.0002 *	.116	—	—	.229
$i = 2$	$t = 5$	1.18	.0000	—.162	—	—	.014
$i = 2$	$t = 10$	1.05	.0001	—.177	—	—	.325

*Indicates statistical significance at the .05 level according to the t-test (two-tailed) or the analysis of variance test.

that the fitting of these equations to our simulated data has not produced any additional *structural* information that is unambiguously reliable. First, the parameters estimated in the various applications of a single regression equation are often substantially different. For example, the partial regression coefficients derived from the application of the expenditure relationship to the urban sector in the Turkish sample reveal that rural votes in the 10th

Table 4.2—Results of the Experiment with Regression Analysis (*Cont.*)

b. Philippine Sample

Relationship and Context	a	b_1	b_2	b_3	b_4	R^2
Urbanization (3.1r)						
$t = 5$	—.495	—.0018 *	.0004 *	.0179 *	.722 *	.919 *
$t = 10$	—.262	—.0018 *	.0006 *	.0251 *	.045	.850 *
Investment (3.6r)						
$i = 1$ $t = 5$	— 91.3	.819 *	—	—	—	.593 *
$i = 1$ $t = 10$	—164.1	1.336 *	—	—	—	.888 *
$i = 2$ $t = 5$	874.9	— .675	—	—	—	.005
$i = 2$ $t = 10$	1,485.9	—1.714 *	—	—	—	.170
Support (3.7r)						
$i = 1$ $t = 5$	.505	.0009 *	— .301	.412	—	.191
$i = 1$ $t = 10$	2.097	.0012 *	—2.69 *	1.427 *	—	.759 *
$i = 2$ $t = 5$	— .221	—.0001	.300	.686	—	.048
$i = 2$ $t = 10$	4.28	—.0001	—5.419 *	2.163 *	—	.738 *
Expenditure (3.8r)						
$i = 1$ $t = 5$	14.98	5.77 *	— 16.2 *	.274	—	.732 *
$i = 1$ $t = 10$	— 24.79	5.97 *	— 17.7 *	.317 *	—	.909 *
$i = 2$ $t = 5$	233.64	—50.19 *	115.3 *	.985 *	—	.734 *
$i = 2$ $t = 10$	198.86	—54.53 *	128.2 *	1.06 *	—	.646 *
Expectations (3.11r)						
$i = 1$ $t = 5$	.815	.0006	.192	—	—	.086
$i = 1$ $t = 10$	.865	.0004 *	.127	—	—	.328 *
$i = 2$ $t = 5$	.483	.0001	.629	—	—	.145
$i = 2$ $t = 10$	1.116	—.0001	—.049	—	—	.116

*Indicates statistical significance at the .05 level according to the *t*-test (two-tailed) or the analysis of variance test.

cycle are nearly two and a half times as important as they are in the 5th cycle, urban votes are less than one-fourth as important, and government revenue is about twice as important. These differences in results across time occur even though the coefficients of determination are very high (R^2 = .947 at $t = 5$, R^2 = .932 at $t = 10$) and even though the parameters of the systems that generated the data and the structure of the systems themselves remain constant over time. In short, the best least-squares estimates in one context are not the best least-squares estimates in another. Any information that does not change from context to context, and is therefore potentially structural rather than behavioral in nature, is imposed on the data in the specification of the form of the equation and not derived from the data.

Second, the fitting of these equations does not unambiguously determine the degree to which the equations or the independent variables within them are structurally correct. Since the regression equations are each derived from structural relationships in the same manner, each regression equation and each independent variable is equally significant in a structural sense. Yet 12 of 36 or 33% of the fitted equations explain less than 50% of the variance in the dependent variable, and 11 of 36 or about 31% of the fitted equations are not statistically significant according to the analysis of variance test. Moreover, 31 of 88 or about 35% of the partial regression coefficients are not significantly different from zero according to the t-test. If R^2 or the analysis of variance test were used to judge the structural significance of the equations, or if the t-test were used to judge the structural significance of the independent variables, a substantial number of errors would be made.

If the behavior of the model is a fundamentally distorted rather than merely a simplified reflection of the behavior of real world systems, these results may be dismissed as irrelevant to the analysis of real-world data. However, at least with respect to the behavior of this model, the reason why regression analysis and most statistical techniques are not *in themselves* sufficient to test hypotheses[140] should be familiar to the reader by now: The behavior of a class of systems does not tell us everything we need to know about their common structure; conversely, a common structure produces different patterns of behavior in different contexts. The fitting of regression equations to data from different contexts produces coefficients that describe these contexts and that may contain clues about structure. These clues are not unambiguous and must be evaluated in the light of other evidence. To an overwhelming extent, however, structural information is imposed on the data rather than derived from it. This is well-known to economists who use regression to estimate parameters for specific contexts, but not to political scientists who use the technique to test general hypotheses or to verify and discover theory.

A Reformulation. In order to use regression techniques to estimate parameters for specific contexts, we must adapt our previous analysis more closely to the structure and behavior of the model. First, let us respecify the regression equations to make them accurate in terms of the model's structure. For the expectation relationship (3.11r), which we shall use as an example, this requires that we introduce the time-lagged variables that appear in (3.11); that we represent the complex term on the right side of (3.11) as a single composite index in order to arrive at an equation that is linear in the coefficients; that we force the regression intercept to a value of zero since it has no counterpart in the process relationship; and that we subtract $E_{i,t-1}$ from both sides of the equation in order to avoid estimating for $E_{1,t-1}$ a regression coefficient that has no counterpart in (3.11). The last operation defines a new dependent variable, $Z_{i,t} = (E_{i,t} - E_{i,t-1})$. These steps produce (3.11s), which is accurate in a structural sense and can be used to estimate the parameter ε:

$$Z_{i,t} = \hat{\varepsilon} X_{i,t} \tag{3.11s}$$

where

$$Z_{i,t} = E_{i,t} - E_{i,t-1}$$

$$X_{i,t} = \left(\frac{C_{i,t}}{N_{i,t}} \frac{N_{i,t-1}}{C_{i,t-1}} - E_{i,t-1} \right) P_{i,t-1}$$

and

$\hat{\varepsilon}$ = the estimate of the parameter ε.

Second, let us redefine the observations to which (3.11s) is to be fitted. If we fit (3.11s) to either the Turkish or the Philippine sample of twenty-five hypothetical systems, we would be attempting to explain *cross-system* variation in $Z_{i,t}$ and would derive one estimate of ε for the sample as a whole. However, (3.11), the process relationship, produces $Z_{i,t} = (E_{i,t} - E_{i,t-1})$ or variation *through time* within systems, and because of the way in which the sample was constructed there is one unique setting of ε for each of the twenty-five systems rather than one setting for the sample as a whole. Consequently, if we want to identify the least-squares estimate $\hat{\varepsilon}$ with the parameter governing the behavior of the system ε, and if we want the statistical explanation of each dependent variable to coincide with the process explanation, then the appropriate units of observation are not systems at one point in time but rather the states of a single system at successive points in time.[141] For convenience, we shall apply (3.11s) to the time series outputs of the Turkish and Philippine reference runs, using observations at fifteen points in time for each system.

The results, as expected, are correct. $\hat{\varepsilon} = .1000$ for both the rural and urban data in the Turkish reference run, and $\hat{\varepsilon} = .1500$ for both the rural and urban data in the Philippine reference run. Furthermore, $R^2 = 1.000$ for each of the four regression equations. In short, when the regression equation accurately reflects the structure of the underlying process relationship, the fitting of the equation produces accurate parameter estimates and structurally meaningful explanations of the dependent variable.

The implications of these experiments are important in defining the role of statistical methods in the study of organized, complex systems. With respect to regression analysis, structural information tends to be imposed on the data rather than derived from it, although regression analysis may be useful in estimating parameters for specific contexts. We should not, however, leave the impression that the estimation of parameters from time series data is a straightforward procedure in the study of complex political systems.

For one thing, errors in the specification of equations and some rather typical properties of social science data, particularly time series data, may invalidate the assumptions of least-squares estimation and give rise to misleading results. These problems have been treated elsewhere.[142] For another, the necessary time series data are often not available, even for a simple model like the model of modernization and mass politics. The appropriate response to these problems, it seems to us, is to put more time and effort into problems of specification, the investigation of properties of data sets, and the collection of time series data. In these important respects, the tasks of the political scientist using regression techniques are similar to those of the political scientist using computer simulation. If we have demonstrated convincingly that the availability of statistical programs is not sufficient reason to deemphasize the detailed consideration of structure, and that the availability of cross-national data is not sufficient reason to deemphasize time series data, one purpose has been fulfilled. Furthermore, if we have demonstrated convincingly that process analysis (whether or not it takes the form of simulation) and not statistical analysis is the prerequisite for understanding the behavior of complex systems, our major purpose has been fulfilled.

Conclusion

In this essay we have tried to define some basic research problems arising from the complexity of political systems, and to explore the potential of computer simulation as a means of grappling with them. Traditional and statistical styles of analysis have tended to underestimate the degree of order and organization underlying the diversity we observe in the behavior of political systems, and these styles have not sufficiently bridged the gap between structure and behavior. Through process analysis and particularly through the formalization of our understanding of important variables and processes into computer simulation models, we can in principle utilize the order of systems to reduce uncertainty about their behavior and to build more rigorous and systematic connections between their structure and behavior. Whether the long-run possibility of useful, empirically tested models can be realized is a question best answered by future experience. However, computer simulation models can be used now to foster coordination and communication among the various areas of specialization in the study of complex political systems. To the extent that our intellectual tasks as well as the systems themselves have the quality of "wholeness" which frustrates partial analysis, this use of computer simulation is significant.

However, computer simulation is still a relatively new and unexplored methodology in political science, and past experience suggests that a new methodology tends to be more frequently misapplied as it diffuses through the profession. By this we mean that the methodology is applied to substantive problems for which it is inappropriate because the limitations of the methodology are not well understood; or even worse, the time, energy, and emotion invested in mastering the methodology bias research priorities to such an extent that it determines the problems considered.[143] With this experience in mind, it behooves us to emphasize the major limitations of computer simulation.

One limitation involves the difficulty or impossibility of reproducing certain aspects of political systems' behavior in a computer simulation model. We cannot reproduce structural and cultural differentiation in the behavior of a model because we cannot create new structural relationships and new state vectors during the execution of a computer simulation program. Similarly, we cannot adequately simulate the role of chance and individuals. Although it is possible to estimate the sensitivity of the outputs of a model to these random and exogenous variations, it is not possible to use the model to explain or predict the nature of these variations, their magnitude, or when they occur.

A second limitation involves the problem of aggregation. At increasingly aggregate levels of analysis the random components in systems' behavior tend to cancel out and the systematic components tend to cumulate, thereby reducing the level of uncertainty. However, to the extent that alternative models of such systems are aggregated, it is difficult to choose between them: Aggregation involves the loss of information that might help us choose among structural alternatives. Moreover, to the extent that a model is aggregated, it distorts the normative questions of distribution by directing attention toward inequality between groups and away from inequality within groups.

A third limitation has so far remained implicit. We have suggested on the one hand that the model used here can be made potentially more realistic by incorporating a large number of phenomena considered to be important in the three approaches to political development. These include information flows, expectations (lead time), and symbolic and communications functions; second-order feedback, rule-application, rule-making, rule-adjudication, and socialization and recruitment processes; and within-nation distinctions representing cultural differences. We have stated on the other hand that as a model becomes more complex, it becomes more difficult to understand its behavior and to find or develop measures of the variables and parameters defined in it. The problem is simply this: Can we develop simulation models of political systems that are sufficiently large and complex to provide reliable information about real-world systems for other than scientific purposes, yet sufficiently small and simple that they can be evaluated and improved scientifically?

Notes

[1] Herbert A. Simon, "The Architecture of Complexity," in L. von Bertalanffy and A. Rapoport, eds., *General Systems*, vol. 10 (1965), pp. 63–4.

[2] David Easton, "An Approach to the Analysis of Political Systems," *World Politics*, vol. 9 (April 1957), p. 383.

[3] George A. Miller, *The Psychology of Communication: Seven Essays* (New York: Basic Books, 1967), p. 49.

[4] The classification of purposes comes from Harold D. Lasswell. See his article, "The Political Science of Science," *American Political Science Review*, vol. 50 (December 1956), pp. 961–79.

[5] See Daniel Lerner, *The Passing of Traditional Society: Modernizing the Middle East* (New York: Free Press, 1964), Chapter II, as well as the studies based on Lerner's work, many of which are cited in the first essay. This citation and the ones that follow are, of course, merely suggestive of the types of studies we have in mind.

[6] Bernard Lewis, *The Emergence of Modern Turkey* (London: Oxford University Press, 1961).

[7] Leicester Webb, "Political Future of Pakistan," *Futuribles*, vol. I (Geneva: Droz, 1963), pp. 295–319.

[8] Kemal H. Karpat, *Political and Social Thought in the Contemporary Middle East* (New York: Praeger, 1968).

[9] Frank Golay, *The Philippines: Public Policy and National Economic Development* (Ithaca: Cornell University Press, 1961).

[10] Karl W. Deutsch, *The Nerves of Government: Models of Political Communication and Control* (New York: The Free Press, 1963).

[11] Gabriel Almond and G. Bingham Powell, Jr., *Comparative Politics: A Developmental Approach* (Boston: Little, Brown, 1966).

[12] See the essays in Lucien Pye and Sidney Verba, eds., *Political Culture and Political Development* (Princeton: Princeton University Press, 1965).

[13] Gabriel Almond and James S. Coleman, eds., *The Politics of the Developing Areas* (Princeton: Princeton University Press, 1960), Introduction.

[14] Richard D. Robinson, *The First Turkish Republic: A Case Study in National Development* (Cambridge: Harvard University Press, 1965).

[15] Phillips Cutright, "National Political Development: Its Measurement and Correlates," in Nelson W. Polsby, R. A. Dentler, and P. A. Smith, eds., *Politics and Social Life* (Boston: Houghton Mifflin, 1963), pp. 569–82.

[16] A study unusual for its explicit treatment of several purposes is Samuel P. Huntington's article, "Political Development and Political Decay," *World Politics*, vol. 17 (April 1965), pp. 386–430.

[17] A somewhat similar theme can be found in Albert O. Hirschman, "The Search for Paradigms as a Hindrance to Understanding," to appear in *World Politics*, vol. 22 (April 1970).

[18] See Lasswell, *op. cit.*, particularly Section IV.

[19] Martin Shubik, in a seminar at Yale, first suggested to us the use of computer simulation models in economics as means of facilitating communication between theoreticians on the one hand and those who collect and utilize economic data on the other.

[20] Easton, *op. cit.*, p. 383.

[21] See Richard Bellman and Robert Kalaba, *Dynamic Programming and Modern Control Theory* (New York: Academic Press, 1965), p. 2.

[22] See Paul A. Samuelson, "Interactions Between the Multiplier and the Principle of Acceleration," *Review of Economic Statistics*, vol. 21 (1939), pp. 75–8. Samuelson's multiplier-accelerator model is also studied in Samuel Goldberg, *Introduction to Difference Equations* (New York: Science Editions, 1961), pp. 5–8, 153–56, 173.

[23] W. Ross Ashby, *An Introduction to Cybernetics* (London: Chapman and Hall, 1961), p. 61.

[24] *Ibid.*

[25] *Ibid.*, pp. 67–68.

[26] Albert Ando, Franklin M. Fisher, and Herbert A. Simon, *Essays on the Structure of Social Science Models* (Cambridge: M.I.T. Press, 1963).

[27] Nonlinear and discontinuous relationships tend to make systems more complex than linear and continuous alternatives. In the system introduced in the next subsection, (3.7) is an example of a nonlinear relationship and (3.12) is an example of a discontinuous relationship. See Table 1.3.

[28] Herbert L. Costner and Robert K. Leik, "Deductions from Axiomatic Theory," *American Sociological Review*, vol. 29 (December 1964), pp. 819–35.

[29] Perhaps the largest computer simulation model of political processes is TEMPER, a model of the international system. See Clark Abt and Morton Gorden, "Report on Project TEMPER" (Unpublished paper, Abt Associates, Inc.) and TEMPER, Vols. 1–7.

[30] Hubert M. Blalock, Jr., *Causal Inferences in Nonexperimental Research* (Chapel Hill, N.C.: University of North Carolina Press, 1964), p. 8.

[31] This is an open rather than closed system since $F_{i,t}$ has an impact on the rest of the system but is not determined by the system. It is a deterministic rather than a stochastic system since there are no stochastic factors. Finally, it utilizes finite rather than infinite time differences. In an unpublished paper Craig W. Kirkwood of M.I.T. reports that a version of the system using infinite differences produces almost exactly the same outputs as the present version.

[32] The program is written in FORTRAN IV and listed in Appendix I of the first essay.

[33] Warren Weaver, "Science and Complexity," *American Scientist*, vol. 36 (1948), p. 538.

[34] *Ibid.*, p. 539. The emphasis is Weaver's.

[35] *Ibid.*, p. 540.

[36] Lerner, *op. cit.*, p. 55.

[37] Inclusion of stochastic processes in the model would complicate the process of theory-building even further, since both the historical and simulated time series would contain random components. The model would have to be run a large number of times with the same inputs in order to generate a sample for each output. The samples would then be compared with the historical data. For a first approximation such as this, the expected payoff is not worth the additional complication.

[38] G. U. Yule and M. G. Kendall, *An Introduction of the Theory of Statistics* (London: Griffin, 14th ed., 1950), p. 314.

[39] The point is made by Guy H. Orcutt, Harold W. Watts, and John B. Edwards, "Data Aggregation and Information Loss," *American Economic Review*, vol. 68 (September 1968), pp. 773–87.

[40] See for example Charles F. Hermann, "Validation Problems in Games and Simulation with Special Reference to Models of International Politics," *Behavioral Science*, vol. 12 (May 1967), pp. 216–31.

[41] Hans Meyerhoff, *The Philosophy of History in Our Time: An Anthology* (Garden City, N.Y.: Doubleday, 1959), p. 19.

[42] *Ibid.*, p. 20.

[43] Stuart Bruchey, *The Roots of American Economic Growth, 1607–1861: An Essay in Social Causation* (New York: Harper & Row, 1968), p. 10.

[44] Henri Pirenne, "What Are Historians Trying to Do?" in Meyerhoff, *op. cit.*, p. 95.

[45] *Ibid.*, pp. 98–99.

[46] Bruchey, *op. cit.*, p. 13.

[47] *Daedalus*, vol. 96 (Summer 1967), p. 946.

[48] *Ibid.*, p. 941.

[49] *Ibid.*, p. 945.

[50] *Ibid.*

[51] See James S. Coleman, *Introduction to Mathematical Sociology* (New York: The Free Press, 1964), pp. 444–47, on "connectedness" of the structure.

[52] Bruchey, *op. cit.*, pp. 13-14.

[53] Technically, S' in our discussion in Section 1 is a nearly *completely* decomposable system; here it is a nearly decomposable system. The difference is explained in Ando, Fisher, and Simon, *op. cit.*, pp. 108–9. For the Ando-Fisher theorem, see *Ibid.*, pp. 92–106.

[54] Pirenne, *op. cit.*, p. 97.

[55] Walter F. Weiker, *The Turkish Revolution, 1960–1961: Aspects of Military Politics* (Washington, D.C.: Brookings Institution, 1963), p. 12.

[56] See the introduction on "The Rise of the New Economic History," in Bruchey, *op. cit.*

[57] Abraham Kaplan, *American Ethics and Public Policy* (New York: Oxford University Press, 1963), p. 98.

[58] *Ibid.*

[59] *Ibid.*, p. 94.

[60] *Ibid.*

[61] *Ibid.*, p. 91.

[62] J. Roland Pennock, "Political Development, Political Systems, and Political Goods," *World Politics*, vol. 18 (April 1966), p. 431. The emphasis is Pennock's.

[63] Sir Geoffrey Vickers, *Value Systems and Social Process* (New York: Basic Books, 1968), p. 113.

[64] *Ibid.*, p. 112.

[65] Robert A. Dahl and Charles E. Lindblom, *Politics, Economics, and Welfare* (New York: Harper & Row, 1963 ed.), p. 27.

[66] *Ibid.*, p. 57.

[67] *Ibid.*, p. 60.

[68] *Ibid.*, p. 61.

[69] *Ibid.*, p. 63.

[70] To draw these isoquants we have had to interpolate among these 441 runs. We wish to thank Nathaniel Beck of Yale for suggesting the use of contour maps to present these data.

[71] See Harold D. Lasswell and Abraham Kaplan, *Power and Society* (New Haven: Yale University Press, 1950), Chapter IV.

[72] See Lasswell, "The Political Science of Science," *op. cit.*; and Harold D. Lasswell, "Technique of Decisions Seminars," *Midwest Journal of Political Science*, vol. 4 (August 1960), pp. 213–36.

[73] Deutsch, *op. cit.*, p. 88.

[74] Cf. A. E. Fitzgerald and David E. Higginbotham, *Basic Electrical Engineering: Circuits, Machines, Electronics, Control* (New York: McGraw-Hill, 1957 ed.), especially pp. 486–516, "Feedback Control Systems."

[75] Deutsch, *op. cit.*, p. 92.

[76] Wilbur Schramm, "Communication Development and the Development Process," in Lucien Pye, ed., *Communications and Political Development* (Princeton: Princeton University Press, 1963), pp. 31–32.

[77] Bernard Lewis, "Recent Developments in Turkey," *International Affairs*, vol. 27 (July 1951), p. 323.

[78] Frank H. Golay, *The Philippines: Public Policy and National Economic Development* (Ithaca, N.Y.: Cornell University Press, 1968), pp. 89f.

[79] Deutsch, *op. cit.*, p. 188.

[80] *Ibid.*, pp. 190–91.

[81] *Ibid.*, p. 111.

[82] *Ibid.*, p. 115.

[83] One consequence of these definitions is that the total net power exercised in an interaction between the government and sector i is equal to $(V_{i,t+1}/V_{i,t} - V_{i,t}/V_{i,t-1})$. If we redefine the net power of sector i to be $(G_{i,t+1}/G_{i,t} - V_{i,t+1}/V_{i,t})$ then the total net power exercised would be $(G_{i,t+1}/G_{i,t} - G_{i,t}/G_{i,t-1})$.

[84] John Kautsky, *Political Change in Underdeveloped Countries: Nationalism and Communism* (New York: Wiley, 1962).

[85] See for example the work of Marion Levy, Jr., Fred W. Riggs, and David Apter.

[86] Almond and Powell, *op. cit.*, p. 30.

[87] *Ibid.*, p. 28.

[88] *Ibid.*, p. 195.

[89] *Ibid.*, p. 198.

[90] *Ibid.*, p. 199.

[91] *Ibid.*, p. 196.

[92] *Ibid.*, p. 199.

[93] *Ibid.*, p. 201.

[94] *Ibid.*

[95] *Ibid.*, p. 29.

[96] *Ibid.*, p. 73.

[97] *Ibid.*, p. 98.

[98] *Ibid.*, p. 103.

[99] *Ibid.*, p. 132.

[100] *Ibid.*, p. 159.

[101] *Ibid.*, p. 166.

[102] *Ibid.*, p. 30.

[103] *Ibid.*, pp. 23–24.

[104] *Ibid.*, pp. 29–30.

[105] *Ibid.*, p. 30.

[106] *Ibid.*, pp. 30–31. The emphasis is Almond and Powell's.

[107] *Ibid.*, p. 31.

[108] *Ibid.*, p. 33.

[109] *Ibid.*, p. 323.

[110] Robinson, *op. cit.*, p. 153.

[111] Seymour Martin Lipset, *Political Man: The Social Bases of Politics* (Garden City, New York: Anchor, 1958), Chapter 3.

[112] "*Development* results when the existing structure and culture of the political system is unable to cope with the problem or challenge which confronts it without further structural differentiation and cultural secularization." Almond and Powell, *op. cit.*, p. 34. The emphasis is Almond and Powell's.

[113] Current work on inductive inference by machine might possibly be developed to bypass the technical barrier.

[114] Pye and Verba, *op. cit.*, p. 513.

[115] Lucien Pye, *Aspects of Political Development* (Boston: Little, Brown, 1966), pp. 104–5.

[116] Pye and Verba, *op. cit.*, p. 517. LaPalombara finds the same phenomenon in unsuccessful attempts to transfer Western administrative forms and structures into non-Western settings. See his essay, "Bureaucracy and Political Development: Notes, Queries, and Dilemmas," in Joseph LaPalombara ed., *Bureaucracy and Political Development* (Princeton: Princeton University Press, 1966 ed.), pp. 34–61.

[117] Pye, *op. cit.*, pp. 104–5.

[118] Deutsch, *op. cit.*, p. 178.

[119] Easton, *op. cit.*, p. 388.

[120] Pye and Verba, *op. cit.*, p. 520.

[121] *Ibid.*, p. 514.

[122] *Ibid.*, p. 515.

[123] *Ibid.*, p. 520.

[124] *Ibid.*, p. 14.

[125] *Ibid.*, p. 15.

[126] *Ibid.*, p. 39.

[127] *Ibid.*, p. 17.

[128] Lucien Pye in Ithiel de Sola Pool, ed., *Contemporary Political Science* (New York: McGraw-Hill, 1967), pp. 192–93.

[129] This is partly a level-of-analysis problem. The most specific discussions of political culture tend to come from political anthropologists who work at the village level. But the relationship between these discussions and the more general, aggregate discussions of political scientists is not often clear.

[130] Carl H. Landé, *Leaders, Factions, and Parties: The Structure of Philippine Politics* (New Haven: Yale University Southeast Asia Studies Monograph no. 6, 1965), pp. 1–3.

[131] L. V. Padgett, *The Mexican Political System* (Boston: Houghton Mifflin, 1966), p. 7. Violence often accompanies the elimination of the despotic local political bosses, the *caciques*. *Ibid.*, p. 83.

[132] S. N. Eisenstadt, "Religious Organization and Political Process in Centralized Empires," *Journal of Asian Studies*, 21 (May 1962), pp. 286–87.

[133] George Foster, "Peasant Society and the Image of Limited Good," in Jack M. Potter, May N. Diaz, and George Foster, eds., *Peasant Society: A Reader* (Boston: Little, Brown, 1967), pp. 304–5.

[134] *Ibid.*, p. 320.

[135] Frederick Frey, *Regional Variations in Rural Turkey* (Cambridge: M.I.T. Center for International Studies, 1966), p. 67; see also pp. 55–58.

[136] See Frederick Frey, *The Turkish Political Elite* (Cambridge: M.I.T. Press, 1965), pp. 387–93; and Malcolm D. Rivkin, *Area Development for National Growth* (New York: Praeger, 1965), Chapter 6.

[137] For example, Hubert M. Blalock, *Social Statistics* (New York: McGraw-Hill, 1960), Chapter 17, or J. Johnston, *Econometric Methods* (New York: McGraw-Hill, 1963) pp. 106–8.

[138] See Johnston, *op. cit.*, pp. 5–6.

[139] Blalock, *op. cit.*, pp. 275–76.

[140] It might be expected that this conclusion does not hold for the causal modelling technique introduced by Simon and developed by Blalock. However, for the causal model $V_{i,t} \rightarrow G_{i,t} \rightarrow Y_{i,t}$, which is typical of these models and which reflects some direct causal links in the model of modernization and mass politics (see Figure 1.3), this is not the case. If the causal model is correct, then (ignoring subscripts) $r_{VY} - r_{VG}r_{GY} = 0$. For the contexts ($i = 1$, $t = 5$), ($i = 1$, $t = 10$), ($i = 2$, $t = 5$), and ($i = 2$, $t = 10$), this difference is in fact .168, .490, .062, and .069 for the sample based on the Turkish reference run and .394, .106, −.165, and −.066 for the sample based on the Philippine reference run. If we arbitrarily adopt the criterion that an absolute difference of greater than .100 is cause for rejection, then the causal model would be rejected in five of eight contexts. In general, causal modelling as a means of studying the structure of systems of this type is limited by the need to assume simple linear causal mechanisms and to assume that errors in these mechanisms are uncorrelated. If the mechanisms are too complex or if the errors are correlated, predictions about the pattern of correlation coefficients cannot be derived. For an introduction see Herbert A. Simon, *Models of Man* (New York: Wiley, 1957), Chapter 2.

[141] Cf. the following: "The relationship between [regression] coefficients [derived from cross-sectional analysis] and those obtained from the change analysis is simple and direct. The cross-section analysis assumes, either implicitly or explicitly, that the causal processes have resulted in an equilibrium state. That is, the implicit assumption in regression analysis is that this is a stable relationship, which would give the same values for the regression coefficients in a later cross-section unless an exogenous factor disturbed the situation." James S. Coleman, "The Mathematical Study of Change," in Hubert M. Blalock, Jr. and A. B. Blalock, eds., *Methodology in Social Research* (New York: McGraw-Hill, 1968), p. 444.

[142] See Johnston, *op. cit.*, Part 2, especially pp. 145–47.

[143] Cf. the "methodological hammer" in Abraham Kaplan, *The Conduct of Inquiry* (San Francisco: Chandler, 1964).

Index

Abello, A. B., 35n., 81n.

Abt, Clark, 173n.

Adaptation function (*see* Structural-functional)

Agricultural product:
  of Philippines (1951–1960), 33, 34
  of Turkey (1950–1960), 26, 28–29

Alker, Hayward R., Jr., xiv, 78n., 79n.
  on mathematical modeling techniques, 3

Allocations, effects of government, 20

Almond, Gabriel, 172n.
  on characteristics of political systems, 146
  on elite bias in interest articulation, 150
  on structural differentiation, 153
  structural-functional theory characterized, 144–147
  (*See also* Powell, G. Bingham, Jr.; Structural-functional)

Analytical contexts, selection rationale, 23

Analytical forms and styles:
  mathematical characterized, 94–95
  simulational, 95
  verbal, 94
  on decomposability, 93

Ando-Fisher theorem:
  defined, 93, 115
  limits in nonlinear system, 119
  related to organized complexity, 115–119

Ando, Hirofumi, 79n.

Ando, Albert, 173n.

Apter, David, 175n.

Aristotle, 13

Articulation, interest (*see* Structural-functional)

Ashby, W. Ross, 82n., 173n.
  on connectedness, 93
  on system size or "largeness," 92

Atatürk (*see* Kemal Atatürk, Mustapha)

Austerity programs, sensitivity analysis of, 43, 45–49
  (*See also* Policy options; Public policy, sensitivity analysis of)

Barber, Clarence L., 81n.

Barton, Thomas F., 174n.

Beck, Nathaniel, 174n.

Behavior, model:
  contrasted with concept of structure, 94–95
    in analytical model, 128–129
    in feedback mechanism terms, 139–141
  contrasted with real systems, 89–90
  defined, 89–90
  function of ensemble of components, 107
  illustrated for "Samuelson Model," 90–92
  long-run relative, 117–118
  sensitivity analysis, 53–54
  small illustrative model, 96
  variations with identical structure, 90–92
  (*See also* Model of Modernization and Mass Politics; Models)

Behavioral revolution in political science, viii

Bell, Daniel, 82n.

Bellman, Richard, 82n., 173n.
  on problem of theory building, 58

Berman, Paul, 78n.
  differential equation model of Lerner's theory noted, 7
  mathematical modeling techniques, 3
  process models, 3

Bertalanffy, L. von, 172n.

Beshers, James M., 79n.

Birth-control programs, sensitivity analysis of, 43–45